PRINCIPLES AND PRACTICE IN BUSINESS AND MANAGEMENT RESEARCH

Principles and Practice in Business and Management Research

Edited by
V. J. WASS
P. E. WELLS

Dartmouth

Aldershot • Brookfield USA • Singapore • Sydney

Published by
Dartmouth Publishing Company Limited
Gower House
Croft Road
Aldershot
Hants GU11 3HR
England

Dartmouth Publishing Company
Old Post Road
Brookfield
Vermont 05036
USA

British Library Cataloguing in Publication Data
Principles and Practice in Business and
Management Research
  I. Wass, V. J.   II. Wells, Peter
  658.0072

Library of Congress Cataloging-in-Publication Data
Principles and practice in business and management research / edited
  by V.J. Wass, P.E. Wells.
      p.   cm.
    Includes index.
    ISBN 1-85521-438-5 : $57.95 (approx.). – ISBN 1-85521-450-4
  (pbk.) : $24.95 (approx.)
    1. Business–Research–Methodology. 2. Management Research-
  -Methodology.   I. Wass, V. J. (Victoria J.)   II. Wells, P. E.
  (Peter E.). 1959-
  HD30.4.P74   1994
  001.42'02465–dc20   94-19808
                                                                       CIP

ISBN 1 85521 438 5 (Hbk)   Printed and bound in Great Britain by
ISBN 1 85521 450 4 (Pbk)   Hartnolls Limited, Bodmin, Cornwall

Contents

v

PART 2   RESEARCH IN ORGANIZATIONS

PART 3   APPLIED RESEARCH

PART 4   WIDER ISSUES IN RESEARCH

Notes on Contributors

Malcolm Anderson is a Research Assistant at Cardiff Business School working in The Business History Unit. He is currently studying the professionalization of British Boards of Directors, 1893-1993, and the related area of the role of the professional accountant in business development.

Fiona Davies is a Research Assistant in the Marketing and Strategy Section of Cardiff Business School. Her current research is in the use of expert systems and neural networks in marketing. She is a co-author of *Computer Modelling and Expert Systems in Marketing*.

Rick Delbridge is a Research Associate at Cardiff Business School. He is a member of the Japanese Management Research Unit and the Centre for Automotive Industry Research. He is currently studying the effect of 'Japanese' manufacturing techniques at the shop floor level and the benchmarking of manufacturing performance.

Michael Healey is a Principal Lecturer at Coventry University. His current research interests include local economic development and local and regional economic information sources.

Ian Kirkpatrick is a Research Associate at Cardiff Business School. His current research interests lie in the field of organizational culture and professionals and management change in the public sector.

Martin Kitchener worked as an internal Management Consultant for a District Health Authority before taking up his present post as a Research Associate at Cardiff Business School. His current research interests include the management of change in the NHS and professional change in both the public and private sectors.

James Lowe is a Lecturer at Cardiff Business School and a member of the Japanese Management Research Unit and The Centre for Automotive Research. He is currently studying the role of the team leader/supervisor in manufacturing industry and benchmarking manufacturing performance.

Paul Nieuwenhuis is a Research Fellow in the Centre for Automotive Research at Cardiff Business School specializing in commercial vehicles and the environmental impact of motor vehicles. He had carried out research and consultancy projects for most of the world's vehicle producers and is co-author of *The Green Car Guide*.

Mike Rawlinson is a Research Fellow in the Centre for Automotive Research at Cardiff Business School. His research interests focus on the automotive components industry and also the introduction of new forms of manufacturing methods.

Paulo Rita, formally a research student at Cardiff Business School, is currently an Assistant Professor in marketing and information technology at the University of Lisbon, Portugal. His research interests include tourism marketing and in particular the role of expert systems and neural networks in assisting the marketing function. He is the co-author of two books on expert systems, *Conceptual Modelling and Expert Systems in Marketing* and *Expert Systems in Tourism Marketing*.

David Stiles is a Lecturer in Marketing and Strategy at Cardiff Business School having previously been a marketing manager for two Building Societies and a consultant for a Government Development Agency. He is currently researching strategy formation and implementation at University Business Schools in the UK and Canada.

Victoria Wass is a Research Associate at Cardiff Business School. An economist by training, she has a long standing interest in issues of labour mobility including redundancy, discrimination, informal care and housing tenure.

Peter Wells has a background in geography and planning and is currently a Research Fellow in the Centre for Automotive Research at Cardiff Business School. His research interests outside the automotive industry include disability and access and the role of contract researchers in universities.

Preface

This book started life as a conference organized by a group of experienced researchers at Cardiff Business School. The purpose was to establish a forum for the exchange of ideas and experiences from a growing number of researchers working on a variety of research projects within the broadly defined area of business and management. The majority of contributions were first presented at this conference

The growth in the population of researchers within Cardiff Business School, postgraduate students and contract research staff, reflects a national trend which has been accompanied by an increase in state intervention in the training of researchers. Arising initially from a concern over postgraduate completion rates, there is a renewed emphasis on equipping students and contract research staff with the skills and supervisory support to establish careers as researchers. The Economic and Social Research Council (ESRC) are at the forefront of promoting these objectives within social science institutions and *Research Training for the 1990s* (ESRC, 1989), recommends a training programme in research methodology which includes philosophical foundations and specific research techniques.

In this book we seek to address issues of research methodology in business and management at both a theoretical and practical level. The book is targeted towards postgraduate students and contract research staff in business and management. Business and management are research intensive subjects and research of high quality is underpinned by an appreciation of the philosophical foundation upon which it is based. More immediately, dissertations, research proposals and publications require an explanation and justification of the methods used to conduct the research. In providing examples of research methods in action, the book is intended as a practical complement to a standard methods text or as an input into a research methods course.

In our opinion, business and management do not offer a distinctive mode of explanation, rather they comprise the application and development of theoretical and empirical knowledge from established disciplines to business and management activity. In drawing from a number of intellectual sources, management research is multi-disciplinary, and often inter-disciplinary, in nature. Consequently, approaches to empirical research are wide-ranging. In addition, the subject area is broad and, uniquely among the social sciences, driven equally by both issues of 'discipline' and by the imperative of providing specific solutions to particular problems encountered within the real world of business and management. In attempting to understand issues which relate to the business and management process, existing theoretical and methodological sources may require development and refinement and the researcher is less able to draw upon an established bank of knowledge or expertise. The supervisor, and colleagues more generally, are unlikely to understand all the theoretical and methodological issues relating to a particular research project. Nevertheless, it became clear at the conference that, despite the breadth of the subject area and analytic frameworks, researchers were primarily concerned with generic issues relating to epistemology of the kind listed at the start of the introductory chapter.

The resolution of epistemological issues in practice are under-represented in the management literature, falling between theory and methodology texts, which are often discipline specific, and reports of empirical research. The consequence of this deficit in the literature is particularly acute given the multi-disciplinary nature of business and management research. In contrast to some traditional disciplines, economics for example, there is no single 'accepted' methodological perspective in business and management research. Rather, methodological perspective is the subject of choice. However, the failure of business and management research to address issues of epistemology undermines the ability of the researcher to make informed choices. This position is exacerbated by an emphasis on applied research, research which seeks to solve specific problems encountered in the business world, which tends to deny the importance of methodology.

In this book, we attempt to bring together the theory and practice of business and management research. In the introduction we provide a classification of research methodologies in terms of (i) philosophical assumptions regarding the nature and explanation of social action upon which they are premised and (ii) data collection and analysis techniques with which they are implemented. These themes are illustrated in the chapters which follow, each of which is an account of a research project in action. The chapters are representative of both the range and distribution of research in business and management. Thus, in each tail of the distribution of research methodologies, we have a single account of a highly quantitative approach which uses a nomethetic methodology and a highly qualitative approach with an ideographic methodology. The majority of business and management research is located between these extremes and uses a multi-method approach, normally in the context of a case study.

We are grateful to our contributors for preparing papers for the conference and subsequently revising them for publication in this book. The contributions themselves have been scrutinized widely by supervisors, examiners, colleagues and conference participants. Each contributor is indebted to colleagues who, on a cumulative basis, become too numerous to mention personally. As editors, we would like to acknowledge our discussions with Ian Kirkpatrick, Tom Keenoy and Mick Silver on the content of the introduction.

Victoria Wass
Peter Wells
1994

1 Research Methods in Action: An Introduction

VICTORIA WASS AND PETER WELLS

Introduction

This book is about the basic issues which all researchers face when seeking to explain social phenomena. A number of fundamental questions are addressed: What is research? What distinguishes academic research from other types? What is the research method (or methods) appropriate for the subject of research? How valid are the results? How are the phenomena explained in terms of cause and consequence? How far can pure academic considerations be compromised by those of practicality, for example, access to data, time and resources constraints? These recurrent themes underpin the contributions in this book, all of which arise out of actual research programmes in the business and management area. Although all the chapters are about specific research projects using specific methods, and as such are useful illustrations of methods in action, they also illustrate that clear-cut answers to the questions raised above are often not possible. There may be no one best way to explain a particular phenomenon. The chapters also illustrate how some aspects of the research process can be 'messy' and apparently unstructured, whatever the methodology used.

The questions raised above are perennial ones in social science research; they express social researchers' concern with the 'scientific' status of their work. Historically, social science has drawn heavily on the physical sciences to inform the objectives, methodologies and evaluation of research. This is reflected in the concern to establish hypotheses as 'laws', the focus on observable variables, and the control of bias in their measurement, and in replicability and generalizability as the main criteria of evaluation. More recently, there have been intense debates on the validity of such an approach in social science research. Thus, in establishing the scientific credibility of research, the question, 'how far can events be predicted on the basis of the research?' is countered with 'is prediction either possible or desirable?'.

It is not our intention as editors to take sides in fractious debates about the qualitative versus quantitative or positivist versus naturalist divides. Rather, we seek here to identify some of the major philosophical and practical themes running through the contributions and to reassure researchers that almost all programmes of work run into difficulties, of both a conceptual and practical nature. In short, all researchers, no matter how disparate the subject of enquiry, face common difficulties.

The common objective of research in social science is to explain social behaviour. It is the interpretation of explanation in this context, and how explanation can be gained through the study of the empirical world, that divides researchers. Opposing positions in this debate are characterized by alternative philosophical assumptions about the nature of human action (ontological assumptions) and about how this nature can be revealed through research (epistemological assumptions). A positivist research perspective is premised on a realist ontology in which actors respond as individuals to external stimuli. The stimuli and the response can be measured and observed objectively; that is observation is independent of subjective interpretation by either the actor or the researcher. Where empirical regularities in responses can be identified, they are seen as both necessary and sufficient for social scientific explanation. The naturalist perspective is based on a nominalist ontology, on the assumption that social reality does not exist outside the consciousness of the subject, and concludes that empirical regularities are meaningless because the external world is subject to individual interpretation. Therefore, empirical regularities are neither a necessary nor a sufficient condition for explanation. Indeed, a naturalist philosophy of science concludes that it is the individual's interpretation which is necessary and sufficient for social scientific explanation and that the purpose of research is to *understand* the process of interpretation for any given subject.

These competing positions in relation to the pursuit of knowledge represent extreme locations on a distribution of research perspectives; intermediate positions are occupied by perspectives which respect both the role of subjective interpretation and of objective measurement in the determination of social action. The precise location of any one research project within this distribution is determined by the relative dominance of either etic explanation (social behaviour is driven by external factors independently of subjective appreciation) or emic explanation (agency determines the reality of the stimulus which produces activity). The middle ground is occupied by perspectives where the independence of external institutions and incentives are recognized but where an individual's response to these external factors is mediated by his or her subjective interpretation of them. This allows for combining methodologies which, it is argued, can generate complementary data about the phenomenon under investigation (see Denzin, 1970; and Smith, 1975). This methodological pluralism has also been justified on the basis of triangulation which seeks to achieve the confirmation of results generated by one technique by those created by another (Denzin, 1970; and Fielding and Fielding, 1986). Reichardt and Cook (1979) argue for a dialectical synthesis through an accomodation between epistemological paradigms, that the differences between competing perspectives reveal different aspects about a phenomenon and thereby generate a more complete picture. In addition, through combining perspectives, weaknesses are minimized. For example, quantitative methods can be used to bolster the reliability and generalizability of naturalistic data (Lecompte and Goetz, 1982; and Herriot and Firestone, 1982).

However, the core philosophical assumptions which underlie positivism and naturalism are unique to each position and conflict with the other. This contradiction is raised by Guba (1985) and would appear to qualify the potential for integration and methodological pluralism:

[I] refute the contention that positivism and naturalism can be compromised in some form of postpositivistic 'grand synthesis' which realigns the basic beliefs of both systems into compatibility ... we *are* dealing with an either-or proposition, in which one must pledge allegiance to one paradigm or the other; there is no compromise (Guba, 1985, p. 80).

In addition, different methods produce data which are qualitatively different and cannot necessarily be triangulated to produce validation (Bloor, 1983).

In practice different disciplines, or school of thought within disciplines, adhere to a particular philosophical approach and set of rules associated with that approach. The results of research are 'accepted' within the context of a particular school of thought because they follow the rules of that school. In choosing to locate a study within a particular paradigm, the researcher is also choosing a philosophical position. This choice is often obscured because, once located within a particular school of thought, there is often no requirement to reflect critically upon the philosophical assumptions which underlie the particular school's mode of engagement. In contrast to traditional social science disciplines, business and management do not comprise a distinct school of thought but rather a distinct subject of study which is informed by theoretical and empirical knowledge from a diversity of academic sources. Hence, in choosing to research in business and management, the researcher is not also choosing a discipline and cannot take as given a particular ontological and epistemological framework. The researcher faces a second decision - on what basis to engage with the subject? The philosophical debate and its implications for research in practice, as it relates to business and management research, is discussed in more detail in the following section. First, however, we discuss the relationship between philosophical issues in relation to knowledge and methodology.

The research methodology is the instrument through which the research objectives are achieved. It represents more than a technique since it reflects the (usually unarticulated) ontological assumptions about the nature of human activity and epistemological assumptions about what constitutes valid knowledge about human activity:

methodology is not just a fancy name for 'methods of investigation' but a study of the relationship between theoretical concepts and warranted conclusions about the real world (Blaug, 1992, p. xii).

According to Rist,

> when we speak of 'qualitative' or 'quantitative' methodologies, we are in the final analysis speaking of an interrelated set of assumptions about the social world which are philosophical, ideological and epistemological. They encompass more than simply data collection techniques (Rist, 1977, p. 62).

Therefore, we seek to emphasize that the choice of research methodology is not a choice made independently of decisions about the theory of human behaviour or of the theory of the scientific study of human behaviour. Research methodology bridges the gap between higher philosophical ideas and the actual research findings.

In this introduction we do not intend to provide an all-embracing 'whirlwind' tour of different research perspectives, or indeed to provide a critique of those approaches. The research process can be daunting enough without our contributing to further to this debate.[1] Rather, the intention is to provide a framework to enable readers to place the subsequent chapters within a wider philosophical context. In doing this we seek to illustrate the importance of philosophical choices and thereby the necessity to make them explicit. Choice of research methodology should not be treated in isolation; in a coherent research programme ontology, epistemology, methodology, research techniques, and even the way in which the research will be presented (see Nieuwenhuis, Chapter 11), should be consistent both with each other and with the particular questions posed by the research. Our second purpose in the introduction is to explain the uncertainty and lack of uniform structure which characterizes research projects in business and management. The sequential model of the research process, whereby the researcher progresses from the literature review and formulating research questions to data collection and analysis on route towards revealing some new 'truth' about the world, is critically assessed in relation to the business and management research project. An overview of individual chapters is provided in the final section of the introduction to enable the reader interested only in a particular area within the subject of management to select the relevant accounts.

Research perspectives: epistemological conflicts in business and management research

The conventional academic motivation for research is a common concern to seek a greater understanding of social phenomena: to establish causal relationships which explain human action in response to external stimuli. Sometimes this is sought through some major conceptual or empirical contribution. More usually the understanding is incremental in character, building on existing knowledge and theories. Nonetheless, research usually involves innovation in some sense. This can take the form of applying existing theories or methods to new aspects of the social world, that is, new data may be tested against existing theories. Alternatively, confirmatory and meta-analysis seek to further understanding through the re-examination of existing data.[2] Too often researchers feel that it is necessary that a major intellectual or conceptual breakthrough is required of them to make the research substantive and innovative enough to merit degree awards. A cursory examination of the history of science would show that theory is often developed at the margins and, in any case, developments in theory are rarely the preserve of one individual.

Management research seeks to describe and explain 'the operation and control of organizations (public and private) in their environmental context' (ESRC, 1993a, p. 1) and is 'a multi-disciplinary area that draws on more established social science disciplines and enhances its relevance to the business community' (ESRC, 1993b, p. 8). Sources of theoretical and empirical knowledge derive mainly from sociology, psychology, economics, social anthropology, political science, mathematics and statistics and are adapted and combined in the context of management problems. One consequence of this diversity of sources is the wide range of research methodologies found under the general heading of business and management research: from the ideographic, e.g. ethnography, to the nomothetic, e.g. the sample survey. As stated above, the management researcher is not constrained by a narrow theoretical and epistemological heritage and as such is able to chose from a range of methodologies and associated data gathering techniques and even combine and adapt methodologies in a single research project to an extent impossible in more established subjects (see Hassard, 1991, for an example of multiple methodology management research). Indeed, it is evident from some of the chapters in this book that individual works will often embody techniques from a variety of research perspectives (see in particular the chapters in Part 2, Research in Organizations). However, philosophical disagreements are present both within and between these academic subjects and generate a constant tension within management research between the prescriptive and predictive qualities of positivism and the inductive and discovering nature of naturalism.

Research in business and management is essentially applied research which takes place in an academic environment and herein lies the source of a second tension. Applied research is driven more by practical and policy problems encountered by practicing managers than through the conventional academic process of theoretical and empirical abstraction. The research findings are targeted primarily towards practitioners whose interest is normally confined to the immediate and particular practical problem under investigation. Basic research, on the other hand, is generated from existing knowledge and is targeted primarily towards the academic world. Such research seeks to generalize beyond the particular and is characterized by critical reflection upon theoretical and empirical sources. The challenge to the business and management researcher is to achieve the objectives of both basic and applied research, 'to produce work that is not only of high academic quality but that is also relevant' (ESRC, 1993c, p. 8).

The sheer scope of possibilities regarding both subject and methodology in business and management research, when coupled with a weak intellectual grounding in the theory and practice of different research methodologies from which to make informed choices, can bewilder the inexperienced researcher. It is all to easy to launch into an empirical study without reflecting upon the philosophical assumptions which underlie the choice of research design and the implications these may have for the findings of the research, the interpretation of the findings and the evaluation of their scientific validity. With this in mind, the broad features of, and differences between, three broadly defined epistemological perspectives - positivism, realism and naturalism - which are relevant to management research are discussed below and summarized in Table 1.1.[3]

The components of these three epistemological perspectives are identified and used as a basis for characterizing and differentiating between them. For example, realism is distinguished from positivism at the philosophical level by the degree to which human response to external stimuli is influenced by subjective perception of those stimuli. At the practical level, sample surveys, using a structured schedule of questions, the answers to which are subject to statistical analysis, distinguish positivist and realist perspectives from those adopting a naturalist epistemological perspective. Most research in the management field tends to draw from more than one ontological or epistemological school, in a more or less successful form of eclecticism, although normally one philosophical perspective is dominant.

Outline of three epistemological perspectives

Positivism is a philosophical position in relation to the pursuit of knowledge which draws from the role model of knowledge creation developed in the natural sciences. The important, or most widely accepted, components of a research methodology underpinned by positivist assumptions are outlined in Table 1.1 and discussed more fully below. A variety of research methodologies purport to be underpinned by a positivist view of social science research but the common foundation for this allegiance is of 'social science as methodologically equivalent to the natural sciences', (Runciman, 1969). The logic of the scientific experiment forms the blueprint for positivist social science research.

The scientific experiment follows a structured circuit whereby an hypothesis about a specific causal relationship between a theoretically dependent object (subject) and a set of theoretically independent objects is deduced from abstract theoretical concepts.[4] Expressing this hypothesis as a researchable proposition (operationalization) requires that the

Table 1.1

A distribution of research perspectives in business and management research

Epistemological perspective	Ontological assumptions	Epistemological assumptions	Scientific objective	Nature of scientific knowledge	Cycle of enquiry	Methodology	Type of data	Techniques for data collection	Bias
Positivism	etic 'realist', real world exists independently of subjective consciousness, this latter is irrelevant to explanation; enquiry can converge on reality	(i) phenomenalism: only that which is objectively observable is valid knowledge (ii) empiricism: explanation comprises of causal laws inferred from empirical regularities; subjects subservient to definition of knowledge, subjective consciousness is meaningless	nomothetic with natural science; abstract from subjective ideosyncracies to uncover general laws; replicability generalizability	privileged, impersonal, value-free, exact, precise, causal, rational, determinate, general	deductive: abstract theories → operational hypotheses → observations ↵ inference using statistical tests 'predictive'	nomethetic e.g. census or sample survey, quasi-experiment, operationalism; outsider looking in: extensive and general	quantitative, systematic and precise; directly observable and measurable	self-completion questionnaire, structured interviews, simulation, use of secondary data	concern to account for measurement error and missing data; use of statistical controls
Realism	real world exists independently of subjective consciousness but experience of the real world is through subjective consciousness	(i) knowledge includes the observable and the intangible (ii) general laws are not deterministic, they only partially explain human action; equally subjective interpretations are partially explained by the external world; human action open to various interpretations; possibility of indeterminates	inclusion of subjective in traditional model of science to uncover general laws and how these are interpreted by subjects; laws are tendancies i.e. not deterministic; often applied research, practioner driven	personal, value-bound, multi-causal, plausible, indeterminate, particular	'retroductive': iterative cycle observation ↕ theory	methodological pluralism, triangulation, interactive, participatory, action research; method determined by subject of research	all data which are relevant to subject; quantitative and qualitative, observable and interpretive	complete tool kit of techniques often in context of a case study	methods are combined with a view to compensate for weaknesses in a single method
Naturalism (naive)	emic 'idealist', real world does not exist outside consciousness of the individual, hence multiple conceptions of reality and enquiry cannot converge on a single reality	(i) phenomenalism: valid knowledge comprises individual comprehension of the 'external' world (ii) empiricism: explanation comprises of causal laws inferred from actors subjective perceptions of their social world; definition of knowledge is determined by the subject; generalization beyond context is meaningless	from hermeneutics to uncover and explain individual conceptualization and internalization of external factors; internal validity, ecological validity	personal, interested, value-bound, uncertain, non-rational, indeterminate, particular	inductive: theory grounded in empirical world observation → reflection → construction of abstract concepts 'descriptive' explanations	idographic e.g. ethnography; insider seeking 'verstehen' with subjects	qualitative, intangible, subjective conceptions and interpretations of actors; intensive and contextual, detailed, penetrating, 'processual'; written texts	participant observation, unstructured interviews, textual analysis	concern to account for reactivity and reflexivity in data; use of reactive and reflective accounts

variation in both the subject and the objects are observable and measurable. The response of the subject to a measured manipulation of one of the independent explanatory objects is observed and recorded.[5] The results are compared with the hypothesis and the theoretical concepts on which the experiment was premised and are either refuted or verified.[6] In the former case, the theory would be reconsidered. The validity of the results are evaluated on the basis of whether or not they could and would be replicated in identical circumstances, replication implies independence from subjective bias, and whether they are generalizable to a wider population. Evaluation generally comprises of a test of whether the difference between the empirical result and the result expected under the null, or negative, hypothesis is over and above that due to sampling error. When the empirical work comprises of values taken from a sample and not a population then, even where the sample is chosen by random selection, it is possible to draw a sample whose characteristics are different from the population from which it is drawn. In order to infer that the result is generated by a real relationship and not a chance occurrence in the chosen sample, i.e., it is *statistically significant* (at a given level), the potential for sampling error must be ruled out. The tests employed to achieve this are the subject of well defined statistical methods (see Silver, 1992). Generalization from a sample to a population is the key and distinctive objective of positivist methods. It is achieved through random selection and through discounting sampling error. Acceptance of the monism of social science research and the scientific experiment is predicated on assumptions about the nature of social action and upon the assumptions about what constitutes valid knowledge about social action. In respect of the first, the existence of a physical and social environment which is independent of subjective consciousness is assumed. Humans respond to an external stimulus like inanimate objects; the external environment is not open to subjective interpretation. A second set of assumptions define what constitutes valid data and what constitutes explanation. Knowledge about human behaviour is confined to activities which are observable because they are measurable. Observation is accorded a central role in the generation of knowledge; theory is rejected or not on the basis of observation. Observation is assumed to be objective. Such objectivity is achieved through its independence from theory, its independence from the presence and subjectivity of the researcher and from subjective interpretation on the part of the actor. Objects of study which cannot be verified through measurable observation are not meaningful for scientific purposes and thus not legitimate subjects for scientific enquiry. Therefore, only situations where social action is observably independent of subjective interpretation are amenable to social research and thus ultimately knowable. Explanation emerges from establishing empirical regularities in the data, in the context of the experiment, a constant conjunction of events. Explanation supported by observation becomes a covering law which can be generalized to predict outcomes outside the specific conditions of the particular experiment.

It is a matter of regret to the positivist that social phenomena are not amenable to investigation using the scientific experiment. There are two main objections to the experiment, both of which have been incorporated into an alternative methodology which nevertheless maintains the logic of the scientific experiment. In the first instance, social behaviour occurs in a social environment and, even where it is possible to observe actors in a laboratory setting, removal from their natural environment will distort their behaviour. What is observed in the artificial environment of the laboratory will be untypical of behaviour in its natural context - the data will lack ecological validity. However, additional difficulties arise when the experiment is taken out into the field. Although the results gain in terms of ecological validity, internal validity is compromised. In a complex social setting, the subject of enquiry will be influenced by many stimuli simultaneously. Outside the laboratory, the independent variables cannot be controlled and manipulated in order to observe their independent effects. Observing the response of the subject to the stimulus and attributing causality to it is invalid because the response may include the effects of the other stimuli. Social scientists have developed techniques to facilitate the application of the experimental methodology to the social setting through the replacement of physical controls with statistical controls. The equivalent of physical control is achieved through multivariate statistical techniques which 'partial out' (in effect hold constant) the effects of 'intervening' variables thus revealing the independent individual effect of the object of interest. However, inconsistencies between the research methodology and the social behaviour being studied which are not solved by multivariate techniques remain and generate bias. The sources of bias reflect the nature of the relationships under study and the inability of a research methodology premised on the scientific experiment to capture this relationship. However, this bias has been interpreted in statistical terms and has given rise to a battery of sophisticated statistical techniques which seek to identify and counter it. For example, multicollinearity is a statistical problem which expresses the inability of an econometric model to handle relationships where the explanatory variables are related to each other as well as the dependent variable although the presence of multicollinearity in fact reflects interdependencies in the social relationships under investigation.

Having more or less successfully adapted the experiment to the field setting, a second objection concerns the use of the experiment itself. There are many situations where an experiment is either impossible or undesirable and where alternative methods of data collection, such as a census or sample survey, which do not require prior assignment to control and response groups, are more appropriate. However, such techniques introduce additional sources of bias including non-response and response error. This latter is of particular significance because of the retrospective nature of survey data. Unlike the experiment, variation is normally observed retrospectively, rather than contemporaneously, and the information recorded by respondents may be affected by 'post hoc' rationalization.

In summary, positivism is a philosophical position which draws from the role model of the scientific experiment. The objective of research is to identify 'laws' which characterize individual behaviour. Knowledge is extended through logical deduction and objective observation and measurement. Data are quantitative and are normally collected from sample populations of the social phenomena under investigation. Hypotheses are tested against data using statistical techniques. Statistical controls replace the physical controls of the experiment in the pursuit of precisely measured objective and unbiased data. Controlling sources of bias impinges upon the principle of falsification (see note 6) since an hypothesis cannot be falsified unless the evidence on which it is to be judged is free from bias. When data are missing or when data do not accord with theoretical concepts, then a result which does not support an hypothesis could have been generated by bias and is not necessarily an indication of contradictory evidence. Wass (Chapter 4) provides an example of aggregate quantitative methods where the main concern is to eliminate sources of statistical bias which would limit the explanatory power of the model against the data.

Naturalism is an anti-positivist position predicated on a set of alternative 'idealist' prior assumptions about the study of social reality, in particular the denial of the independence of the social world from subjective interpretation. As with the positivist perspective of social science research, dissatisfaction with the scientific experiment forms the benchmark for the development of alternative methodologies. However, here the disagreement is a more fundamental one. The entire logic of the scientific experiment is rejected as a model with which to conduct social research. Instead, a hermeneutic view about what constitutes knowledge (data and explanation) is adopted in which data are defined as subjects' comprehension of their social world and explanation is defined as the interpretative understanding of the causes of action on the part of the subject. Weber (1947) distinguishes this form of 'explanatory' understanding, when the motivation and reasoning behind the action of the subject is uncovered, from 'observational' understanding which characterizes positivist explanation.

Again a variety of research methodologies claim to be based on the philosophical assumptions of naturalism, the most fundamental of which is the centrality of the actor's interpretation in explanation. Consequently, naturalistic research displays a commitment to describing and explaining behaviour from the subject's point of view or 'seeing through the eyes of the people you are studying', Bryman (1988, p. 61). The priority given to the subject in the study of the subject's behaviour is such that the subject determines what constitutes knowledge; the subjects' determination of reality is treated as 'objective' data. The objective of empirical research is to uncover the subjects' conceptualization and interpretation of their social environment. This position is in direct opposition to that of positivism where prior epistemological assumptions and objectives determine what is knowable about a subject. Some of the implications of this dichotomy in approach, in terms of the role of data, the type of data, methodology and data gathering techniques are outlined below.

The over-riding significance of the subject in explanation precludes the specification of hypotheses prior to research. Ideally, research is conducted inductively whereby abstract theoretical constructs are formulated at the end of, and on the basis of, the field work. Theory is 'grounded' in the empirical world in order that it reflects actors' own perceptions and not the prior constructs of the academic world (Glaser and Strauss, 1967). Additionally, and unlike deductive methodologies, inductive research is open to new and unanticipated forms of response (ibid).

Alongside the naturalists objection to the imposition of a priori theoretical constraints on observation, is a concern to minimize the impact of data collection on the behaviour of the subject. Hence, unstructured techniques which are sensitive towards and flexible to the response of the subject are used in preference to the experiment and quasi-experiment characteristic of positivist research.

The context of actions are of critical importance in the understanding of actions and the objective of enquiry is to capture the 'holism' of the action. As such, description is accorded a significant role in data and explanation. Going beyond what positivists understand by description, detailed accounts of subjects, their environment and their behaviour which, as far as possible, are consistent with the perceptions of the participants are synonymous with explanation. In contrast to information generated from an experimental or survey methodology, data about the perceptions and interpretations of actors in a particular context are qualitative and most appropriately collected using unstructured techniques such as participant observation or unstructured interviews. In addition, since the social world is experienced by the subject as an ongoing process, a subject's response is not a discrete action but rather a continuing process, and the data must capture this longitudinal element. Consequently, closeness to the social world of the subject and attention to detail characterize the research methodology.

Ideographic methodology is premised on emic explanation of human behaviour and therefore its research objective is to uncover the process of interpretation and consequent action at the level of individual meaning. We have seen that this objective precludes the use of the experiment or methodologies based on the experiment. As a result, the criteria by which research findings are evaluated are different from those of the experiment. Greater priority is accorded to ecological validity: the closeness of the data to the behaviour of the subject, and internal validity: the identification of the correct cause and effect.

Does the rejection of the experiment imply that naturalism is not scientific? In its broadest sense, science is defined as the ascertainment of knowledge through observation. How valid a set of research findings, in terms of their scientific credibility, depend upon how they measure up to what is assumed to constitute knowledge. Thus, a positivist perspective, premised on an etic view of the world and the logic of the experiment as an appropriate means of revealing this view, evaluates the scientific validity of research findings on the basis of their replicability and generalizability to wider populations. On the basis of an opposing naturalist view about the nature of human behaviour and how to reveal it, research findings generated from a naturalist methodology are evaluated on the basis of their ecological and internal validity. Validity in these terms implies generalizability through grounded theory. The construction of abstract concepts from close contextual observation of the empirical world enables generalization through theoretical abstraction from the specific social context to other similar contexts (Mitchell, 1983). Hence, a naturalist epistemology posits not merely an alternative methodology but also a qualitatively different conception of what constitutes scientific knowledge and, therefore, science itself.

Both research perspectives are concerned to account for distortions in the gathering, analysis and interpretation of data through the application of rigour in their work and thereby achieve scientific validity. Though, given different interpretations of science, the sources of potential distortion are accorded different priorities. For positivism, these distortions generate bias and invalidate the results. The objective of the research methodology is to eliminate sources of bias in order to uncover the 'truth'. The sources of bias which are of primary concern here are those of measurement error in variables and missing information. Some of the techniques available to minimize and manage bias are described by

Wass in Chapter 4 of this book. For the naturalist, 'bias' is a natural feature of the phenomenon under investigation. Rather than seeking to purge 'bias' from the data, the researcher seeks to recognize and reflect upon the effect of the researcher on the behaviour of the subject (reactivity) and the ability of the researcher to 'see through the eyes of the subject' and thereby uncover the subject's true perceptions. Delbridge and Kirkpatrick (Chapter 2) discuss the problems of reflexivity and reactivity in participant observation.

Realism seeks to reconcile the realist (etic) and idealist (emic) understanding of human action: recognizing the existence of an external reality, its subjective interpretation and the role of human agency in affecting the external social world. The above accounts presented highly stylized 'stereotypical' interpretations of the two extreme positions in relation to the definition of and pursuit of understanding human behaviour. In practice, most research projects draw on a mix of positivist and naturalist epistemologies and methods. For example, even in the quantitative project reported in Chapter 4, Wass, in seeking to explain the labour market behaviour of redundant miners, attempts to account for their subjective interpretation of their future job prospects. In a similar fashion, case studies will often be compared with other case studies or other members of the sample (defined in terms of a cluster of key characteristics) in order to assess the representativeness of the findings to the wider population.

If synthesis between apparently opposing philosophical paradigms is occurring in practice, and if, as Giddens (1984) argues, there is an underlying relationship between methodology and epistemology, then some sort of reconciliation at the philosophical level is required.[7] A realist interpretation of science may offer this possibility.

In terms of the distribution of research perspectives devised in Table 1.1, every research project reported in this book can be classified as realist since none subscribe either to the crude positive or naturalist positions. That is, each recognizes the role of both etic and emic explanation to a greater or lesser degree. However, this classification reflects a broadness in the definition of philosophical realism adopted here rather than a commonality of philosophical choices. Many philosophical positions are compatible within the realist definition of science and therefore it is necessary to distinguish between positions across the distribution according to whether they approach a central position from, or diverge from it towards, either positivist or naturalist extremes.

Realism, from a positivist perspective, is able to integrate etic explanation with a degree of subjective interpretation. The real world comprises tangible objects which exist independently and prior to subjective comprehension of them. However, the possibility of subjective interpretation of the real world and the impact of meaningful interpretation on action are recognized. As a result, the inevitability and certainty of human responses are rejected in favour of responses mediated by subjective interpretation. Under these assumptions, causal laws are no longer deterministic of action but rather become 'tendencies' which influence action. Although positive realism recognizes the role of interpretation, the scientific objective is merely to control for it along with other intervening variables. Subjective interpretation is treated as a competing hypothesis in the explanation of a particular activity which, in order to achieve internal validity, must be ruled out through statistical control. Where necessary, qualitative research techniques are incorporated into the research design in order to achieve this. Nevertheless, the purpose is to account for the impact of subjective factors on behaviour and not to understand the process by which that impact occurs.

A naturalistic interpretation of realism, 'critical realism', has philosophical roots in transcendental realism (Lovering, 1990) and, as might be expected, emphasizes the subjects' experience of the external world in explaining activity. However, unlike naturalism, it recognizes the partial independence of the external world from subjective comprehension. Hence, there is an acceptance of the idea of general covering laws but a rejection of their identification in practice because general laws are seen as contextual. The importance of subjective mediation of events and structures renders identification of general laws meaningless. Instead, the objective of the social science project is to demonstrate explanatory mechanisms which link a diverse empirical reality via an intervening contextual layer, which is time and space specific, to deeper social structures. It is the intersection of the external and subjective which lie at the centre of analysis. Since, the particular configuration of structures cannot be determined a priori, ideographic techniques predominate in the research design.

The coexistence between positivist and naturalist philosophical beliefs, which implicitly underlies the above realist accounts, is predicated on an alternative definition of science: a view which reinterprets laws as tendencies which are context specific; that is they are subject to 'restricted determinism' in determining social action (Kaplan 1964, p. 122). In this way the role of meaningful interpretation is preserved alongside recognition of the role of causal mechanisms.

Of course, if one believes in a divorce between methodology and epistemology, then reconciling epistemological conflicts is not necessary before combining techniques. This view is often expressed in the form that the research design should be determined by the research problem itself, 'the problem under investigation properly dictates the methods of investigation' (Trow, 1957, p. 37). This is particularly relevant to applied research where the connection between empirical research and a particular discipline or paradigm is less evident. The choice of research design then becomes a technical decision whereby the strengths and weakness of various techniques, in relation to the research problem, are optimally combined (see Hakim, 1989). Bryman (1988), although not directly concurring with this view, observes that in practice researchers do not formulate a view of the philosophical assumptions which underlie their research proposal in advance of choosing the techniques with which to carry it out. He concludes that they are not therefore basing their decision on epistemological and ontological choices. In contrast to this, we would argue that although not explicitly stated, and probably not consciously thought out, research questions and methodological choices are predetermined by an implicit commitment to a particular view of science on the part of the researcher, the supervisor and the intellectual discipline from which the research derives. Eilon (1974, quoted in Gill and Johnson (1991), p. 9) uses the words 'habit' and 'conviction' as opposed to conscious and reason to describe the choice of research methodology. Table 1.1 suggests that research techniques are not autonomous neutral devices for generating knowledge, rather they come as part and parcel of a wider philosophical package. Therefore, we would seek to encourage the researcher to be sensitive about the philosophical assumptions which underpin a research project and the implications they may have for the findings and conclusions of the enquiry. While we remain open minded to the philosophical question of what constitutes knowledge, we argue that it is incumbent on the researcher to acknowledge explicitly the philosophical choices associated with the choice and combination of method and to ensure, at the very least, consistency between techniques in pursuit of the research objectives. After all, the 'synthesis' achieved through realism's redefinition of science makes it possible to justify a research design drawing from more than one philosophical paradigm.

We have already noted that management draws on a range of social science disciplines. The theoretical and epistemological eclecticism that this implies has lead to a trend towards methodological and technical pluralism in management research (see for example, Burrell and Morgan, 1979; and Hassard, 1991). The use of a mixed method research design, while offering the opportunity to combine the strengths of different methods and limit the weaknesses, may run into problems where different elements of the process do not fit together comfortably. This will occur where different elements of the research process derive from opposing epistemologies. Whereas, different research methods may reveal different aspects of a phenomenon, and this constitutes a major strength if the research objective is to gain a comprehensive picture, the findings may not be consistent with each other. For example, consider a study which uses a naturalistic research methodology to develop research hypotheses and then adopts a survey methodology to test these hypotheses. If positivist methods reject the hypotheses, how are the results to be interpreted? In terms of the methodology by which they were generated, the hypotheses are valid. In terms of an alternative methodology which is used to test the results, they are invalid. This is a problem which multi-method research fails to address. Neither do we offer a solution other than to suggest that results generated by multi-method research require an interpretation which is sensitive to their particular underlying views of science.

Despite embracing a range of research perspectives which largely reject the scientific experiment as an appropriate methodology for social science research, the management research project is nevertheless conceptualized on the basis of the scientific experiment. It therefore comes as no surprise that the actual practice of carrying out a research proposal in social science is less orderly and predictable than in natural science. In the next section, we discuss some of the difficulties the management researcher is likely to encounter.

The research process

The sequential model

We begin this section with the idealized model of the research process. In Figure 1.1, the research process is characterized by a logical six-stage sequence derived from various 'how to do research' text books (see for example, Rummel and Ballaine, 1963; Bell, 1987; and Howard and Sharp, 1983). Before discussing the limitation of this model of research, the six stages identified in Figure 1.1 are outlined.

Stage 1	Pre-research reading
Stage 2	Formulation of research questions
Stage 3	Choice of methodology
Stage 4	Fieldwork
Stage 5	Data analysis
Stage 6	Writing up of results

Figure 1.1   Stages in the research process

Stage 1. The first stage comprises reading and reflection on the subject in general and on specific theories which might be deployed to explain social phenomena for the case under consideration. The researcher here is expected to get to know the literature, to be informed of the work of peers, and thus to locate his or her own efforts within a wider academic tradition.

Stage 2. Having become immersed in the subject and contemporary interpretations on how that subject can be revealed and explained, the researcher is expected to formulate specific research questions or hypotheses which will form the basis of subsequent empirical investigations.

Stage 3. A period is then spent deciding how those questions might be addressed. The issue is to decide how the social phenomena under consideration are to be measured and analysed in a way which is both rigorous and useful. This is often a critical stage in that the methodology adopted must be capable of addressing the sort of questions raised in Stage 2.

Stage 4. The researcher may then proceed to actual fieldwork. In a long research programme, of the kind often associated with a traditional Ph.D, it may be possible to undertake a pilot study or trial to test the practicality of the research method chosen. For those working on a more compressed time scale, this may be something of a luxury and any problems which emerge will have to be tackled as the research progresses. It is at this stage that most of the primary data (i.e. original data created by the researcher) are actually defined and collected.

Stage 5. After the data gathering period, the researcher then has to reflect upon and analyse that data. The information gathered may have to be sifted, with some simply discarded as inappropriate. Frequently there is a need to manipulate the data in some way, perhaps to eliminate unwanted bias or to show certain relationships between variables.

Stage 6. Finally the research needs to be written up. Some form of printed document is still by far the most usual expected output from a research programme, and for many researchers this is the most difficult stage of all.

While there are clear procedural advantages in thinking of research in terms of discrete sequential stages, the actual experience of researchers is often quite different. The linear process depicted in Figure 1.1 is not inevitable, even where a nomothetic methodology is adopted, but especially where the research is ideographic in nature. For example, within the positivist perspective, this model is inappropriate for confirmatory analysis, meta-analysis and mathematical models research which do not use primary data. Within the naturalist perspective, the research questions are formulated during, rather than prior to, fieldwork and data analysis. The response is not necessarily to devise a more appropriate linear model as we make clear below.

Frequently those just embarking on research feel that discrete stages are completed in order and, when a research project does not follow such a tidy pattern, researchers may feel discouraged. This is a clear danger ignored by textbooks which advocate a highly disciplined and 'step-by-step' approach. Equally, researchers' own reports of their work often follow the stages outlined above even though in practice the compartmentalization of activities which follow a logical temporal pattern may not have occurred. The feedback process whereby hypotheses are amended on the basis of the findings, or further data collection is found to be necessary, are not always reported. This process of 'sanitizing' and structuring the final report may well be responsible for the continued use of the rational sequential research model in management research. Our experience suggests that stages 1 through 6 take place 'in parallel', regardless of the research perspective adopted. For example, research questions may exist prior to any reading but their development may be informed by the literature, research questions may arise in the process of the fieldwork or analysis, and may require an adaptation of methodology, and reading should continue throughout the duration of the study. Despite our efforts as editors, the chapters of this book also do not report all the adaptations, blind alleys and negative findings encountered in the research.

Each of the six stages of research identified above contain potential problems, not least as a result of the artificial division into separate stages. In Stage 1, there may not be a suitable body of work for the researcher to build upon, especially if the subject of research is particularly new or ignored in the literature. Certain contributions from other literatures may be relevant, but the researcher has to interpret those contributions in the light of his or her own theoretical perspective and in relation to the phenomena under investigation. Moreover, if there is a literature outside the area currently understood by the researcher, then finding it may not be a simple process. Thus, the more innovative the research, the more difficult it is to locate that research in a wider academic tradition. Equally, importing concepts and traditions from outside the mainstream of the literature also increases the likelihood of the work being rejected by established academics who may not recognize the validity of the literature to the subject in question. Consequently, where the researcher is working wholly within an established field, the advice to build on existing work may lead to more incremental and 'safer' research. Such research may be less interesting and innovative in terms of ideas.

In Stage 2, it is supposed that research questions arise out of reflection on the literature, usually guided by the research supervisor. There is no guarantee that appropriate questions will emerge or that specific testable hypotheses will be generated and, for research adopting an ideographic methodology, it is not even the case that such questions should be asked in advance of the empirical part of the work. Interesting and useful research questions arise in the course of the fieldwork.

Stage 3 represents the methodology stage. The implicit assumption of the sequential model is that particular methods or techniques may be taken 'off the shelf' as tools to do a particular job. Yet the ways in which we seek to observe the social world are themselves a product of prior judgements regarding the nature of the social world and the nature of researching it (Burrell and Morgan, 1979). As such, methodologies cannot simply be regarded as neutral or value-free means of measurement. It was argued in the previous section that researchers have to understand the epistemological foundations of the methodologies they employ: the essential point being that methodologies must be appropriate both in terms of theoretical positions and the subject under investigation. Two key features should be emphasized here: first, the choice of methodology will influence the character of the findings and, secondly, there are limits to the extent to which diverse methodologies may be integrated within one research project because the epistemological foundations of different methodologies may conflict. This is not to advocate a slavish adherence to a specific pre-determined method and an unwillingness to innovate, but rather a choice of research method (or methods) which take in account its philosophical foundations and practical implications.

In Stage 4, the actual fieldwork is carried out. For many projects, data gathering may well be an ongoing process. Indeed, the research may actually be instigated because of the identification of a piece of information during fieldwork which sheds new light on the subject. We would argue that business and management research will often involve a process of simultaneous developments in which theory, method and actual fieldwork progress iteratively rather than in sequence. The gathering of data will often merge with the analysis stage.

This divergence between the sequential logic of the research process and the typical irregularity of practical research can leave the researcher concerned at having to change from their structured research plan as they encounter practical difficulties. The researcher feels that it reflects badly upon the research: in effect amounting to a failure to conduct the earlier stages properly. Again, we would seek to alter this impression, and encourage researchers to be more prepared to be flexible in the course of their work. If one approach fails to yield enough answers then it may or may not be appropriate to consider another. In any event, the researcher must reflect upon, and provide an explanation for, why the method failed to achieve the desired result. Even a negative finding can be said to add to the fund of knowledge on a subject.

Stage 5 is also unrealistic in that it assumes that the desired answers will emerge in an unproblematic manner from a contemplation of the data. Even when using the hypothetico-deductive approach whereby information requirements are determined at Stage 2, data may not accord precisely with theoretical concepts, thus posing problems for its analysis. From a naturalist perspective, the precise specification of data requirements in advance of collection leads to research which is too narrow. In effect researchers will only see what they want to see and actually miss a vital part of the phenomena they are investigating. The choice about which data to collect, and in what form, can only be made incrementally as the project progresses.

As was suggested above, Stage 6 can often represent the most difficult stage of the research. At the writing stage the implicit conflicts have to be faced and the choice of methodologies made have to be justified. Researchers who have started with unrealistic expectations, for example that the research would progress in fairly uncomplicated stages, feel obliged to fit their findings into a pre-determined structured account: to disguise the apparently chaotic and unstructured nature of their explorations.

An important factor in choice of research method, and one which is often overlooked, is the target audience. As Nieuwenhuis argues (Chapter 11) the actual output expected of the research greatly influences the sort of research undertaken. Most chapters report academic research for a Ph.D which has an initial target audience of three academics - the supervisor and two examiners. The nature of the information required and methodologies are in general well known, as is the style of presentation. However, if the 'research training' approach is to be followed, then researchers need to be prepared to meet different requirements, if only because the time and attention that can be devoted to an academic Ph.D can rarely be repeated later in an individuals' career. Universities, and in particular business schools, face increasing demands for 'wider relevance' (ESRC, 1993a, p. 4) and Ph.D theses and academic journals are not major mechanisms for disseminating business and management research to the practitioner community. The contribution from Nieuwenhuis reflects the increasing importance of more customer/practitioner orientated research in business schools. This type of research demands both rigour and an ability to produce results quickly. The information demands are quite different from those associated with academic research and the style of presentation very distinctive.

Thus, we would argue that research projects rarely move as smoothly and sequentially as the idealized model of research would suggest. The diversity of research practices and subjects evident in the management field, reflecting deep-seated differences of opinion on explanation of social phenomena, makes the description of a generalized model of research an exercise of only limited application.

Research methodologies in practice

The chapters in this book are all illustrative of actual cases of research, except for the last two (Nieuwenhuis, Chapter 11; and Wells, Chapter 12). In these two chapters, wider themes are explored by researchers with several years of research experience. The book is divided into four parts, in which contributions are grouped under common themes:

Part 1. Managing bias in three research methodologies
Part 2. Research in organizations
Part 3. Applied research
Part 4. Wider issues in research

However, the classification is not a definitive one. All the chapters deal with bias to some degree and two of the chapters grouped under organizational research are also examples of applied research. The themes contained in each of these parts are discussed in turn below.

Part 1   Managing bias in three research methodologies

Research methodologies are concerned to eliminate or otherwise account for possible sources of distortion in data since the presence of such are seen as undermining the validity and generalizability of the research. This concern is reflected in three chapters which each use a very different methodology.

The three contributions show that the concern to identify and account for sources of distortion cut across epistemological boundaries. However, key differences emerge in the importance accorded to different sources of distortion. For those working with a nomothetic methodology, bias is understood as any systematic influence on the recorded response where that influence is thought to be unrepresentative of a more general condition. That is, the data themselves are biased. Equally, responses which do not correspond to the research questions, however accurately they are recorded, contain bias. The concern is to eliminate or control for sources of statistical bias. For those adopting an ideographic framework, it is neither possible nor desirable to eliminate distortions from the data.

Instead researchers are concerned to recognize and describe conceptual, cultural, and social bias within the individual researcher when recording and interpreting the data.

In Chapter 4, Wass seeks to establish the reliability of data on redundant miners derived from structured postal questionnaires. A variety of statistical techniques are used to control potential bias in the data collected which might limit its generalizability to other groups of workers. For Anderson (Chapter 3), the main source of bias is the partial nature of the information which remains intact after many years. In this case, the data refer to accounting and other corporate records and the problem, in terms of the robustness of the methodology, is that the bias in the data is essentially unknown. Where a more interactive research methodology is adopted, such as participant observation, the reflexivity of the researcher is the most important source of bias. Chapter 2 (Delbridge and Kirkpatrick), illustrates a view of research which embraces the unique and unrepresentative. The challenge to the researchers here is to recognize and account for their own bias in collecting and interpreting the data.

An important conclusion raised by these contributions is that academic research is not necessarily negated by bias. Rather, the researcher must demonstrate awareness of the sources of bias and where possible attempt to reduce the extent of bias and account for the impact of remaining bias on the research findings.

Part 2 Research in organizations

It is often the case in business and management research that organizations are the subject of research. In practice, much research on organizations combines both aggregate methodologies of the type used in the Aston Studies (Pugh and Hickson, 1976), with detailed intensive case study work, e.g. Pettigrew and Whipp (1991). Three case studies are presented in Chapters 6, 7 and 8. Initially in Chapter 5, however, the use of interviews in organizational research is discussed with reference to a number of research projects. Here Healey and Rawlinson compares structured and unstructured interview techniques in terms of their merits and weaknesses in particular settings and within particular research methodologies. The interview is a means of collecting data within organizations which is normally associated with a realist research perspective although, as a result of its flexibility, it is compatible with nomothetic and ideographic methodologies. Specifically, the level of structure in an interview and the sample size increase in line with the importance attached to the objective of population generalizability. Typically structured interviews are used when intermediate sample sizes are selected, say between 10 and 30 cases; larger sample sizes are more likely to be approached with a self-completion questionnaire. Structured data facilitate the comparison of responses over the sample and can be used to reveal aggregate relationships. Unstructured interviews are used as a technique within an ideographic methodological framework where internal validity is a priority. Reflecting realist foundations, the interview is often used as part of a multi-method research design: maybe to validate earlier postal questionnaires, or explore in more depth some of the main themes which have emerged from the postal questionnaire. Alternatively, but again within a quantitative framework, interviews may be used as an aid to drafting a questionnaire in order to identify relevant topics. They are also an important technique for collecting qualitative data as a supplement to, or an alternative to, participant observation. Bias, in the form of population representativeness - selection of organization and selection of individuals within the organization - and reflexivity on the part of the interviewer, are also relevant considerations.

The subject of research in Chapter 6 is corporate culture where the problematic definition and measurement of the subject has implications for the methodology. Stiles combines some unusual techniques which seek to reveal and subsequently measure employees subjective perception of their workplace. Although the study comprises an intensive investigation of strategic change in two business schools, the nature of the approach is relatively quantitative; perceptions are described by ranked sets of personal values.

In Chapter 7, Lowe reports the investigation of one organization, a car plant. In comparing the jobs of supervisors under mass production and lean production techniques, a variety of very different research techniques (and by implication methodologies) are employed to investigate different aspects of the research problem. Questionnaires and structured interviews are used in a benchmarking exercise to assess how far the production process has progressed towards the lean production model. This provides the context from which to assess the changing role of supervisors within the plant. Unstructured interviews and participant observation are used to acquire information on the role played by supervisors under this new regime.

The case study reported in Chapter 8 (Kitchener) takes place in a hospital which is undergoing change in the context of internal markets in the NHS. As a result of competition within the market place of the NHS, hospitals are looking to the ideas and techniques of marketing to achieve competitive advantage. Structured and unstructured interviews are used to observe and explain the response of two hospitals, in terms of implementing marketing strategies, to this new commercial environment.

Part 3 Applied research

A question often asked by researchers is 'how innovative must my research be?'. Innovation in terms of the development of theory is more highly regarded by the academic world than innovation in terms of new data or the application of theory. However, as the two contributions in this part show, for business and management research (especially in the area of marketing) a greater importance is attached to research which has 'real world' applications. Both contributions describe the development of an 'expert system' for use in the business sector. The expert system brings academic knowledge to managers. The development of expert systems derives from systems theory in which elements of the real world are isolated and modelled with a view to providing description, explanation and prediction for direct application to the business community. The methodology is positivist but, the emphasis here is on operationalism rather than statistical methods, that is devising workable contructs from abstract concepts. Minimizing construct bias is the key to achieving reliability and validity in the results.

The first contribution by Rita (Chapter 9) describes the inductive process by which knowledge is acquired to develop an expert system for marketing tourism. Following on from the development of the product, Davies (Chapter 10) describes a research design used for validation of an expert system with reference to the potential market, this time for the financial sector.

These two research projects, are representative of the growing importance of applied research within business schools where the underlying purpose of the research has more to do with delivering practical solutions to specific problems encountered in the world of business than with traditional academic notions of extending human knowledge.

Part 4   Wider issues in research

The last section of the book reflects a concern to step back from the details of individual research projects and methodologies. Both contributions are more discursive and address rather different themes. The essential point of both contributions is that researchers must look up from the detail of the project and consider the wider context within which they are working. For those in a business and management environment, the demands of a purely 'academic' nature are matched by demands from the business and management world. If the concept of research training is to be taken seriously then researchers need to be prepared for the wider world outside academia. In particular, they need to be able to communicate their research findings to business and management practitioners. This issue is addressed in Chapter 11 by Nieuwenhuis who argues that the researcher must consider the final audience for the work when deciding on a methodology.

Different audiences have different requirements in terms of the research product. Three distinct target audiences are identified whose expectations and understanding of both the subject of the research and the research process itself are different. Implications of these differences for the research methodology and the final output of the research are examined. For the student researcher, the process of literature review and supervision will normally be sufficient to enable the researcher to gain an understanding of the nature and quality of the methodology required and the way in which the research should be presented. However, for other audiences, the requirements are different and it is not sufficient to assume that researchers will somehow absorb the correct presentation style. Given the importance of publications to a researcher's career and the opportunities and desirability of disseminating the findings of business and management research, it is clearly important to address the relationship between methodology, presentation and audience.

Finally, Wells (Chapter 12) examines the question of ethics in business and management research. The ethical framework of academic research is located within the context of established codes of practice to which the legal and medical professions are bound. The academic researcher has to have regard to basic moral values which are deeply embedded in the academic system. For instance, plagiarism is regarded as inimical to quality research; the researcher must make clear the extent to which the work is original and give sufficient credit to other sources as appropriate. However, the author seeks to extend the debate on ethics in research to consider wider issues including the sources of funding, the subjects of research and the social implications of the research findings generated by the research.

Notes

1. The debate between quantitative and qualitative research methodology is covered in the literature see for example, Brewer and Hunter, 1989; Bryman, 1988; Burrel and Morgan, 1979; Gill and Johnson, 1991; Lessnoff, 1974; Morgan, 1983; and Sayer, 1984.
2. The research projects reported in the chapters of this book all use primary data (historians consider archival documentary evidence as a primary source). Although similar questions arise in research which uses secondary data, there are differences in relation to the role of the researcher and the methods used and secondary data are inimical to naturalist research.
3. Table 1.1 is devised to summarize the most important elements which define and characterize a particular research perspective and not as an exhaustive and definitive methodology classification.
4. In circumstances where unidirectional causation between variables cannot be assumed, it is not appropriate to describe variables as dependent and independent. Instead, variables are distinguished according to whether they are endogenous, i.e. determined by and within the model, or exogenous to the model.

5. This book is concerned with empirical research. There is a type of research in economics in which an economic relationship is represented by a mathematical model and where the proof of the model comprises the research. This kind of research is based entirely on deduction, i.e. data play no role in the verification of the model's solution. More commonly, the solutions generated by these mathematical models are treated as hypotheses and are tested against observation as in Wass, Chapter 4.

6. The Popperian principle of falsification which natural science has, in general, adopted defines a theory as a proposition which is falsifiable with reference to the empirical world. The object of research is to falsify hitherto established general laws. General laws hold until they are falsified and since the future is not known, general laws cannot be accepted only not rejected. Hence, the hypothesis to be tested is the null (negative) hypothesis which states that there is no difference, or relationship, between x and y and a null hypothesis which is rejected on the basis of evidence is not equivalent to the acceptance of the alternative hypothesis. In practice, however, a general law which is not refuted is understood to be accepted.

7. 'Social sciences are lost if they are not directly related to philosophical problems by those who practice them' Giddens (1988).

References

Bell, J. (1987), *Doing Your Research Project*, Open University Press, Milton Keynes.

Blaug, M. (1992), *The Methodology of Economics,* Cambridge University Press, Cambridge.

Bloor, M. (1983), 'Notes on member validation', in R. Emerson (ed.), *Contemporary Field Research: A Collection of Readings*, Little Brown, Boston.

Brewer, J. and A. Hunter (1989), *Multimethod Research: A Synthesis of Styles*, Sage Library of Social Research, Vol. 175, Sage, California.

Bryman, A. (1988), *Quantity and Quality in Social Research*, Unwin Hyman, London.

Burrell, G. and G. Morgan (1979), *Sociological Paradigms and Organizational Analysis*, Heinemann, London.

Denzin, N. (1970), *The Research Act: A Theoretical Introduction to Sociological Methods*, Aldine, Chicago.

Eilon, S. (1974), Seven faces of research, *Omega*, Vol. 2, No. 1, pp. 1-9.

ESRC (1993a), *Summary of Statements of Evidence Submitted to the Commission on Management Research.*

ESRC (1993b), 'What's wrong with management research?' *Social Sciences,* No. 19, p. 8.

ESRC (1993c), 'Management Commission plans new forum', *Social Sciences,* No. 21, p. 8.

Fielding, N. and J. Fielding (1986), *Linking Data*, Sage University Paper Series on Quantitative Research, Vol. 4, Sage, California.

Giddens, A. (1984), *The Construction of Society*, Polity Press, London.

Gill, J. and P. Johnson (1991), *Research Methods for Managers*, Paul Chapman Publishing, London.

Glaser, B. and A. Strauss (1967), *The Discovery of Grounded Theory*, Aldine, Chicago.

Guba, E. (1985), 'The context of emergent paradigm research' in Y. Lincoln (ed.), *Organizational Theory and Inquiry: The Paradigm Revolution*, Sage, California.

Hakim, C. (1989), *Research Design*, Contemporary Social Research, Vol. 13, Routledge, London.

Herriot, R. and W. Firestone (1982), 'Multisite qualitative policy research: Optimizing description and generalizability', *Educational Research*, Vol. 12, pp.14-9.

Howard, K. and J. Sharp (1983), *The Management of a Student Research Project*, Gower, Aldershot.

Kaplan, A. (1964), *The Conduct of Inquiry: Methodology for Behavioural Science*, Thomas Y. Crowell, New York.

Lecompte, M. and J. Goetz (1982), 'Problems of reliability and validity in ethnographic research, *Review of Educational Research*, Vol. 52, pp. 31-60.

Lessnoff, M. (1974), *The Structure of Social Science*, Allen & Unwin, London.

Lovering, J. (1990), Fordism's unknown successor: a comment on Scott's theory of flexible accumulation and the re-emergence of regional economies, *International Journal of Urban and Regional Research*, Vol. 14, No. 1, pp. 159-74.

Mitchell, J. (1983), 'Case and situation analysis', *Sociological Review*, Vol. 31, No. 2, pp. 186-211.

Morgan, G. (ed.) (1983), *Beyond Method*, Sage, London.

Pettigrew, A. and R. Whipp (1991), *Managing Change for Competitive Success*, Blackwell, Oxford.

Pugh, D. and D. Hickson (1976), *Organizational Structure in its Context: The Aston Programme I*, Gower, Aldershot.

Reichardt, C. and T. Cook (1979), 'Beyond qualitative and quantitative methods', in T. Cook and C. Reichardt (eds.), *Qualitative and Quantitative Methods in Evaluation Research*, Sage, California.

Rist, R. (1977), 'On the relations among educational research paradigms: from disdain to detente', *Anthropology and Education Quarterly*, Vol. 8, No. 2, pp. 42-9.

Rummel, R. and W. Ballaine (1963), *Research Methodology in Business*, Harper & Row, New York.

Runciman, W. (1969), *Social Science and Political Theory*, Cambridge University Press, Cambridge.

Sayer, A. (1984), *Method in Social Science*, Hutchinson, London.

Silver, M. (1992), *Business Statistics*, McGraw-Hill.

Smith, H. (1975), *Strategies of Social Research: The Methodological Imagination*, Prentice-Hall International, London.

Trow, M. (1957), A comment on participant oberservation and interviewing: a comparison, *Human Organisation*, Vol. 16, No. 3, pp. 33-5.

Weber, M. (1947), *A Theory of Social and Economic Organization*, Free Press, Chicago.

Part 1

Managing Bias in Three Research Methodologies

2 Theory and Practice of Participant Observation

RICK DELBRIDGE AND IAN KIRKPATRICK

Introduction

This chapter is based around the decisions and experiences that we confronted during the course of our doctoral studies. The postgraduate researcher has always to make decisions about the nature and style of his or her research. These decisions will concern the subject of the research, where and how to carry it out and so on. More fundamental is the question of how the epistemological assumptions of one's research determine which methods of data collection are used. In its very essence the passage of study involved in gaining a doctoral degree is of a very personal nature. The answers that we gave ourselves to the initial questions of 'what?', 'how?', 'where?', etc. are influenced by our own personal values. At the heart of these decisions however is something more than just our own common sense reasoning and idiosyncrasy. In our view *any* research methodology should reflect a rational response to the specifics of the research questions and objectives being posed, the relevant material already to hand and the research setting. This chapter will outline the epistemological beliefs that led us independently to select

35

participant observation as the data collection technique for our different studies.

To demonstrate this process of choice, as well as describing the theoretical and practical implications of using participant observation, the methodological choices made by the authors in our own research are explained.

Specifically, the two doctoral projects which used participant observation as a primary data collection technique are discussed. The first of these looked at the issue of understanding the culture of organizational bureaucracy. Much of the literature on this subject suggests that people working in organizations are either governed by structure, or that they negotiate and determine that structure freely through their own actions and definitions of the situation (Silverman, 1970). This research used a case study of an academic library to demonstrate how different types of bureaucratic rules and routines were actually used by staff. Did these rules determine people's behaviour, or was it more the case that people determined whether or not the rules were followed, or both? To answer these questions it was necessary to gain access to the actor's point of view: that is, to understand the organization from the perspective of those who worked in it. For this reason a multi-faceted research methodology was adopted in which the researcher combined real life observations with retrospective interview accounts.

The second research project had a similar but slightly more practical objective: to understand how new production methods such as Just in Time Management (JIT) and Total Quality Management (TQM), that are being transferred from Japan as manufacturing 'best practice', were implemented, understood, experienced and negotiated by workers on the shop floor. This in turn sought to extend the understanding of the reality of the application of these techniques outside the specific socio-cultural environment of Japan. In this project participant observation was the primary data collection technique. The researcher spent a period of three months actually working on the shop floor of a European-owned auto components plant in South Wales and one month on the shop floor of a Japanese-owned consumer electronics plant in the West of England.

Both research projects will be referred to throughout this chapter. In the first instance however, it is necessary to discuss the scientific status of participant observation and its roots in what is commonly termed the interpretative paradigm. The following section of the chapter looks at some of the issues involved in *doing* participant observation and in managing field relations. Finally, the chapter considers how data collected using participant observation is interpreted and analysed. Here the problems surrounding 'grounded theory' and the status of explanation in qualitative research, are also discussed.

Theoretical background

Definition of terms

Despite numerous attempts by methodology textbook writers to agree on a definition, there is still some confusion over what the term 'participant observation' actually means. In sociology, it is widely used as a catch-all term to describe a variety of qualitative research techniques or 'field strategies' (Denzin, 1970). These strategies are seen as sharing a common objective which is to 'describe and analyse the culture and behaviour of humans and their groups from the point of view of those being studied' (Bryman, 1988, p. 46). Alternatively, anthropologists have argued that participant observation is more appropriately defined as a data collection technique within ethnography, and not an all-embracing panacea for qualitative research as sociologists have implied (Hammersley and Atkinson, 1983). Throughout this paper we will use the 'anthropological' definition of participant observation.

Participant observation is defined here as a data collection technique within ethnography. Specifically it implies a field strategy of 'immersion' in the research setting, with the objective of 'sharing in people's lives while attempting to learn their symbolic world' (Silverman, 1985, p. 104). Participant observation shares with other ethnographic data collection techniques, such as straight observation, interviewing and hermaneutic text analysis, a concern with understanding the perspectives of social actors and a respect for the empirical world under study.

Prior to discussing some of the practicalities of *doing* participant observation it is necessary to define and outline the intellectual (epistemological) assumptions which lie at the heart of ethnography, and therefore behind participant observation.

The interpretive paradigm: the problem of understanding

When considering the intellectual underpinnings of participant observation a useful place to start is with Weber's notion of 'understanding' (*verstehen*). According to Weber (1949), all forms of social science must achieve both an *understanding* and *explanation* of the particular phenomena under investigation. Accordingly, 'sociology' is defined as 'a science which attempts the interpretive understanding of social action in order to arrive at a causal explanation of its cause and effects' (Weber, 1947, p. 90). In this way, when discussing the issue of understanding we are asked to differentiate between the social and the natural sciences in terms of their qualitatively distinctive research subjects. In the social sciences one must strive to understand how complex forms of social activity are defined (by actors) in terms of their own (subjective) meanings. This is because, 'Whatever the type of activity, it has consistency only to the extent that its individual or collective agent gives it meaning' (Freund, 1979, p. 168). In other words, all human action possesses an internal logic (meaning) which must be understood in order to make that action intelligible. In the social sciences, the subject matter has a subjective comprehension of its own activity (Gill and Johnson, 1991).

In the natural sciences the observer is spared the complexity of understanding because the phenomena under investigation are passive objects without an internal logic of their own. In stark contrast, within the 'observational field of the social sciences, social reality - has a specific meaning and relevance structure for the beings living, acting, and thinking within it' (Schutz, 1962, p. 59). This is a 'field' in which the research subjects are social agents, actively engaged in the 'accomplishment' of their world (Mehan, 1979). It is precisely because our research 'subjects' are defined as agents who 'act toward things on the basis of the meanings the things have for them' (Blumer, 1969, p. 2) that the task of understanding is so important. This understanding, moreover, has explanatory power simply because knowing what people's motives (meanings) are often helps to explain their behaviour. To sum up, in the social sciences we cannot hope to adequately explain the behaviour of social actors unless we at least try to understand their meanings.

Not only is meaning a core element of all forms of social activity, and therefore of social interaction, but it is also contextualized. In other words, meaning can only make sense in its context. Thus the same set of beliefs may mean one thing in context A, and another in context B where the physical and social situation is qualitatively different (Garfinkel, 1967). In this way individuals and groups are seen to act according to the meanings they ascribe to things and their 'definition of the situation'. Employees from a typical accountancy firm for example may act differently in the presence of a senior partner in and out of work time depending on how they 'typically' define these situations as being either formal or informal. To conclude, in order to 'scientifically' explain social phenomena via an understanding of meanings, it is essential to account for the contextual and historically located basis of those meanings.

How do we 'understand' meaning?

Having defined our task as 'understanding' meaning the question remains: *how* is such an understanding to be achieved? As we mentioned earlier, the particular research methodology used is always a response to the specifics of the research questions and objectives adopted by the researcher. Consequently, for our purposes, we must discover a methodology appropriate for understanding the meanings of social action.

In this section, through a discussion of positivism, we argue that ethnography is the most appropriate methodology to meet the objective of achieving an understanding of social phenomena. Although we adopt a critical stance towards positivist methods, this is not to say that we reject them completely. These methods, like any others, are relevant when used at the *appropriate level*, i.e., to answer the specific questions in the specific research setting chosen by the researcher.

In order to develop an 'interpretive understanding of human action' it is essential to ground our conclusions (second order concepts) as closely as possible in the real perceptions and viewpoints (first order concepts) of the informants. This involves 'being true to the nature of the phenomena under study' (Matza, 1969, p. 5), and adopting an 'attitude of "respect" or "appreciation" toward the social world' (Hammersley and Atkinson, 1983, p. 6). In a nutshell, if we want to understand meaning then we must base our understanding on how social actors *themselves* define and perceive meaning. Given this requirement, we must reject positivist approaches to epistemology and method for a number of reasons.

A key assumption of positivism (as it refers to social science methodology) is that all 'scientific' analysis should involve the deductive testing and verification (or falsification) of *a priori* hypotheses. Such hypotheses seek to explain and predict what happens in the social world by searching for regularities and laws which describe causal relationships. Theories are therefore tested (or measured) rigorously through the standardization of data and data collection techniques which strive to eliminate bias and therefore underscore the validity of any subsequent results. Returning to our earlier questions about understanding, one might ask how it is possible to understand meanings if we start by imposing an *a priori* framework on them which ignores the perceptions of the social actors involved? Logico-deductivist methods (positivist) are surely inappropriate for the investigation of meaning (understanding) when they fail to consult the data prior to developing hypotheses. There is bound to be a very real danger that meanings, as understood by the subjects of research, are missed or worse still, 'The verifier may find that the speculative theory has nothing to do with his evidence, unless he forces a connection' (Glaser and Strauss, 1967, p. 29).

A further problem with logico-deductivist methods is the widespread use of questionnaires to measure sets of pre-defined categories which supposedly exist out there in the *real* world. Without getting too involved in a discussion of the pros and cons of questionnaires, it is pertinent to say that besides the problem of distorting meanings (mentioned above), there is also the issue of their failure to capture the contextual nature of that meaning. When emphasis is placed on theory verification (the main purpose of questionnaires) at the expense of theory generation, then there will also be a tendency to generalize across contexts. This also acts to reduce levels of complexity and variety which a greater sensitivity to context might reveal. We argue that such complexity needs to be understood if one is to develop plausible explanations of social action.

Having rejected positivist methodologies in our quest for understanding, what are the alternatives? As referred to earlier, ethnography is a methodology encompassing qualitative research in both sociology and anthropology, and has the objective of grounding interpretations in the perceptions of research subjects. Broadly speaking it aims to achieve an understanding of the,

> actions and interactions of respondents, by virtue of grasping and comprehending the culturally appropriate concepts through which they conduct their social life (Halfpenny, 1979, p. 808).

In theory at least, ethnography is the appropriate method for understanding meaning. Since it follows an inductivist approach to social science research the emphasis is on 'grounding' second order concepts (Schutz, 1962), or theories (Glaser and Strauss, 1967), in the empirical world of meaning rather than artificially imposing constructs to be tested. Meaning is not distorted when the ethnographic researcher adopts a stance of 'respect for the empirical world under study' (Blumer, 1969), and as far as possible allows the subjects to speak for themselves.

This concern with grounding research also explains why ethnographers place so much emphasis on the observation of natural phenomena. By observing the researcher,

> is not bound in his field work by pre-judgements about the nature of his problem, by rigid data gathering devices, or by hypotheses (Denzin, 1970, p. 216).

Through immersion in the field and by observing social action in its context the researcher tries to *understand* meaning rather than artificially construct meaning.

The status of interpretive data

The process of data collection within ethnography is not trouble-free and there are both practical and conceptual concerns. The information a researcher obtains from participant observation is varied and complex - not to mention the sheer volume of data that is generated. Consequently, it is typically necessary to classify the data both formally and analytically. In order to cope with this problem, the researcher is likely to spend some time organizing the way data is stored and indexed (discussed below in data management). Besides the issue of how one physically organizes the data, there are also questions about how the researcher defines what data is. Put another way, should the researcher record everything he or she sees and hears, or is it better to adopt a more focused and selective approach? The answer to this question depends on how the researcher copes with reflexivity and the position he or she adopts in the debate between pure description and grounded theory (see below).

A further issue is whether in the process of collecting data the observer should attempt to adjudicate between different statements or observations. Should the researcher take informant's statements to be an explanation of behaviour or should he or she treat everything as a subjective 'display' of cultural knowledge? In our opinion the latter view, which is preferable, would force the observer to adopt an 'open but sceptical acceptance' (Werner and Schoepfle, 1987, p. 61) of both his or her observations (interpretations), and of native statements. In situations where native accounts or observations differ the observer simply asks a 'more interesting and insightful question' which is 'why the views are opposing, contradictory, or anomalous?' (Werner and Schoepfle, 1987). Although we recognize these different approaches, in our research, we have treated all data as 'displays' of cultural knowledge which have validity in their own terms. This does not imply that one should ignore the context in which the data was collected (i.e., who said or did whatever), or that the researcher should not try to account for their impact (see our discussion of reflexivity below). The key point is that we consider bias to be a problem of analysis and not something integral to the data itself.

Given this espoused approach towards data collection, what are the different categories of data one would expect to obtain through participant observation?

- primary (on the spot) observations of events, activities etc. This would include observations of what was said and the language used.
- secondary observations of events (anecdotes etc. from informants). These are statements by informants suggesting their interpretations of events removed in time and space.
- the observers' interpretations of what is observed (the above). This is discussed below (writing descriptions) as 'second order concepts'.
- experiential data on the feelings and perceptions of the observer, i.e. what it's like!
- observations of changing field relations, including attempts by the observer to account for his or her impact on the situation.
- self-reflective information. Accounts of how the observer's values have intervened during the data collection process.
- structural information about communicative networks, contexts etc. Also historical information about the informants themselves.
- information about the material artifacts of the culture.

The problem of bias in participant observation

Before we move onto our practical discussion of participant observation as a data collection technique further mention needs to be made of the problematic theoretical status of observation.

Ethnography has been criticized for sharing with positivism a 'joint obsession with eliminating the effects of the researcher on the data' (Hammersley and Atkinson, 1983, p. 14), i.e., the belief that it is possible to gain access to a body of 'natural' data uncontaminated by the values or presence of the researcher. This view fails however to recognize the reflexive nature of all social research. Because we are part of the social world we are studying we cannot detach ourselves from it, or for that matter avoid relying on our common sense knowledge and life experiences when we try to interpret it. Consequently, we cannot avoid affecting the outcomes of the social situations we are studying, especially if the researcher is an actual participant. If all research is reflexive, the question of bias changes from 'how do I detach myself from the data both physically and psychologically?'. To 'how do I minimize or account for my impact on that data?'. Rather than constantly refer to some higher set of universal judgemental standards, we should trust our own common sense and 'work with what knowledge we have, while recognizing that it may be erroneous and subjecting it to systematic inquiry where doubt seems justified' (Hammersley and Atkinson, 1983, p. 17).

Although reflexivity shifts our attention away from questions of eradicating bias to questions of how we explain the effect of the observer, it leads to some confusion over what role the researcher involved in participant observation should adopt. Some (including Hammersley and Atkinson) use reflexivity almost as a blank cheque for the researcher to see him or herself as the research instrument 'par excellence'. More precisely they propose that the researchers adopt a proactive 'experimental' role within the field of observation rather than a passive one in which he or she attempts to become a neutral vessel of cultural experience. If we accept the principle of reflexivity with all its implications for our impact on the data, then surely the role we adopt in participant observation vis-a-vis that data depends on how far the observer decides to adopt a proactive role, while at the same time being able to account for his or her impact on the data being collected. This leads to a distinction being made in the ethnographic literature between observation as a means of theory generation (Glaser and Strauss, 1967), and observation as a way of achieving 'accurate' cultural descriptions which approximate as closely as possible to the 'insider's view' (Geertz, 1973). In this paper we make no attempt to take sides in this debate. Rather, we aim to outline the parameters of participant observation within which, depending on the objectives of the research (see final section), a number of approaches are possible.

Managing fieldwork: *Doing* participant observation

While participant observation has been discussed in many publications what it actually involves often remains unclear. It has been suggested that this is partly because practitioners of participant observation have resisted formulating definitive procedures and techniques and have regarded its practice as artful and inappropriate for linear, mechanical presentation (Jorgensen, 1989). Moreover, when participant observation is considered in 'researcher's handbook' style publications a very diverse set of considerations are typically introduced. This is because the actual practice of participant observation research is dependent upon many constraints and external factors beyond the control of the researcher which are often impossible to foresee. For this reason 'how to do it' articles are not useful beyond a certain level. However, it is important for the researcher to be aware of as many of the problems that may befall them as possible in order for steps to be taken to minimize such difficulties where appropriate.

Our experiences have taught us that the key to successful participant observation is flexibility, to be able to deal with contingencies. One old prescription for fieldwork includes the advice 'behave like a gentleman, keep off the women, take quinine daily and play it by ear' (Evans-Pritchard, quoted in Bell and Encel, 1978). Social research can be very complex and messy. The researcher is exposed to a minefield of political activity in the research setting and a false move can ruin the opportunity for effective collection of meaningful data. Our fieldwork underlined to us the importance of 'playing it by ear', as for the rest of Evans-Pritchard's advice...We concur with Buchanan et al (1988) who advize that:

> the researcher should adopt an *opportunistic* approach to fieldwork in organizations. Fieldwork is permeated with the conflict between what is theoretically desirable on the one hand and what is practically possible on the other. (*Ibid,* p. 53)

As well as the difficulties in balancing conflicting pressures there are further theoretical problems with the process of carrying out participant observation research. One must consider the impact of the presence of the researcher, and how that can be affected, and the problem of objectivity. Also, there are other more practical problems such as the need to form relationships with the subjects of the research and data collection and management issues. These problems are considered below.

The impact of the observer

The effect an observer may have on the research setting is potentially large. Any outsider entering into a social group may change the nature of that group. Such effects are particularly likely when the newcomer is actually present. In other words distortion is most likely at exactly the time the researcher least wants it. This is exacerbated when the reason for the outsider's arrival (i.e. the study of members of the social setting) is explained in research instances. Researchers are often perceived as management tools/spies and as such are not trusted by workers/subordinates. Moreover, the subjects of the research may act differently when under scrutiny. There are a variety of techniques employed by researchers to deal with these problems. Some carry out covert participant observation where their true identity is kept secret from most, if not all, members of the research setting. The ethical nature of such research has been called into question. Our research took the form of overt participant observation but it is always possible that not everyone knows who you are and what you are doing even if it is not deliberately kept secret. In researching overtly there is the opportunity to formally or *informally* interview people without arousing suspicion. It also gives the researcher the chance to dictate, at least in part, where they will be and what they will be doing. Participant observation alone in a store room would yield limited data.

Aside from the decision regarding overt versus covert research, participant observation in practice can take different forms. Often the particular characteristics of the research setting will dictate how it is managed. It may not for example always be possible to act as a full participant. This could be due to a lack of skill or specific competence on behalf of the researcher, a dearth of opportunities while actually in the research setting, or a restriction on activity imposed by those acceding entry to the locale. For example, in the Japanese-owned plant some of the research took the form of pseudo-participant observation because the dexterity required to manage an operator's full load was beyond the capabilities of the researcher. On other occasions the sheer speed of the line precluded the researcher's inclusion. In contrast, during the library study it was possible for the observer to actually participate because the level of skill competence required to operate issue/return terminals was minimal. This had obvious benefits, most notably, being able to simulate learning 'on the job' like an assistant trainee. It also however had its drawbacks. As a participant who knows the job, the observer was often relied on to stand in during periods of high user demand. Consequently, the observer unconsciously changed the outcome by helping to avert what might have been mini crises. Practical constraints can restrict the researcher in terms of how far he or she is able to 'fade into the background' and adopt a 'fly on the wall' approach to observation.

As we have noted above, not all participant observers have sought to minimize their effects on the research setting. However, we feel that whilst one must acknowledge the possibility that the presence of the researcher will contaminate the data one must seek to understand the nature of this impact and attempt to keep it to a minimum wherever possible. Deliberately creating situations can result in further stimuli whose effects must be understood and will complicate already highly complex phenomena.

There are factors which can help to minimize the biases unavoidably incurred. If the research period is lengthy it is impossible for people to constantly keep up an act. As Becker (1970) notes:

They [ie the people a field worker studies] are enmeshed in social relationships important to them, at work, in community life, wherever. The events they participate in matter to them. The opinions and actions of the people they interact with must be taken into account, because they affect those events. All the constraints that affect them in their ordinary lives continue to operate while the observer observes. (*Ibid*, p. 46)

If one understands the nature of the potential bias then this can be used to inform the analysis and interpretation of the data. In seeking to minimize the effect of their own presence, the researcher often has to act almost as a chameleon in adopting different stances, values and perspectives dependent upon the specific context. Allied to this, in restricting the impact of his or her presence, the researcher may want to appear unimportant and largely naïve. Expressing genuine interest and curiosity, but appearing uninformed, can reduce the need those being studied feel to act differently. This, as with much else, requires a 'feel' for the situation because appearing 'stupid' will strip the researcher of credibility. The researcher will typically have to display a different level of understanding (and perhaps feign different political allegiances) depending on who is present. During the library study, the observer's ability to play the chameleon role was crucial. It soon became obvious that management (senior librarians) and staff (library assistants) had built up different expectations and perceptions of the observer's role. The former saw the observer as an internal consultant gathering information on plans for cultural change, while the latter took the view that he was a neutral vessel who would tell the 'truth' about 'what's really going on here'. In this situation, being able to come across as sympathetic to both groups helped the researcher maintain balanced field relations and at the same time collect useful data.

The problem of objectivity

Since the researcher is a part of the social world that is being studied and has intrinsic values and beliefs from which they cannot successfully detach themselves absolute neutrality is impossible to achieve. From conception through implementation to analysis and interpretation, an individual researcher's personal sympathies and values will affect the research process. That is unavoidable and therefore complete/perfect 'objectivity' is unachievable. The task of the researcher is to ensure that such biases do not render their work unscientific and useless. Ultimately, it is the individual's honesty and integrity in reporting the facts accurately, and interpreting them as truthfully as they can, which must safeguard against accusations of bias. One technique to attempt to limit the problems of blinkeredness in the research is to understand the nature of our own biases through rigorous self analysis. In other words, through 'self observation' and examination, we can avail ourselves of our own ethnocentric bias and use that understanding to help interpret our research findings. Another technique sometimes used is to treat *all* data as 'anthropologically strange' and attempt to record and analyse everything that happens, even what appears to be obvious and mundane. The logistical problems in handling the bulk of data generated are obvious.

With the very nature of participant observation research, typically incorporating long periods of intensive field work, it is very difficult for an attentive researcher to be unaware of things that are important and do not fit the preconceptions they may have had. As Becker (1970) notes:

> the field worker typically gathers his data over an extended period of time, in a variety of situations, using several different ways of getting at the questions he is interested in, all of these reducing the danger of bias. Because he observes over a long time, he finds it hard to ignore the mass of information supporting an appropriate hypothesis he may neither have expected or desired ... (*Ibid*, p. 52).

One particular method that can help guard against 'seeing only what the researcher wants to see' is to enter the setting with a *tabula rasa* approach whereby the area of investigation is delimited as far as possible and interesting themes are sought. In the research in the factory settings an in-depth review of the broader industrial sociology literature was avoided so that the researcher involved could identify events which took place that were actually important *during the research* rather than merely checking on things others had previously (in a different time and context) found relevant. In carrying out research in this manner the individual is always aware of the setting from an observer's viewpoint; always at the back of one's mind is that feeling of 'looking out for things'.

An alternative to maintaining a detachment from the social setting and its members is when researchers 'go native' or 'become the phenomenon'. This, if successfully achieved, enables the researcher to write from personal experience about the phenomena under study.

In our research we maintained a certain detachment. While getting out of bed at seven o'clock and making windscreen wipers for three months gives an insight into the lives of factory workers, the simple knowledge that it is only a period of time before one can return to 'normality' in itself ensures that the experience is not the same as a typical shop floor worker.

This detachment, lost when researchers turn native, also facilitates the rational and thoughtful collection of data. Since participant observation research is inductive the process can be very flexible. With no hypotheses to test the researcher is free to track the issues that arise during the actual research programme. As such then, this research is often unstructured which facilitates a true understanding of what is going on and why rather than the pre-determined generation of answers to potentially useless questions.

Building relationships

To have any chance of minimizing the effects of the researcher actually being in the social setting it is essential to form relationships with fellow members. Moreover, inserting oneself into a foreign and strange place can be a very isolating and lonely experience. The period of research in the South Wales company began on January 2nd which meant a long journey back from the festivities of the previous night. On arriving in a dark, sodden and wind-swept valley train station (and unable to find the town let alone a phone box), it was tempting to get on the next train home and forget the whole thing. The next day, at eight o'clock, it was down onto the shop floor amongst strangers, safe only in the knowledge that a mistake in what was said, or even an accidental misinterpretation, could ruin the entire research period at a stroke. There is real pressure and intensity in field work of this nature, particularly in the initial stages where the researcher must informally 'negotiate' his or her entry into the social setting.

The process of forming relationships will depend on individuals, and for this reason amongst others, some people will be better at carrying out this form of research. Of course, the building and sustaining of informal, 'friendly' relations is also imperative as a channel of research data. Not surprisingly, the arrival of unknown outsiders with the intent of studying people's actions is often treated with extreme suspicion. It takes time, and the familiarity that brings, to try and overcome these reservations. While the actual experience of carrying out tasks is potentially very useful in reaching an understanding of the research setting, the *participation* of the researcher also helps break down barriers between the student and the studied. During the factory studies, several people explicitly told the observer that once they had seen him working on the line day in, day out they had come to have some respect and belief in what he was doing. One must also realize that not everyone will speak to you, and forcing the issue will potentially do great harm. Perhaps the most effective tool of a participant observer is to become known as a 'good bloke' or 'one of the girls'. This can only be achieved through long periods of time spent very carefully building relationships. In one of the factory cases, the observer entered into a tight-knit Welsh valley community and soon got involved in long conversations about families, both his and theirs. As Wax (1960) has noted:

> If I invade another human's privacy with long lists of questions, I will learn little unless I am genuinely curious; it is no more than common courtesy to reciprocate by satisfying the curiosity of my informant. (*Ibid*, p. 93)

Really speaking such attention to detail and sincere interest can only be maintained if the researcher is comfortable in the social setting, genuinely committed to the project, and enjoys this form of research.

Trust and mutual honesty must be cultivated. Once this has been achieved, the researcher can gain from these informants an improved understanding of what is happening and why. In getting to know your 'fellow workmates', important insights can be gleaned. One must utilize the time of the research period to the full in reaching the *understanding* which is vital. Assimilating as much as possible of the environment of the research setting is especially important for success in the interpretation and analysis stages of the project. For example, the specific nature of the surrounding valley community and its people had basic implications for the nature of management-worker relations. Blum (1952) has noted the 'high degree of consciousness' that is required of researchers:

> Besides insight into personal relationships, the researcher must know something about the position of the people in the community and in the

factory, the role they play, and the reactions of other people to them. Only a careful evaluation of information in the light of these factors can indicate their real meaning and significance as research data. (*Ibid*, p. 38)

The difficulties in forming and maintaining relationships are often due to the conflicting pressures that a researcher experiences. One must seek to remain loyal and honest to all the different actors in the social setting. Sometimes this can be very hard. In the two factories studied there was considerable pressure on occasions to 'side' with management or workers. Similar pressures arose during the library study, forcing the observer to adopt the role of chameleon. This gets more complicated when one becomes aware of different cliques and sub-groups as one is further accepted into the group. The approach, in practice, will depend on the context of observation, which will shift from day to day.

Data collection and presentation

As we have discussed above there are several forms of data that can be collected during a period of participant observation research. Most of these forms rely on some form of record being kept on a day-to-day basis. Whilst our research was overt, it is unwise to spend all day wandering around with a pen and a piece of paper. People are typically likely to speak and act more 'honestly' and openly if they are not constantly being visually reminded that what they are saying and doing is being recorded. For this reason note-taking is often kept to snatched moments in the toilet or some other place out of view. A potential problem comes should the researcher be caught making these surreptitious notes. This may give an impression of dishonesty and secretiveness which could erode the relationships built. While on the shop floor in the factory, notes were not taken except in secret, but during the interviews with managers the recording of data was explicit. Often the respondent would say something like, 'this isn't for your notes but ...', or, 'don't write this down but ...'. In such instances it is important to *appear* to comply and consequently a good memory is useful. In contrast, during the library study notes were taken overtly. At first the observer adopted a strategy of secretly taking notes (hidden away behind bookshelves) until he decided that in the library context this might be counter-productive, i.e., being perceived as a management spy. After a while overt note-taking was accepted as 'normal', thus making life a lot easier and having the obvious advantage of being able to record informant's statements *verbatim*. Another problem encountered during the factory study and to some extent in the library, occurred when the respondents wanted to read the notes. In such circumstances having tiny and illegible handwriting is a boon!

Typically such notes refer to specific events and/or statements from informants. At the end of each day comes an opportunity to record personal observations and perceptions of a more general nature. Make no mistake this can be hard work. After a day on the line it is often difficult (impossible on some occasions) to find the motivation and energy to write for another hour or two. As one tired Ph.D researcher put it,

> Picture the participant observer, after a gruelling eight hours on the production line, slumped in a kitchen chair in his modest apartment, oil and metal chips dripping and dropping from his trouser cuffs into his shoes and over the linoleum, his face sagging into a plate of beans that he is too tired to eat, and with the immediate job before him of recording in his work diary the events and feelings of a day that he would like to forget. (Roy, 1952)

Every effort should be made to record things as soon as possible since the longer after an event it is recorded the greater the likelihood of bias toward greater ethnocentrism (see Shweder and D'Andrade, 1979). It is useful if as much information as possible regarding the research is recorded. This should ideally include notes on exactly what form the data took, how it was collected, and the relevant actors' perceptions and actions. Ultimately, as with many things when they leave the pages of a textbook and meet reality, there is a pay-off between what is desirable in theory and achievable in practice.

Certainly any researcher is likely to have a great deal of raw data by the time the research period is concluded. While some form of preliminary analysis may take place during that period, it is not usually until the researcher has left the research locale that the processes of interpretation and analysis begin in earnest. There are many texts which give recommended ways of dealing with the data developed, the advice is generally little more than rational common sense and we will not concern ourselves with it here.

We would like to make one point about the presentation of data and how a particular style can preclude certain accusations of bias. While there are normally constraints on space in publishing material, the doctoral thesis has greater flexibility. If the researcher, in writing up his or her work, is to persuade the reader that the interpretations made are justified and 'honest' then it is useful to present the data in a relatively uncontaminated state. In this way, it can be demonstrated *why* the researcher came to draw the conclusions made and *how* understanding was achieved.

Interpretation and analysis

Description

So far we have considered the theoretical (epistemological) status of ethnography and discussed some of the practical issues involved in *doing* participant observation. However, once data has been collected and organized, how is it then used? More specifically, how do we move on from the actual task of doing participant observation to the interpretation of data, the writing of descriptions and, if desirable and feasible, the generation of theory? In this final section, we will attempt to address these questions, which are inextricably linked to wider issues of epistemology and practice.

As we have argued, our main objective in doing empirical research was to achieve an understanding of social phenomena. Perhaps the best way of testing whether or not this objective has been met is in the writing of 'adequate' descriptions. These descriptions must be accurate and loyal to the subject under study. They should be derived from 'insider' accounts and reveal something of the rich tapestry of contextualized meanings, what anthropologists call a 'thick description' (Geertz, 1973). In this final section, we will discuss briefly some of the key difficulties involved in writing description, looking at two interrelated problems of interpretation and theory and explanation.

Interpretation

As was hinted at earlier in our discussion of reflexivity, our interpretations of what is observed are inevitably 'presumptive'. In short, they are 'second order concepts' or 'typifications' generated by the observer in his or her attempt to understand the social world. As such, these concepts will be 'infected' by the observers' own values and his or her interpretation of what the informant(s) 'really' meant. This fact should not, however, come as any great surprise. In all human interactions words are no more than signifiers or 'vibrations of air' whereas:

> Meanings are interpretations of these patterned vibrations in the receiver's mind. Since no human beings have exactly the same life experience, none of the interpretations by the receiver are exactly the same as the meanings intended by the transmitter. There is enough slack in the system of human communication to justify the assumption that it is never perfect. (Werner and Schoepfle, 1987)

The realization that we can never duplicate exactly what people mean, and the associated problem of introducing our own values during interpretation, should not deter us from generating second order concepts. If it did, it would not be possible to do research at all. Moreover, it is a widely accepted reality that, 'any intellectual analysis entails some abstraction and some movement away from the "purely" phenomenal' (Rock, 1973, p. 20). The question is therefore not, 'How do I duplicate exactly what informants meant?' But rather, 'How do I generate second order concepts which are as close as possible to the meanings held by social actors?' The whole point of ethnography is, 'to make concepts both analytic and sensitizing' so that they help 'the reader see and hear vividly the people in the area under investigation' (Glaser and Strauss *op cit*, p. 39).

There are a number of ways in which our descriptive concepts can be made more 'analytic and sensitizing'. As mentioned above (during our consideration of the theoretical status of observation), although we can never fully eradicate our personal values from the process of interpretation, we can try and account for them through 'self-reflection'. At a different level, if we follow our objective of locating observations in their context, then we will also be one step nearer to generating concepts which are closer to the empirical data.

This chapter has argued in favour of treating observational data as displays of cultural knowledge. In this sense we are not in the business of adjudicating between *right* or *wrong* statements or observations, but of treating everything as relevant in its context. This also ties in with the need to record and understand diversity. If there is a disagreement between informants' statements/perceptions, then our task is surely to explain that disagreement, and not decide which one is correct or incorrect. In all these ways it should be possible to keep our concepts as closely aligned to the perceptions of the social actors as is possible and desirable.

Approaches to validation

Besides these epistemological guidelines a number of techniques for strengthening description have also been suggested. A few of these, including informant verification, triangulation, and the use of simple counting procedures, are worth mentioning briefly.

Firstly, let us consider informant verification. This has been widely advocated as a technique for testing the accuracy/validity of second order concepts, i.e. by asking the informant, 'Is this an accurate description of what you said and did?'. On the surface informant verification seems like a good way of adding rigour to our descriptive concepts. It should however always be treated with caution, especially when it is used exclusively as a test of validity (Bloor, 1983). Problems arise because informants are being asked quite unrealistically to verify a researcher's second order concepts when these very concepts are removed in both time and space from the circumstances of their production.

Similar problems occur when popular techniques of research triangulation are used, despite the fact that this is widely advocated by organization theorists (Eisenhardt, 1989). Triangulation is also an attempt to validate descriptive concepts by cross referencing between different sources of data (and ways of interpreting that data). As a consequence the researcher risks turning into an 'ironist' (Garfinkel, 1967) who tries to adjudicate between different accounts, but also fails to realize how these accounts are uniquely situated and as such relevant to their context.

A further validation technique is that of using simple counting procedures (Silverman, 1985). As a means of systematically presenting the whole of the data, simple counting can have the effect of reassuring the reader that descriptive concepts are rigorously produced. In so doing however one must be careful to count only what is countable, i.e. avoid the temptation to develop artificial categories or equivalence classes just for the sake of counting. This technique also works well in conjunction with analytic induction, a method which seeks to systematically account for deviant cases in order to reinforce second order concepts.

To summarize, when writing descriptions we should be aware that our second order concepts are inherently 'presumptive'. At the same time however it is possible to find limited ways of validating descriptions and keeping them as close to the data as possible.

Theory and explanation

One of the strongest criticisms of ethnography is that it is overtly 'descriptive' and, as a consequence, fails not only to test, but also to develop explanatory theories. Many ethnographers would simply reject this criticism on the grounds that it relies on a set of (positivist) assumptions about social research which they would not accept. In contrast others argue that ethnography, far from being atheoretical, can actually produce sound explanations for social phenomena. Below we give a brief description of both these positions, what we describe as the 'hard liners' and the 'theorists'.

Hard Liners: Ethnographic description writing has been criticized as empty reportage, not far advanced from high quality journalism

(Moerman, 1974). Ethnographers would argue however that this critique fails to understand the difficulties involved in producing an accurate description. Indeed, far from being a straightforward process of empty reportage, 'Asking the question, "What is going on here?" is at once disarmingly simple and incredibly complex' (Rist, 1984, p. 161). Moreover, ethnographers would probably reject as 'positivistic' the assumption that all description is simply the first stage to producing explanation. Proper description they argue, can also have an explanatory force. That is, when looking at the 'methods members use to accomplish the world for what it is', we are in effect 'attempting to generalize about social life ... about the sort of "apparatus", the "sense assembly equipment", that human beings use to construct and sustain their everyday lives' (Cuff and Payne, 1978, p. 178). In this sense, ethnographers would argue quite convincingly that adequate description is not just the forerunner of explanatory theory generation, but is in itself a justifiable objective of social research.

Theorists: In contrast to the views outlined above, some argue quite forcefully that ethnographic research can indeed develop explanatory theory. The most well-known proponents of this view are Glaser and Strauss (1967) who advocate a grounded theory approach. As an ongoing process, they argue, the researcher engages in the analysis and verification of concepts which cumulatively develop into fully blown substantive theories. These theories can then be generalized through comparative research into more general *formal* theories. Central to this idea of grounded theory is the establishment of rigorous *ideal-type* models which are closely aligned with the empirical world and not deductively imposed onto it. In order to achieve this rigour some of the methods discussed need to be employed, including analytic induction and simple counting procedures. The resulting theory which emerges from research in perhaps a single case study is not judged according to the criteria of 'typicality', but rather in terms of its theoretical logic (Mitchell, 1983). In short, ethnographic description forms the basis for rigorous theoretical concepts which emerge *from*, rather than being imposed *upon*, the data.

Concluding remarks

In this paper we have demonstrated how participant observation (ethnography) was the most appropriate choice of methodology to deal with research which aims to understand complex social relations and organizational processes. Furthermore, we strongly refute the notion that this choice was in any way purely ad hoc or unscientific. We have also demonstrated that participant observation is not a 'soft' option. While we acknowledge that there are problems of both a theoretical and practical nature - in particular those of reflexivity and the minimization and understanding of bias - we firmly believe that participant observation has an important role to play in the task of understanding social phenomena.

Our discussion of *doing* participant observation has shown how the researcher needs to adopt a contingent and flexible approach. There are few rules or guidelines to rely on when out in the field, rather the emphasis is on learning by experience and thinking on one's feet. Although it can be stressful and hard work participant observation is both a highly rewarding and personally enriching method of research. To all those who are still undecided about whether or not to choose this approach our advice is simply: 'go out there and do it'.

References

Becker, H. (1970), *Sociological Work: Method and Substance*, Aldine, Chicago.

Bell, C., and S. Encel, (eds.) (1978), *Inside the Whale: Ten Personal Accounts of Social Research*, Pergamon Press, Oxford.

Bloor, M. (1983), 'Notes on member validation' in R.M. Emerson (ed.), *Contemporary Field Research: A Collection of Readings*, Little, Brown, Boston, pp. 156-72.

Blum, F.H. (1952), 'Getting individuals to give information to the outsider', *Journal of Social Sciences*, Vol. 8, pp. 35-42.

Blumer, H. (1969), *Symbolic Interactionism*, Prentice Hall, New Jersey.

Bryman, A. (ed.) (1988), *Quantity and Quality in Social Research*, Unwin Hyman, London.

Bryman, A. (1989), *Research Methods and Organizational Studies*, Unwin Hyman, London.

Buchanan, D., D. Boddy, and J. McCalman, (1988), 'Getting in, getting on, getting out and getting back' in A. Bryman (ed.), *Doing Research in Organizations*, pp. 53-67.

Cuff, E.C. and G.F.C. Payne, (eds.) (1979), *Perspectives in Sociology*, Allen and Unwin, London.

Denzin, N.K. (1970), *The Research Act in Sociology*, Butterworth, London.

Eisenhardt, K.M. (1989), 'Building theories from case study research', *Academy of Management Review*, Vol. 14, No. 4, pp. 532-550.

Freund, J. (1979), 'German sociology at the time of Max Weber' in T. Bottemore and R. Nisbet, (eds.), *A History of Sociological Analysis*, Heinemann, London.

Garfinkel, H. (1967), *Studies in Ethnomethodology*, Prentice Hall, New Jersey.

Geertz, C. (1973), *The Interpretation of Cultures*, Basic Books, New York.

Glaser, B. and A. Strauss (1967), *The Discovery of Grounded Theory*, Aldine, Chicago.

Gill, J. and I. Johnson (1991), *Research Methods for Managers*, Paul Chapman, London.

Hammersley, M. and P. Atkinson (1983), *Ethnography: Principles in Practice*, Tavistock, London.

Halfpenny, P. (1979), 'The analysis of qualitative data', *Sociological Review*, Vol. 27, No. 4, pp. 799-825.

Jorgensen, D. (1989), *Participant Observation: A Methodology for Human Studies*, Sage, California.

Matza, D. (1969), *Becoming Deviant*, Prentice Hall, New Jersey.

Mehan, H. (1979), *Learning Lessons: Social Organization in the Classroom*, Harvard University Press, Cambridge, Mass.

Mitchell, J.C. (1983), 'Case and situation analysis', *Sociological Review*, May, pp. 187-211.

Moermon, M. (1974), 'Accomplishing ethnicity' in Turner, R. (ed.) *Ethnomethodology*, Penguin, Harmondsworth.

Rist, R.C. (1984), 'On the application of qualitative research to the policy process: an emergent linkeage', in Barton, L. and S. Walker, (eds.), *Social Crisis and Educational Research*, pp. 153-70, Croom Helm, London.

Rock, P. (1970), 'Phenomenalism and essentialism in the sociology of deviance', *Sociology*, Vol. 7, No. 1, pp. 17-29.

Roy, D. (1952), *Restriction of Output in a Piecework Machine Shop*, Ph.D dissertation, University of Chicago, Chicago.

Schutz, A. (1962), *Collected Papers 1: The Problem of Social Reality*, Martinus Nijhoff, The Hague.

Schweder, R.A. and R.G. D'Andrade (1980), 'The systematic distortion hypothesis', in R.A. Schweder (ed.) (1980), *New Directions for Methodology of Social and Behaviour Science*, Jossey Bass.

Silverman, D. (1970), *The Theory of Organizations*, Heinemann, London.

Silverman, D. (1985), *Qualitative Methodology and Sociology*, Gower, Aldershot.

Wax, R.H. (1960), 'Reciprocity in field work' in R.J. Adams and J. Heiss (eds.), *Human Organization Research: Field Relations and Techniques*, pp. 90-8. Dorsey, Homewood, Ill.

Weber, M. (1947), *A Theory of Social and Economic Organization*, Free Press, Chicago.

Weber, M. (1949), *The Methodology of the Social Sciences*, Free Press, New York.

Werner, O. and G.M. Schoepfle (1987), *Systematic Fieldwork*, Vol 1, Sage, London.

3 Research Methods in Accounting History

MALCOLM ANDERSON

Introduction

'Any subject of historical research must be approached by employing research method(s) considered appropriate to the facts being sought and the issues being investigated' (Previts, Parker, Coffman (PPC), 1990b, p. 144). Hence, this chapter initially reviews six main subject areas for research in accounting history - biography; institutional history; development of accounting thought and practice; general history; databases; and historiography, before considering methodological questions.[1] Three methodological perspectives (traditional, critical and positive), within which to conduct such research into accounting history are identified, though these are not intended to be exhaustive.[2] The traditional school is geared towards describing past events and practices. The critical perspective attempts to explain such events and practices; through the study of accountancy in its historical context. The positive approach to accounting, like the critical perspective, is of more recent origin, but has grown in importance in the last few years. It seeks to test theoretical models against the empirical world using classical statistical techniques.

Research in each of the three fields outlined above, utilizes distinctive methods. Traditionalist, fact-finding research uses archive and other primary-source material, in its attempt to describe events of the past. Typically three sources are used: (a) original accounting records; (b) treatises; and (c) other contemporary documents. The critical perspective attempts to widen the focus, to place events and practices of the past into their broader social, economic, political and environmental context. Researchers in this field typically draw on theories from other academic disciplines, particularly sociology and philosophy, in order to interpret primary data. The positive school, one of analytical hypothesis-testing, and based on the scientific experimental model, uses a battery of quantitative techniques to test theoretical models.

Having outlined three competing methodological traditions commonly used in accounting history, the mechanics of the implementation of a given strategy are highlighted in a detailed case-study of a research project currently being undertaken at Cardiff Business School. The objective of this research is, broadly speaking, to seek a greater understanding of the role played by qualified accountants in business development in Britain, in the late nineteenth and twentieth centuries. The research methods employed have necessarily been conditioned by the chosen areas of focus of this study. In wishing to chronicle the numbers of accountants moving from the profession to industry, numerical techniques were required. Seeking an explanation for such movement led to the need to consult qualitative data. Hence, within one project, completely different research methods are deemed appropriate. This chapter illustrates how unstructured and innovative the research process can be. Specifically, this project: (a) does not follow the methods text-book model of a research project; (b) combines research methods which do not fit neatly into any one methodological approach in accounting history research; and (c) develops ideas inductively thereby attracting criticism for its lack of theoretical rigour, especially in the accounting world. However, it does illustrate the ways in which methods from different methodological frameworks can be brought together in order to bring a further dimension to the research.

Throughout, the chapter seeks to highlight limitations in the implementation of accounting history research methods. One phenomenon which undermines the generalizability of research is the presence of bias. Two types are discussed. First, there is bias resulting from the 'selective survival' of material over time. This raises the question of how representative are data which are but a fraction of the whole information set. Secondly, biases of interpretation, resulting from the backgrounds and prejudices of the researcher are considered. The scope for minimizing each source of bias is outlined, though where this is not possible, an attempt is made to account for the impact of the bias on the research findings.

The uses and practical applications of historical accounting research are not considered, as this is well-recorded elsewhere (see Edwards, 1989a, 1989b; Parker, 1981).

The scope for research in accounting history

The subject matter of accounting history can be broadly divided into six main areas - biography; institutional history; development of accounting thought and practice; general history; databases; and historiography, though 'often a study draws upon and is identified with other areas' (PPC, 1990b, p. 137).[3]

Biographical research looks at the influence of individuals on the development of accounting thought, practice and institutions. Source material in this area includes personal correspondence, archive material and published works and speeches. In conducting such research, the scholar must attempt to analyse the major factors influencing the individuals' thought process, e.g. family background, education, social and political institutions, etc. PPC note the fragility of biographical research, in the sense that 'it relies on a single source' (ibid.), the subject, although it does utilise a wide range of primary and secondary supporting material. Examples of biographical research include Edwin Waterhouse's *Memoirs* (Jones, 1988); 'Truth in Accounting: The Ordeal of Kenneth MacNeal' (Zeff, 1982); and *Accounting Thought and Education: Six English Pioneers* (Kitchen and Parker, 1980).

The development of accounting firms and institutions are typical examples of research in institutional history. Conducting such research necessitates consulting records, correspondence, publications, press reports, memoranda, internal/management/departmental reports, minutes of board meetings and evidence given to various committees by representatives of particular bodies, for example, Company Law Amendment Committees. PPC argue that, 'assessing and analysing institutions' social and political environments are important dimensions' (1990b, p. 139). Histories of most of the major accountancy bodies have been written - e.g. ICAEW (Howitt, 1966), CIMA (Loft, 1990) and Society of Incorporated Accountants and Auditors (Garrett, 1961) - as have many histories of firms or 'house histories', e.g. Curtis, Jenkins, Cornwell & Co. (Cornwell, 1991); Pannell Kerr Forster (Medlam, 1980) and Thomson McLintock & Co. (Winsbury, 1977). A more ambitious version of this type of study is Edgar Jones' examination of Ernst & Whinney, which places the development of the firm in a macroeconomic context (Jones, 1981).

Scholars in the area of the development of accounting thought attempt to 'identify, articulate and explain the role that individuals, institutions and ideas have in developing and disseminating knowledge' (PPC, 1990b, p. 140). Some historians have conducted research on particular periods, for example Kojima and Yamey (1975), investigated the evolution of accounting thought in the Middle Ages. Others have tended to look at particular accounting concepts, and have attempted to analyse the factors influencing and inducing change over time (e.g. LIFO valuation, Davis, 1982). With respect to accounting practice, examples of work include 'The Development of Group Accounting in the United Kingdom to 1933' (Edwards and Webb, 1984) and *Company Legislation and Changing Patterns of Disclosure in British Company Accounts 1900-1940* (Edwards, 1981).

General history 'adopts an extensive temporal perspective focusing on issues such as practice in a particular country, the development of a nation's accounting profession over several centuries, or the progress of a whole sector of the discipline, such as cost accounting' (PPC, 1990b, p. 142). Pioneering works in this field include Littleton's *Accounting Evolution to 1900* (1933) and *A History of Accounting in America: An*

Historical Interpretation of the Cultural Significance of Accounting, by Previts and Merino (1979). Such general studies provide the researcher with a basic understanding, a broad overview, to allow him/her to home in on specific micro issues of interest.

Databases provide useful information to assist in other historical research. Examples include chronologies, e.g. Gibson (1988) *Chronological List of Books and Articles on Australian Accounting History* and bibliographies, e.g. Parker (1980) *Bibliographies for Accounting Historians*. Such research is a means for further research, by providing 'descriptive information about events, dates, times, groups of items, sources and related publications' (PPC, 1990b, p. 144) and is not an end in itself.

It is possible to sub divide each of these five research areas into private or public sector, and further, according to whether the focus is on either financial accounting or management accounting. Broadly speaking, to date, most research has considered financial accounting in the private sector. Few scholars have dedicated themselves to management accounting and even fewer have looked into government accounting, central or local. The possible time period to undertake research in accounting history is vast. Some of the earliest work has focused on the development of accounting in Mesopotamia six thousand years ago. Work on very early times is fairly scattered; more work has been done on accounting practices in the classical period, with there having been a heated debate whether the Romans used double entry book keeping.

A more recent area of research is historiography; the study of the writing of history. That it is new is hardly surprising, given that it is only post-1970 that academic research in accounting history has been vigorously undertaken. Examples include Gaffikin's 'The Archaeology of Accounting History' (1988) and Baladouni's 'The Study of Accounting History' (1979).

Methodological paradigms in accounting history

Three different methodological frameworks relevant to research in accounting history are considered; the traditional school, the critical perspective and the positive approach.

The traditional school

Much accounting history research has been geared towards describing and interpreting the past. This comprises the traditional school of research, which has generated data regarding different forms of accounts and accounting practice over time. In order to understand the past, there is a need to discover the events of the past. The discovery stage must involve a comprehensive study of original accounting records, accounting treatises and contemporary documents, which provide material relating to the usage of accounting; each of these three sources are discussed at length in this section. 'The discovery stage in the study of accounting history is essential for us to avoid the erection of theoretical superstructures on inadequate foundations' (Napier, 1989, p. 239).

The scrutiny of original documents is a highly time-intensive activity. This may explain the neglect of certain areas of research, such as nineteenth and early twentieth century company accounting practice and English and Scottish accounting methods between 1500 and 1850. Necessitating archival visits, research of original manuscripts is a slow process and a substantial amount of time must be invested to gain an insight into the accounting practices and methods adopted by a few companies. The difficulties encountered with archival research are numerous. First, there is the well-documented problem regarding access to private archives (for a useful archival guide, see Richmond and Stockford, 1986). There are problems for the researcher in deciding how representative are records of companies which have survived in archives to the present day (this is considered in greater detail later in this section). More specifically, it is clear that it will only be surviving companies who have archives and broadly speaking, the majority of these will be the larger and more successful companies.

Given that in some archives, libraries or records centres, there are restrictions on the number of items that can be consulted, the researcher must devise clear objectives. Hand lists should be obtained, in advance wherever possible, giving details of all the material available in the archive for a particular company. In some cases, deciphering what is relevant from what is irrelevant, based on entries on these lists, can be difficult. The researcher must adopt a detective-type procedure, based on the elimination of certain material, in order to focus on that which is of more direct relevance. Having said that, there is always the danger of finding fascinating material and losing sight of the objectives of the current project. In this respect, self-discipline is required, although interesting material should be noted for future reference.

Archival research demands patience and certainly cannot be hurried. Clearly such a time-intensive activity will raise funding requirements, unless local repositories are available. In many cases, a preliminary visit would be advisable, to devise a research plan and to check availability of material, items to consult, etc., for a future, longer visit.

With regard to the fundamentals of archival research, several points should be borne in mind. First, there is a marked tendency for archives to be open non-standard hours. Secondly, some institutions limit the number of researchers admitted in one day and the number of items that can be consulted in any one visit. Such regulations should be checked in advance. Thirdly, with any research project being undertaken in another institution, the availability of photocopying facilities is of great importance and should be clarified. Fourthly, the potential research outlet should be discussed in negotiating access to the archive, to ensure that results can be published. Some bodies will be sensitive regarding the publication of certain material, where it is even made available to the researcher.

Highlighting some of the difficulties of primary research should not undermine the importance and utility that archival studies can contribute to the enhancement of knowledge, particularly in the relatively youthful discipline of accounting history. Without the continuation of such work, the vibrancy of the discipline will be severely diminished.

The desire of the researcher to offer generalizations must be tempered when only a small number of records have been consulted. Until the researcher can be reasonably confident that practices disclosed by a few companies are representative of the population, generalization must be avoided. However, one means of understanding individual companies accounting systems and practices is to adopt a case-study approach, which necessitates consulting original documents.

One of the problems in any historical project is that of completeness. Given that only some of the records the researcher wishes to study will actually have survived, those that remain will only reveal a partial picture. The diligent researcher must, therefore, be aware of the limitations that 'selective survival' places on the research and attempt to account for the impact of this bias on the findings of the project. Surviving records can, however, be a mine of information. Book-keeping techniques, the subject matter of accounting, i.e. what is accounted for and accounting choices taken, e.g. valuation methods adopted, can all be revealed by studying a set of accounts.[4] One of the problems of the analysis of such accounts has been the tendency of scholars to judge past accounts on present criteria. Specifically, historians must guard against making judgements about the usefulness of past practices in terms of what is considered to be best practice today. For example, the lack of attention paid to valuation methods, such as making provisions for doubtful debts or depreciation, matters little when the purpose of the accounts is to keep track of physical goods, rather than to measure profit. Having said that, present practice can nevertheless serve as a useful yardstick for the purpose of identifying differences which will be comprehensible to readers.

Whilst the study of original, or primary accounting records, 'provides us with the raw data of history ... other sources to help us understand the past [include] ... treatises on accounting ... [which] help to illuminate practice and allow us to judge practices of their period in terms of textbook methods and assumptions' (Napier, 1989, p. 242). Clearly in attempting to use treatises to understand the past, the researcher must be aware of the relationship between the written texts and actual practice. Chatfield (1977, pp. 52-61) asserts that treatises positively assisted in spreading accounting practice. Did they reflect practice or did they influence practice? Were they used as teaching manuals, as works of reference or in some other manner? Such texts frequently contained model sets of accounts, which Edwards (1937) has argued were drawn from actual businesses. It seems probable that such treatises had a dual effect; they reflected practice and also helped to advance the diffusion of accounting practices.

Research utilizing the major auditing treatises has been undertaken by Chandler, Edwards and Anderson (1993). We look at the objectives of company audits, in addition to evidence given to government committees;

reports in contemporary journals, particularly *The Accountant* and secondary sources to challenge conventional wisdom. We suggest that statement verification was the primary audit concern in relation to large public companies as early as the 1830s, though fraud detection received more attention later in the nineteenth century. The conventional view saw auditors as *initially* being concerned with fraud detection, and that it was not until the 1930s that greater emphasis was devoted to the verification of financial statements (Chandler, Edwards and Anderson, forthcoming).

A third means of understanding the past is to consult contemporary documents, e.g. government reports, Acts of Parliament, law cases, literary references, etc. The researcher must make a conscious cost-benefit decision, on how far to probe such sources. Research by Edey and Panitpakdi (1956) and Edwards (1980) has focused on the legal framework in which accounting operates. Napier warns of the dangers of exaggerating 'the significance of legal requirements, or their absence' (1989, p. 243). He cites Edey and Panitpakdi, who, 'tend to view the relative absence of accounting provisions in general British company law as pointing to a laissez faire approach by the State in the latter part of the 19th Century' (ibid.). Napier and Noke (1988) argue that when legislation regarding particular types of business, e.g. railways and banks, is consulted, the State appears to have had a 'much more interventionist attitude to accounting ... than seems to be implied by the relative absence of accounting requirements from general company legislation' (ibid.). Such an example is an illustration of the importance of the cost-benefit decision, in deciding how far certain sources should be looked into. The failure to consult specific Acts of Parliament in this case, leads the researcher, who cites Edey and Panitpakdi, to draw an inaccurate picture of the role of the State regarding accounting requirements. To avoid such information biases from impacting on research output, the researcher must identify all potential sources that relate to the project before the cost-benefit decision is made. Whilst it is impossible to consult all material, assuming that such sources are either known or available, it is imperative that the researcher attempts to account for the impact of information bias and bias accruing from not being able to obtain documents, on the research findings.

Napier (1989, p. 243) warns of the dangers of using material in an antiquarian manner:

> To give a hypothetical example, an antiquarian might be interested with merely identifying every reference to accounts in the plays of Shakespeare, while an historian would attempt to integrate these references with a knowledge of contemporary accounting practice and theory in order to draw conclusions as to how well Shakespeare knew his accounting.

There are inherent dangers in taking sources at face value because bias and differing levels of understanding of writers, the financial press and professionals, must always be appreciated. As Napier explains, 'the attitude of these [*The Times* and *Financial Times*] newspapers to accounting at any particular time must reflect only a partial (and, quite probably, a biased) view of overall social viewpoints' (ibid.).

Some of the problems alluded to in this section, namely, generalization, understanding the past in terms of the present and antiquarianism, have led to a recent trend in accounting history, which attempts to place events in their historical context. This approach is now considered.

Critical perspective

The critical perspective is a major recent development in the study of accounting history, which attempts to place the subject more firmly in its historical context. As Napier (1989, p. 244) has pointed out, 'this approach to accounting history owes its name to the title of a paper by Hopwood (1983): 'On Trying to study Accounting in the Contexts in which it Operates''.

The main argument of these researchers is that we should not regard accounting as a neutral, technical process, but that we should view it as one element in a complex process involving social, political, economic and organizational factors which are often in direct conflict with one another. Hopwood (1987, p. 207) has challenged conventional wisdom that sees 'accounting change as a process of technical elaboration and, almost inevitably, improvement'. Such 'Accounting Darwinism' (American Accounting Association, 1977) assumed that the best firms would use the best methods ensuring that procedures gradually achieve higher and higher levels of sophistication.

Advocates of the critical perspective sometimes see accounting history as consisting of a series of discontinuous events. 'The seeds of present practices and explanations cannot necessarily be detected in the past: accounting becomes what it was not' (Napier, 1989, p. 244). This is sometimes referred to as The New Accounting History and its proponents have appealed to theories put forward by a variety of writers and philosophers, foremost among whom is Michael Foucault (1970; 1972; 1977; and 1980). His influence works on several levels, but is based on the existence of power-knowledge relationships.[5] Foucault introduces the notion of a discourse of accounting, which is 'a language expressed in terms of accounting that, as it changes through time, enables us to see, within accounting, different phenomena, and by seeing them to control them' (Napier, 1989, p. 245). He argues that 'we can understand the development of modern societies in terms of power, and the shift in its mode of exercise' (Miller and O'Leary, 1987, p. 238). Foucault identifies a broad shift in power around 1800, from sovereign power to disciplinary power. Sovereign power is 'seen as arbitrary but at the same time limited' (Napier, 1989, p. 245), relying at some stage on seizure 'of things, of bodies and ultimately of life' (Miller and O'Leary, 1987, p. 238). Disciplinary power, in contrast, penetrates all areas of life through numerous regulations and administrative tools, achieving 'the calculated management of social life' (ibid.).

Power-knowledge relationships have been used by several writers in the accounting history field (see Hoskin and Macve (1986 and 1988); Loft (1986 and 1988) and Hopwood (1987)). Hopwood highlights the usefulness of the Foucauldian perspective in his reinterpretation of research into the eighteenth century potter Josiah Wedgwood, originally undertaken by McKendrick (1970). Reacting to adverse market conditions in 1772, Wedgwood reviewed his prices and costs, to identify product lines where there was scope for price-cutting. As a by-product of this review, the master potter unveiled fraudulent behaviour by his

London agent and inefficient practices being undertaken by his employees were exposed.

Hopwood (1987, pp. 214-218) sees the unanticipated nature of the consequences of the discovery of accounting by Wedgwood as being central to 'the notion of accounting's becoming what it was not. One aspect of this is "putting accounting where accounting was not"' (Napier, 1989, p. 245). Whilst a concept of cost was embodied in the discourse of commerce and trade, no accurate techniques of cost finding existed in 1772. But,

> once [costs had been] constructed, ... Wedgwood had a powerful instrument for observing the organisation in economic terms. His strategic conception of the role which records could play in the management of crisis had resulted in a means by which he could penetrate the inner workings of the organisation. A new visibility had been created. The organisation had been colonised by economic facts ... An accounting eye had provided Wedgwood with a new means for intervening in the organisation. And intervene he did (Hopwood, 1987, p. 217).

Foucault introduced two further concepts, genealogy and archaeology, which provide a useful framework for scholars who seek to contextualize accounting history. Genealogy creates a role for history which attempts to 'make intelligible the way in which we think today by reminding us of its conditions of formation' (Miller and O'Leary, 1987, p. 237). This is undertaken, not to look for a single point in history as being the origin of current practices and concepts, but rather to identify the interaction of a complex of events that have given rise to the current state of affairs. Genealogy involves opening out our history from purely accounting to include the social context, in particular national conditions, political objectives of different regimes, the development of similar disciplines and historical chance.

Archaeology relates to the way in which our historical research should be undertaken. As Napier (1989, p. 246) explains,

Our attention should be directed towards the emergence of forms of discourse, and their grounding in institutional and legal criteria and pedagogical norms. An archaeology, in the Foucauldian sense, is an attempt to isolate the conditions that make practices and discourses possible, aiming to reconstruct the basis on which practice is formed, functions and has its effects. Genealogy, however, focuses on the discontinuities and transitions whereby practices take on new significances as they become involved in new purposes.

Whether the Foucauldian philosophy will be successful in increasing our understanding of accounting history remains to be seen, given its recent origin. Recent papers on the accounting profession have brought a more explicit sociological dimension, though not necessarily Foucauldian, to the study of accounting history (see papers by Macdonald (1984); Loft (1986) and Willmott (1986)). Such approaches require readers to come to terms with 'concepts and disciplines quite distant from accounting' (Napier, 1989, p. 247), particularly philosophy and sociology. Some academics find the critical perspective to be obscure and prefer a positive approach to accounting history. Such an approach is now considered.

Positive approach

A third 'positive' approach to accounting, which views the 'objective of theory as explaining and predicting accounting practice' (ibid.) has increased in importance in the last decade. One of the major strengths of this approach is its testability against empirical data, by using statistical hypotheses testing of models.[6] Much reliance is placed on economic theories, which are themselves drawn largely from the neo-classical perspective. The importance of this is clear, given the (sometimes harsh) criticism of some traditional research as fact-finding antiquarianism. In addition, 'the problems addressed are likely to be of contemporary relevance (although this might reflect the demand for positive explanations of certain current phenomena rather than anything intrinsic to positive accounting theory)' (ibid.).

The problems with quantitative research are well-known, but in relation to accounting history are threefold. First, there are raw data problems. There are inherent difficulties in taking data at face value. It is frequently argued that such problems are overlooked by positive scholars, who see their role as one of interpretation of the actual numbers, rather than saying what those numbers ought to be. From my own research, using the *Stock Exchange Year Book*, there are difficulties in using data on non-tangibles, capital employed, loan capital, profitability, dividend payments and financial ratio analysis (see Armstrong, 1991, p. 15, for a discussion). A second problem, which is common to accounting history research generally, and one which we have already discussed, concerns attempting to understand the past in terms of the present. Using quantitative methods, positive theorists are prone to viewing the past in ways in which they can model, with the use of contemporary theories and analytical tools. A third area of concern regarding the application of quantitative techniques to accounting history relates to the historical environment. This draws attention to the fact that statistics may be unable to capture the real explanatory factors in a process. For example, accounting regulation and legalistic developments are responsible for much of the financial disclosure and accounting practices adopted by companies. Chow (1982) chose a period of non-regulation (1926) to examine US firms' incentives to pay for auditing. As Benston (1979-80) argues, it would seem likely that mandatory audit requirements would distort the market-determined economic models of auditing. The study is valid, in the sense that regulatory factors do not limit the outcomes, but it is limited, in that the time-period covered is conditioned   by the prevailing environment. Other examples of work in this area are Brown and Easton (1986); Dillon (1984); and Watts and Zimmermann (1979).

A reconciliation of the three approaches

Having outlined three different frameworks for research, it must be emphasized that they need not be seen in isolation, though often are, by their various proponents. In many research projects, there is room for more than one approach. The positive and critical approaches both rely on data drawn from the traditional, fact-finding school. Without discovering the events of the past, there is no possibility of understanding the past. As Napier (1989, p. 250) argues, 'the contextualisers are likely

... to rely on the traditionalists to generate much of the raw data for their theorizing', though the collectors themselves do attempt to interpret their findings. Those who favour such interpretational history, which seeks 'to evaluate relationships and provide interpretations in the manner of a social science' (PPC, 1990a, p. 2), must rely on the fruits of narrative research, which itself aims 'to establish and/or describe items of fact' (ibid.). Advocates of the New Accounting History are rather harsh on earlier writers. They seem to assume that no one before has made any attempt to place observed events into their environmental, historical, social or economic context. Whilst it is a recent phenomenon for sociological and philosophical theories to be used in the accounting history literature, the assertion that the traditionalists failed to contextualize is far from the truth.

The role of accountants in business development

This research project looks at the role of professional accountants in business development over the period from the mid-nineteenth century to the present day. The influence of accountants in the growth and subsequent decline of the British economy is an area that has received little attention, hence the impetus for this study, which broadly fits into the traditional school of accounting history research.[7] Our research combines qualitative and quantitative techniques and illustrates how 'messy' the research process can be. We neither adopt a text book model, nor work in an area that has been the subject of previous research. The parallels between the general research methods employed in this project and those in ethnographic research, particularly participant observation, are most marked. Both involve the gathering of vast amounts of information; then the researcher faces the task of making sense of this information set, in order to generate explanatory theories. Whilst many historians are critical of research which lacks theoretical rigour at the outset, without such fact-finding research, the theorists would lack the material on which to theorize. Our experience emphasizes that the implementation of research methods is often an uncertain and disjointed process; a process involving risk, both in terms of academic credibility and also time. The former relates to criticisms of antiquarianism, while the latter refers to the vast amount of time invested in a project which carries no guarantee of uncovering anything of interest. This time-element is of great significance given the increasing pressures being placed on the academic community to increase research output. The failure to produce publishable material from such projects, can also have serious implications for future research funding applications.

The reasons for attempting to combine qualitative and quantitative dimensions were twofold. First, we wished to generate a broad picture of the numbers of professional accountants who entered business across the time period and secondly, to attempt to find out the reasons for such moves and the influence of accountants in their new environment. This project conforms with PPC's contention that 'evidence as to the use of quantitative approaches to support historical interpretation is becoming more frequent' (1990b, p. 148). This section highlights the two aspects of the project; the statistical method is outlined first.

A pilot study was first undertaken (see Matthews, 1993) and a method was then adopted which utilized the *Stock Exchange Year Book* (SEY) as a data source. The value of the SEY is acknowledged by Armstrong (1991, p. 14), 'although these records only give details on publicly quoted companies - more specifically those traded on the London Stock Exchange ... they are nonetheless a priceless source for the business historian'. We generated random samples of quoted companies with headquarters in England or Wales, from the SEY, across our sample years of 1891, 1911, 1931, 1951, 1971 and 1991. These dates were chosen to correspond with The Census of Population. However, subsequent research has shown the Census figures to be unreliable in measuring accountants, largely due to the changing classification of 'accountant'.[8]

Having generated random samples of companies for each of the years selected, we used a spreadsheet statistical package to manage the data. Whilst being primarily interested in directors, we have been able to build up a comprehensive database on Lotus 123, of the companies in each 20 year sample. The data includes name, address, business, SEY classification, authorized capital, profitability, date registered, recent dividend history, auditors, office bearers and their qualifications. Having input this data onto the spreadsheet, we sorted the office bearers alphabetically and obtained a printout. For each office bearer, we designated with appropriate letters whether they were chairman (C), managing director (M), secretary (SN for secretary not sitting on board; SE for one who does) and other directors (D).

The alphabetical lists of directors from 1891-1991, built up from our random samples of quoted companies, were then compared with lists of members of professional accountancy bodies, held at the British Library. This was a considerable administrative exercise and necessitated checking our list of in excess of two thousand names, for each sample year, against the lists of each society. Bearing in mind that the major accountancy bodies of today (e.g. ICAEW, ACCA, CIMA) have formed as a result of mergers, the laborious nature of this process can be appreciated. For example, in 1931, eight different bodies' Lists of Members were checked against the sample of directors for that year. We used the *Directory of Directors* to sort out problems regarding Christian names, addresses, etc., of directors with popular names.[9]

Once we had identified professionally qualified accountants, we were then able to calculate the proportion of qualified accountants in our sample of directors. This is shown in Table 3.1. The data on chairmen, managing directors and secretaries, was also used to calculate the percentage of our sample in each of these three positions respectively, who were professionally qualified accountants. This also allowed us to examine what percentage of companies had an accountant director. Clearly, from Table 3.1, it can be seen that there has been a massive increase in the representation of accountants at board level over the last 100 years. Indeed, by 1991, slightly more than four in five companies had at least one accountant director. The object of this chapter is not to interpret the results of our findings, but to highlight the methods used. However, the rise of accountants in the boardroom would not be significant if other professions demonstrated a parallel increase. How can the rise of other professions be measured?

Having built up a database, we measured the rise of all professions by analysing the qualifications of directors given in the SEY. Further research is currently being undertaken in this area, but preliminary results show that the rise of the accountant at board level is only eclipsed by the growth in the graduate qualification. One of the problems with this statistical exercise is the 20 year intervals. Whilst we have discovered a strong upward trend, the short-term variations in board representation cannot be deduced from such a study. An analogy would be looking at GDP growth and missing the effect of the trade-cycle. What we are striving to find out, is whether there has been a steady growth, or whether accountants have become board members in clusters, for example, when the company has been in distress, or when a takeover is looming.

Table 3.1

The Involvement of Qualified Accountants in Business Development 1891-1991

Year	1891	1911	1931	1951	1971	1991
Companies in sample	541	437	340	340	322	324
Directors in sample	2651	2011	1653	1592	1870	2084
Per cent of companies with an accountant director	4.0	7.6	19.1	39.1	65.8	82.1
Per cent of managing directors who were accountants	0.0	2.2	2.6	4.8	13.8	19.3
Per cent of secretaries who were accountants	7.1	7.3	14.3	29.0	41.7	47.4
Per cent of chairmen who were accountants	0.8	0.6	4.6	7.6	13.6	20.7
Per cent of company directors who were accountants	0.8	1.7	3.8	9.4	15.2	22.0

Given that we have been able to show that accountants have become increasingly prominent on the boards of directors of quoted companies, we must address two fundamental questions. Why were accountants brought onto the board and what did they do? Clearly statistics cannot answer such questions, hence the rationale for bringing in a qualitative dimension to the study. One of the ways in which we have attempted to tackle this problem is to trawl through the five volumes of Jeremy's *Dictionary of Business Biography* (DBB), which gives biographical notes on prominent businessmen, including over 40 accountants. Reading through these provides a basis for seeking further references to chronicle individual's associations with companies, outside their duties as public accountants working in private practice. The DBB provides a wealth of information on the different personalities, reflecting the interests of the biographer, hence it is usually necessary to consult the sources cited to seek additional material.

Having targeted certain companies and individuals which seemed to warrant further research, we turned to company histories. References for these can be found in Debrett's *Bibliography of Business History* and the University of Glasgow's Business Archives Council Library Catalogue (available on microfiche). Both are useful sources; the latter is more comprehensive, giving company and subject classifications, whereas Debrett's gives a sector breakdown. One common problem is the difficulty of deciding from the author, title and number of pages in a book, how relevant or useful such a text will be. The problem is insoluble, though the number of pages can be a useful barometer of the depth of the book. Also, having identified certain authors who include accounting material in their histories, other texts written by them can be scanned.

Problems in conducting company history research, using secondary sources are numerous. First, there is the difficulty of obtaining material. Many historical texts cannot be found on the shelves of university libraries, which either necessitates taking recourse to inter-library loans or visiting libraries where they are available; the latter incurs considerable expense. Secondly, the diligent researcher must attempt to assess how representative one history is of the population. This is the problem of generalization from an inadequate factual base, outlined earlier. One partial solution to this is to consult many histories, to attempt to view the overall picture from many different angles. Clearly though, such a strategy will be bounded by financial and time constraints. A third problem concerns the identification of bias in company histories and attempting to take them into account, in order to build as an objective a portrait of the company as is possible. This is extremely difficult. The use of *Accountancy and the British Economy 1840-1980*, by Edgar Jones (1981), will serve as an example. Jones claims that Whinney, Smith and

Whinney (WSW) was a typical nineteenth century accounting firm, which was heavily involved in insolvency work. This finding, from Jones' breakdown of the fee income of WSW (data on other firms is as yet unpublished), has become the 'conventional wisdom'. However, the 1867 Select Committee on Limited Liability recorded that two of the predecessor firms of WSW had 'cornered the market in liquidations', being responsible for administering 61 out of 259 liquidations proceeding in 1866. The dangers of a 'conventional wisdom' developing from one piece of research are clearly evident. In company histories, the danger is magnified in the sense that the researcher often has to take material at face value due to lack of knowledge of the subject matter. Hence, certain interpretational biases cannot be picked out.

A fourth problem, recurrent in accounting history generally, concerns the fact that records of past events are incomplete. Moreover, the records of more successful firms are more likely to have survived than the records of those that have failed. In terms of company histories, there will perhaps be a marked tendency for the histories of successful firms to be written; often such histories are written to commemorate anniversaries. Related to this point, but more specifically with regard to archival work, is the problem of selective survival of material; sturdy bound ledgers are more likely to have survived and been protected by archivists and librarians than loose leaf documentation, which is often of much greater interest.[10] This is to be lamented, given that it is usually the working papers that are of greater interest (see Napier, 1989, p. 240).

Having outlined some of the difficulties of secondary source research, the advantages of such an approach are now considered. First, the coverage of industries and individual accountants is vast. Hence, by reading 60 or 70 company histories, a broad overview of the role of different accountants operating in different sectors can be achieved. Secondly, whilst it is a lengthy process to read a large number of histories, it is less time-intensive than visiting a large number of company archives, assuming that the researcher can gain access to these. A useful text which lists company archives and what they contain is *Company Archives: The Survey of the Records of 1000 of the First Registered Companies in England and Wales*, authored by Richmond and Stockford (1986). Thirdly, this secondary source-type of research may be the only avenue available to undertake. Where no archive material is available, or where interview or questionnaire analysis is precluded, due to the time period under consideration, reliance may have to be placed on such a method. Fourthly, the bibliographies of company histories can be useful in providing further references for additional research.

Consulting company histories, the DBB and histories of accounting firms, enables us to obtain a clearer picture of the role played by accountants across the period from 1840 to date. Clearly, as we have seen, reliance on secondary source evidence alone has limitations. However, incorporating other research methods into the analysis, overcomes many of these and brings a further dimension to the work.

Conclusion

This chapter has focused on research issues in accounting history; a discipline which has seen a surge in academic interest following the first International Congress of Accounting Historians, in Brussels in 1970. Scholars have tended to work in six main areas: biography; institutional history; development of accounting thought and practice; general history; databases; and historiography, though these are not rigid demarcations.

The second part of the chapter dealt with a critique of three competing methodological perspectives, within which accounting history research is conducted. Whilst the traditional, critical and positive approaches appear to differ markedly, a reconciliation of the schools of thought was offered, based on the dependence of the latter two methods on the fact-finding and data collection role of the traditional school.

To illustrate that accounting history research can draw on aspects from different methodological frameworks, a research project which looks at the role of accountants in business development was outlined. This work combines qualitative and quantitative methods and demonstrates that the research process is often imperfect and need not necessarily follow text book models. The limitations of historical enquiry were addressed in different contexts throughout the chapter. In particular, the impact of bias on the findings of a given project was highlighted. Two types of bias - incompleteness resulting from selective survival of material and biases of interpretation - were outlined. Strategies for minimizing such bias were offered, though given that it is qualitative data being dealt with, no rigorous techniques similar to those adopted in the quantitative field have been developed, hence the researcher must be more cautious. Such limitations should not be glossed over, they should be acknowledged and an attempt made to quantify their impact on the research findings.

Notes

1.   For a general discussion of historical methodology see, Muller (1967); Postan (1971); and Carr (1962). These authors address a wide range of issues including ideas of fact, impartiality, historical truths, assumptions and narrative.

2.   Conscious of Parker's (1993) criticism of Previts, Parker and Coffman (1990a, 1990b) this paper intentionally concentrates solely on work written in English.

3.   This useful classification is provided by Previts, Parker and Coffman (1990b).

4.   Papers by Parker (1991) and Marriner (1980) look at some of the ways in which accounts can be misleading to the historian.

5.   Neimark (1990) provides a useful critique of Foucault's influence on critical accounting.

6.   Necessarily, the results of such positive research projects will be conditioned by the assumptions made and the framework of the explanatory model employed. Such assumptions inherent in the research methodology should be made explicit and the ways in which they impact on the results must be addressed. For a critique of the positive approach, see Christenson (1983); Lowe, Puxty and Laughlin (1983); and Tinker, Merino and Neimark (1982).

7.   This discovery-type research project is an illustration of the limitations of categorizing accounting history work into different areas. It is partly traditional, in that it attempts to address issues hitherto neglected; it employs some simple statistical techniques and it seeks to contextualize the role of accountants in business development, though not within a Foucauldian or sociological framework.

8. It should be noted that the inaccuracy of the Census in counting the number of accountants does not impinge on the reliability of our study. Matthews (1993) discusses an alternative method of enumerating the number of accountants by summing the total memberships of the major accountancy societies, though this is an imperfect solution, given dual memberships, the retired and those members who reside overseas.

9. For a director with a popular name (e.g. John Smith), when checking in the accountancy societies Lists of Members, the *Directory of Directors* would be consulted, to check his qualifications, his board appointments and also to obtain an address for him, to ensure that this corresponded with the SEY entry (i.e. that it was the same John Smith who was a director of one of the companies in our sample).

10. A store room of large bound ledgers may be of little use in answering any of the major questions worrying accounting and business historians. They might only prove that the company operated a system to keep track of goods, act as a memory aid and enable the final accounts to be prepared. The first two are of limited interest to today's researcher and the third of little interest if the published accounts themselves are available.

References

American Accounting Association (1970), Committee on Accounting History, *The Accounting Review*, Vol. 45 (Suppl.).

American Accounting Association (1977), Committee on Concepts and Standards for External Financial Reports, *Statement on Accounting Theory and Theory Acceptance*, American Accounting Association, New York.

Armstrong, J. (1991), 'An introduction to archival research in business history', *Business History*, No 1, pp. 7-34.

Baladouni, V. (1979), 'The study of accounting history', Working Paper No. 19, in Coffman, E.N. (ed.), *The Academy of Accounting Historians Working Paper Series*, Vol. 1, The Academy of Accounting Historians.

Benston, G.J. (1979-80), 'The market for public accounting services: demand, supply and regulation', *Accounting Journal*, Winter, pp. 2-46.

Brown, R.L. and S.A. Easton (1986), 'Weak form efficiency in the nineteenth century: A study of daily prices in the London market for three per Cent consols 1821-1861', Working Paper No. 26, Monash University, Australia.

Carr, E.H. (1962), *What is History?*, Macmillan, London.

Chandler, R.A., J.R. Edwards and M. Anderson (1993), 'Changing perceptions of the role of the company auditor, 1840-1940', *Accounting and Business Research*, forthcoming.

Chatfield, M. (1977), *A History of Accounting Thought*, Krieger, Huntingdon, New York.

Chow, C.W. (1982), 'The demand for external auditing: Size, debt and ownership influences', *The Accounting Review*, April, pp. 272-291.

Christenson, C. (1983), 'The methodology of positive accounting', *The Accounting Review*, No. 1, pp. 1-22.

Cornwell, S.V.P. (1991), *Curtis, Jenkins, Cornwell & Co. A Study in Professional Origins 1816-1966*, Garland, New York.

Davis, H.Z. (1982), 'History of LIFO', *The Accounting Historians Journal*, Spring, pp. 1-23.

Dillon, G.J. (1984), *The Role of Accounting in the Stock Market Crash of 1929*, Business Publishing Division, College of Business Administration, Georgia State University.

Directory of Directors (various years), Thomas Skinner, London.

Edey, H. C. and P. Panitpakdi (1956), 'British company accounting and the law 1844-1900' in A.C. Littleton and B.S. Yamey (eds), *Studies in the History of Accounting*, Sweet & Maxwell, London, pp. 356-379.

Edwards, J.R. (1980), *British Company Legislation and Company Accounts 1844-1976*, Arno Press, New York.

Edwards, J.R. (1981), *Company Legislation and Changing Patterns of Disclosure in British Company Accounts 1900-1940*, ICAEW, London.

Edwards, J.R. (1989), 'Ignore history at your peril', *Accountancy*, May, pp. 184-185.

Edwards, J.R. (1989), *A History of Financial Accounting*, Routledge, London.

Edwards, J.R. and K.M. Webb (1984), 'The development of group accounting in the United Kingdom to 1933', *The Accounting Historians Journal*, Spring, pp. 31-61.

Edwards, R.S. (1937), 'Some notes on the early literature and development of cost accounting - II', *The Accountant*, 14 August, pp. 225-231.

Foucault, M. (1970), *The Order of Things*, Tavistock Publications, London.

Foucault, M. (1972), *The Archaeology of Knowledge*, Tavistock Publications, London.

Foucault, M. (1977), *Discipline and Punish*, Allen Lane, London.

Foucault, M. (1980), *Power/Knowledge*, Harvester Press, Brighton.

Gaffikin, M.J.R. (1988a), 'Legacy of the golden age: Recent developments in the methodology of accounting', *ABACUS*, No. 1, pp. 16-36.

Gaffikin, M. (1988b), 'The archaeology of accounting' in Craswell, A. (ed.), *Collected Papers of the Fifth World Congress of Accounting Historians*, The University of Sydney.

Gaffikin, M. (1987), 'The methodology of early accounting theorists', *ABACUS*, No. 1, pp. 17-30.

Garrett, A.A. (1961), *History of the Society of Incorporated Accountants and Auditors, 1885-1957*, University Press, Oxford.

Gibson, R.W. (1988), 'Chronological list of books and articles on Australian accounting history', *Accounting History Newsletter* (AAANZ), Winter.

Hopwood, A.G. (1983), 'On trying to study accounting in the contexts in which it operates', *Accounting, Organizations and Society*, pp. 287-305.

Hopwood, A.G. (1987), 'The archaeology of accounting systems', *Accounting, Organizations and Society*, pp. 207-234.

Hopwood, A.G. and H. T. Johnson (1986), 'Accounting history's claim to legitimacy', *The International Journal of Accounting*, Spring, pp. 37-46.

Hoskin, K.M. and R.H. Macve (1986), 'Accounting and the examination: A genealogy of disciplinary power', *Accounting, Organizations and Society*, pp. 105-136.

Hoskin, K.M. and R.H. Macve (1988), 'The genesis of accountability: The West Point connection', *Accounting, Organizations and Society*, pp. 37-73.

Howitt, H. (1966), *The History of the Chartered Accountants in England and Wales 1870-1965*, William Heinemann Ltd., London; reprinted by Garland Publishing, London and New York, 1984.

Jeremy, D.J. (ed.) (1984-86), *Dictionary of Business Biography*, I-V, Butterworths, London.

Jones, E. (1981), *Accountancy and the British Economy 1840-1980: The Evolution of Ernst & Whinney*, Batsford, London.

Jones, E. (ed.) (1988), *The Memoirs of Edwin Waterhouse: A Founder of Price Waterhouse*, Batsford, London.

Kitchen, J. and R.H. Parker (1980), *Accounting Education and Thought: Six British Pioneers*, ICAEW, London.

Kojima, O. and B.S. Yamey (eds) (1975), *A Notable and Very Excellente Woorke*, Daigakudo Books.

Lister, R.J. (1984), 'Accounting as history', *The International Journal of Accounting*, Spring, pp. 49-68.

Littleton, A.C. (1933), *Accounting Evolution to 1900*, American Institute Publishing Company Inc., New York.

Loft, A. (1986), 'Towards a critical understanding of accounting: The case of cost accounting in the U.K., 1914-1925', *Accounting, Organizations and Society*, pp. 137-171.

Loft, A. (1988), *Understanding Accounting in its Social and Historical Context: The Case of Cost Accounting in Britain 1914-1923*, Garland Publishing, New York.

Loft, A. (1990), *Coming Into the Light*, CIMA, London.

Lowe, E.A., A.G. Puxty, and R.C. Laughlin (1983), 'Simple theories for complex processes: Accounting policy and the market for myopia', *Journal of Accounting and Public Policy*, pp. 19-42.

Macdonald, K.M. (1984), 'Professional formation: The case of Scottish accountants', *British Journal of Sociology*, June, pp. 174-189.

Marriner, S. (1980), 'Company financial statements as source material for business historians', *Business History*, No. 2, pp. 203-235.

Matthews, D. (1993), 'Counting the accountants: A trial balance for 1911', *Accounting, Business and Financial History*, forthcoming.

McKendrick, N. (1970), 'Josiah Wedgwood and cost accounting in the industrial revolution', *The Economic History Review*, pp. 45-67.

Medlam, W. (1980), *Pannell Kerr Forster. A History of Pannell Fitzpatrick & Co.*, Pannell Kerr Forster, London.

Miller, P., T. Hopper, and R. Laughlin (1991), 'The new accounting history: An introduction', *Accounting, Organizations and Society*, No. 5/6, pp. 395-403.

Miller, P. and T. O'Leary (1987), 'Accounting and the construction of the governable person', *Accounting, Organizations and Society*, pp. 235-266.

Muller, G. (1967), 'History as a rigorous discipline', *History and Theory*, No. 3, pp. 299-312.

Napier, C.J. (1989), 'Research directions in accounting history', *British Accounting Review*, 21, pp. 237-254.

Napier, C.J. and C.W. Noke (1988), 'Accounting and the law: An historical overview of an uneasy relationship'. Paper presented at the Deloitte Haskins & Sells/ICAEW Accounting Research Synopsium, 26 September.

Neimark, M. (1990), 'The king is dead, long live the king!', *Critical Perspectives on Accounting*, 1, pp. 103-114.

Parker, R.H. (1978), 'British men of account', *ABACUS*, June, pp. 53-65.

Parker, R.H. (1980), *Bibliographies for Accounting Historians*, Arno Press, New York.

Parker, R.H. (1981), 'The study of accounting history' in M. Bromwich M. and A.G. Hopwood (eds), *Essays in British Accounting Research*, Pitman, London, pp. 279-293.

Parker, R.H. (1991), 'Misleading accounts? Pitfalls for historians', *Business History*, No. 4, pp. 1-18.

Parker, R.H. (1993), 'The scope of accounting history: A note', *ABACUS*, No. 1, pp. 106-110.

Postan, M.M. (1971), 'The historical method in social science', reprinted in *Fact and Relevance: Essays on Historical Methods*, Cambridge University Press, Cambridge.

Previts, G.J., L.D. Parker and E.N. Coffman (1990a), 'Accounting History: Definition and Relevance', *ABACUS*, No. 1, pp. 1-16.

Previts, G.J., L.D. Parker and E.N. Coffman (1990b), 'An accounting historiography: Subject matter and methodology', *ABACUS*, No. 2, pp. 136-158.

Previts, G.J. and B.D. Merino (1979), *A History of Accounting in America: An Historical Interpretation of the Cultural Significance of Accounting*, Ronald Press, New York.

Richmond, L. and B. Stockford (1986), *Company Archives: The Survey of the Records of 1000 of the First Registered Companies in England and Wales*, Gower Publishing Company, Vermont, USA.

Spicer, E.E. and E.C. Pegler (1923), *Audit Programmes* (6th Edition), H.F.L. Publishers Ltd., London.

Stacey, N.A.H. (1954), *English Accountancy: A Study in Social and Economic History*, Gee, London.

Stock Exchange Official Intelligence (various years), London.

Stock Exchange Official Year Book (various years), Macmillan, London and Basingstoke.

Stock Exchange Year Book (various years), Thomas Skinner, London.

Tinker, A.M., B.D. Merino and M.D. Neimark (1982), 'The normative origins of positive theories: Ideology and accounting thought', *Accounting, Organizations and Society*, pp. 167-200.

Watts, R.L. and J. Zimmermann (1979), 'The demand for and supply of accounting theories: The market for excuses', *The Accounting Review*, April, pp. 273-305.

Willmott, H. (1986), 'Organising the profession: A theoretical and historical examination of the development of the major accountancy bodies in the U.K.', *Accounting, Organizations and Society*, No. 6, pp. 555-580.

Winsbury, R. (1977), *Thomson McLintock & Co. - The First Hundred Years*, London.

Zarach, S. (ed.) (1987), *Debrett's Bibliography of Business History*, Macmillan, Basingstoke.

Zeff, S.A. (1982), 'Truth in accounting: The ordeal of Kenneth MacNeal', *The Accounting Review*, July, pp. 528-553.

4 Minimizing and Managing Bias in a Mail Survey: A Study of Redundant Miners

VICTORIA WASS

Introduction

In any research project there is a hierarchy of objectives, the first and foremost of which relates to the purpose of the research in terms of expanding knowledge about a social phenomenon. The research methodology is the instrument through which the research objective is fulfilled. The objective of the research methodology, whatever the objective of the research, is to achieve high quality information, that is data, which are free from bias in relation to the social phenomenon under investigation. In this chapter attention is drawn to some of the potential sources of bias in the collection and analysis of data collected by means of a postal questionnaire survey and some of the techniques available to identify and control for them are outlined.

The objective of this research project was, broadly speaking, to investigate the effects of colliery closure on the local labour market. In particular, we sought to explain the differential risk of redundancy and unemployment across a group of miners affected by colliery closure and the implications of any differential for labour market adjustment. To this end, information about personal characteristics and labour market outcomes of redundant and relocating miners was collected. A nomethetic methodology, specifically a sample survey, was used and conducted by means of a postal questionnaire.

The chapter begins by explaining the choice of research methodology in relation to the theoretical perspective underlying the study. The discussion which follows describes how the methodology was implemented with a view to achieving relevant and high quality data.

The choice of research methodology

Background to the research

Between April 1985 and April 1986, the National Coal Board (NCB) had closed 11 collieries in the coal field of South Wales, 32 nationally, with the direct loss of 6,000 and 48,000 jobs respectively. Redundancy was non-compulsory, in the sense that miners had the right to remain in the employment of the NCB through relocation to an alternative working colliery. The redundancy scheme, the Redundant Miners Payments Scheme (RMPS), was characterized by self-selection and differential compensation. Redundancy compensation compared favourably to that available in other sectors and was widely regarded as generous. RMPS was not unique; since the Redundancy Payment Act of 1965, an increasing number of companies, including nationalized industries, were adopting voluntary, or more accurately self-selection, redundancy schemes in preference to compulsory redundancy. Increasing levels of redundancy compensation were an inevitable consequence of this trend. The stated objective of the redundancy legislation of the 1960s and 1970s was, and continues to be, to raise labour mobility. In 1985, male unemployment rates were approaching 16 per cent nationally: 25 per cent in the South Wales coal field. The coincidence of redundancy and mass unemployment calls into question whether, at the level of the macro economy, this objective is being realized. At the microeconomic level, it is the relationship between redundancy and unemployment for the individual which is important. Is there a disfunctionality between the objective of the redundancy legislation and the outcome of the legislation in practice? Are those workers most likely to experience unemployment also those most likely to become redundant?

Theoretical perspective

Research questions appear to arise naturally from the subject of the research but the researcher does not enter the field with a blank mind. Which questions s/he seeks to answer depends not only upon the subject of the investigation, but also on an existing understanding of how social phenomena can be explained and revealed. This latter depends upon prior choices about the theoretical approach to the research subject (ontology) and the theoretical approach to research (epistemology). Often these choices are not made consciously but nevertheless they have major implications for the nature of research undertaken and the answers generated.

A neoclassical economic theoretical perspective was adopted in this study. Labour market outcomes are explained in terms of individual circumstances and behaviour in response to labour market incentives. Outcomes are predicted in advance of the research through a process of logical deduction and are tested against observations in the empirical world.

The research methodology is nomethetic - an adaptation of the experimental model from natural science for use in a non-experimental social science context. The methodology includes a set of criteria by which to evaluate the findings in relation to the research hypotheses. Bias in the data is a particular concern. Where data are in some respect incomplete or inadequate in relation to the research hypotheses, i.e. they are biased, then inferences about the hypotheses cannot easily be drawn. In the second part of this chapter, attention is focused on identifying and controlling for sources of bias.

Neoclassical economic theory as an explanation of redundancy and unemployment Human capital theory seeks to explain labour market outcomes in terms of investments in human capital or training (Becker, 1975). A development of this theory which distinguishes between skill types, in terms of whether they are specific to a particular firm or transferable to other firms, is used to model redundancy and recruitment and generates the following predictions: in the absence of differential redundancy payments, workers' propensity to select themselves for discharge will depend inversely on the level of firm specific skills they possess. In the external labour market, redundant workers will be hired in inverse proportion to their skill specificity within a skill level. Hence, mobility is more likely to be required of workers who are most mobile. Differential redundancy compensation complicates this outcome because compensation is positively related to specific skills. Rights to specific skills are terminated on redundancy and compensation is related to the loss which results. Where the incentives generated by extra-statutory redundancy payments dominate human capital incentives, then redundancy reduces labour mobility.

Methodology in relation to theoretical perspective The framework of the human capital model and the underlying neoclassical market lends itself to a nomethetic methodology The predictions generated deductively from human capital theory were developed into hypotheses to test against information about miners affected by colliery closure and their experience of redundancy. For example in mining, specific skills are important, they are not easily transferable to other industries. Specific skills are acquired on the job, rather than through formal training, and therefore acquisition of specific skill is determined by length of service. If compensation is paid according to loss of specific skills, and specific skills are acquired through service, then the structure of redundancy payments will reflect service. Since redundancy compensation was high, compensation will dominate positive aspects of job attachment in the miners' redundancy decision. The hypothesis is therefore that longer serving workers will be concentrated among redundants. Furthermore, workers whose skills are firm specific (workers with long service) are less mobile, because their skills are less transferable, and will be at greater risk of experiencing unemployment.

The type of data needed to test such hypotheses are factual, collected from miners affected by colliery closure, and concern personal characteristics, the redundancy decision, job search behaviour, mobility in the external labour market and the experience of unemployment. Although the primary focus of the study was the role of specific skills in determining redundancy and labour market outcomes, information concerning a large number of other variables, variables which influence outcomes independently of skills, was required in order to isolate the partial independent effect of skills. Multiple regression techniques were employed to do this. In order to use such techniques, a relatively large number of observations were required. Such data are appropriately collected by means of a sample survey. Generalizability from the study to the wider population of redundant workers was an important objective of the study; the closure of Markham was one of a larger number of colliery closures, and an even larger number of plant closures and rationalizations, where redundancy had been organized through self-selection and extra-statutory redundancy payments. Under certain conditions, which are discussed in the following section, the survey method offers the possibility of generalization .

The choice of research methodology and associated research methods have been explained in terms of the subject of the study and the philosophical assumptions which relate to both the nature of understanding the subject and the nature of researching it. The focus of the chapter now turns to how the research objectives were achieved within this methodological framework.

The research methodology in practice: identifying and controlling for bias

Non-response is recognized in the literature as the major difficulty affecting social surveys and in particular the postal questionnaire survey. A great deal of attention has been devoted to developing techniques which reduce bias caused by non-response. The literature has concentrated in particular on procedures which raise response rates (see Scott, 1961; Kanuk and Berenson, 1975; and Dillman, 1978 for examples), procedures which detect non-response bias (see Ferber, 1948; Lehman, 1963; Oppenheim, 1966; Filion, 1975, Hansen and Hurwitz, 1946; Larson and Catton, 1959; Donald, 1960; and Kish, 1965) and techniques which compensate for the effects of non-response through the weighting of responses (see Donald, 1960; Filion, 1975; Moser and Kalton, 1985; and Holt and Elliot, 1991). However, the focus on non-response as a source of bias appears to have been at the expense of consideration of other potential sources of bias. The accuracy and reliability of results and the validity of inference depends upon the minimization and management of *all* potential sources of bias. When the research design, by which we mean the collection of techniques which comprise the research project, is considered in its entirety, from selecting the survey technique to the analysis and interpretation of responses, non-response becomes only one of many potential sources of bias.

It is never possible to eliminate all potential sources of bias and therefore to establish beyond doubt the validity of research findings. However, attention given to identifying and controlling for bias allows the researcher to get as close as possible to this objective. The importance of, and techniques available for, the identification and control of bias are explained and illustrated in this chapter, as in Donald (1960) and Filion (1975), by drawing examples from a single completed mail survey. The approach, nevertheless, is generalizable across social survey research; the sources of bias identified in this study, non-response and sample and variable censorship, are commonly encountered.

In the discussion below, the research design is divided up into six distinct stages where the potential sources of bias, and techniques for dealing with them, are discussed separately for each stage. This distinction is an artificial one but is made for purposes of clarity of explanation. The integrity of the research design is emphasized throughout the chapter. Table 4.1 reports a summary of the potential sources of bias in each of the six stages. These are elaborated in the discussion below.

1. Data Collection in relation to research objectives

The choice of survey technique is essentially an exercise in constrained optimization. The nature of the information required is determined by the objective of the research and constrained by the resources available to pursue this objective. From a sample of about 500 individuals,

Table 4.1
Potential sources of bias in a mail survey

Steps in research design	Potential bias	Explanation	Implications
1. Selecting a survey technique	Construct bias	Arises if the data gathering process is not consistent with both the purpose of the research and the nature of the data	Response bias; collection of irrelevant data
2. Design of the survey	Response bias Non-response bias	Arises from wording and sequence of questions Arises from non-response	Poor quality responses low response rate, unreliable and invalid responses
3. Selecting a sample design	Sampling bias	Arises if the sample of individuals studied are not representative of the population about which information is desired	Link between the sample and population broken; lack of generalizability, results apply only to sample
4. Return of completed questionnaires	Non-response bias	Arises where only a proportion of those mailed return the questionnaire and where non-respondents are not a random selection of the sample	Respondents not representative of sample; results apply only to respondents; lack of reliability and lack of generalizability
5. Data analysis	Mis-specification bias	Arises where the statistical technique used to explain the data is inappropriate in relation to the objectives of the research and to the type of data collected	Estimated parameters biased and/or tests of significance misleading
6. Interpretation	Lack of internal and external validity	Arises where conclusions are not qualified on the basis of remaining sources of potential bias	Uncertainty regarding the reliability, validity and generalizibility of conclusions

information was required of a factual nature concerning the personal characteristics and circumstances of respondents, their employment histories and, in particular, their post-closure labour market experiences. The resources comprised of a grant of £1000 and six months for field work. A single postal survey comprising a self-completion questionnaire was judged to be an appropriate method to collect this information given available resources.

It is important at the outset to recognize the limitations, in relation to the research objectives, imposed by the choice of techniques. A postal survey limits the areas which can be researched and the type of information which can be ascertained. In the first instance, a self-completion questionnaire offers only standard pre-determined replies and does not afford the researcher the opportunity to explain or expand upon areas of interest. Denied the opportunity of interaction with respondents, a researcher can include only straightforward clear questions relating to actual events and experiences. While this is suitable for ascertaining information regarding labour market outcomes over a large number of respondents, it is less appropriate as a means of enquiring about complex labour market processes, attitudes and interpretations and the psychological impact of job loss. Secondly, respondents are forced to describe their experiences in terms of a selection of answers pre-determined by the researcher. As a result, their experiences may not be recorded accurately, 'the several different angles from which most questions are, and legitimately can be, answered are to a large extent concealed' (Kahn, 1964). In particular, their experiences are unlikely to be as simple, precise and standard as they appear. Lastly, relevant and available information not foreseen by the researcher, and therefore not included in the questionnaire, goes uncollected.

To some degree these pitfalls are minimized by the use of a pilot study, the inclusion of open-ended questions and follow-up interviews with a sub-sample of respondents. Interview material can be used to supplement information collected from the questionnaire and thus compensate for some of its deficiencies. In addition, any inconsistencies in the data collected by each method provide an indication of the presence of response error.

A more important difficulty concerns the time interval between the survey and the behaviour being studied. Information was sought, *at the time of the survey*, about the miners' response to colliery closure *at the time of the closure* and their own assessment of job prospects *at the time of their redundancy*. This relies upon the ability of respondents to accurately recall events and feelings which had occurred up to two years previously and during a period of considerable disruption and hardship. It is unlikely that their recollection of this information will remain unaffected by their subsequent experience. This form of response error, where past perceptions and feelings are modified in the light of experience, is called 'post hoc rationalization bias' or 'self-justification bias' and may be expected to be greater than any response error caused by contemporaneous prejudices. According to Dex (1991), the accuracy of recall data appears to be confined to factual information. Self-justification bias lies largely outside the control of the researcher and the presence and effects of such bias are to a great extent unknown. As a result, information based on recall should be relied upon only as a last resort and should be limited to factual information.

A further inconsistency between the objectives of this research and the nature of data collected concerns the survey's focus on the effects of colliery closure on the individuals directly affected when in fact the repercussions are experienced by the entire colliery community. Individuals do not operate in isolation from their domestic and social environment and their own responses to colliery closure cannot fully be understood in abstraction from their wider circumstances. For example, an individual's response to unemployment should be located in the context of the household's response to his/her displacement (Morris, 1987). Placed within this context, the individual faces different constraints, incentives and choices. The quantitative nature of this study together with limited resources, both financial and time, precluded the detailed analysis of the household response to the men's redundancy. However, it was possible to collect data concerning some aspects of the inter-relationship between the men's labour market choices and their household circumstances from a survey of the men. In particular, the effect of dependants on the behaviour and labour market outcome of the head of household were incorporated into the analysis.

Having established the information necessary to test the research hypotheses, and chosen a survey technique to collect it, the next phase of the research design was to construct a questionnaire which would generate this information: that is, would elicit reliable and valid responses.

2. Survey design

The objective of this phase of the research design was to generate the greatest number of high quality responses. This can be achieved if careful attention is given to the design of the questionnaire, for example its length, wording, sequencing of questions and layout, and to the administration of the survey, including preliminary notification, explanatory letters from the research team, personalization, and follow-ups of non-respondents.

The quality of responses depends on the minimization of response bias and requires careful wording and sequencing of questions: responses being highly sensitive to both (Kalton and Schuman, 1982, p. 52). Obviously, questions which are potentially ambiguous, vague, embarrassing or loaded should be avoided. A great deal of advice is available regarding questionnaire design (see, in particular, Dillman, 1978, Moser and Kalton, 1985; and Kalton and Schuman, 1982). To minimize response bias due to poor questionnaire design, the questionnaire should be pilot tested. The pilot study is critical in achieving the optimum use of language and sequence of questions, it is, according to Moser and Kalton (1985), the essence to a good questionnaire.

In the pilot study of the miners' survey, a draft questionnaire was administered to 25 men affected by colliery closure. These men were from a neighbouring colliery which had closed around the time of the closure of Markham colliery and were not included in the final sample. The respondents were interviewed after they had completed the questionnaire and asked to comment on each of the included questions and also on potential questions. A number of questions were amended as a result. For example, two questions which enquired about the men's personal finances were changed out of respect for respondents' privacy.[1]

In addition, it became apparent that an extra pre-coded response was required in answer to the question, 'Which of the following reasons explain why you did not undertake retraining?' to include those men who were not aware that this opportunity was available to them. This turned out to be an important finding of the survey.

Even after careful construction and thorough piloting, one needs an indication of the quality of responses. It is possible to judge the consistency, or reliability, of responses by comparing an individual's answers to repeated or similar questions. For example, respondents were asked in two separate questions about the methods of job search they had used. This revealed two anomalies (out of 110 responses) and the resulting net error, revealed in the distribution of responses to these questions, was judged to be negligible. Assessing the validity of responses is more difficult and requires a cross-check with an independent source of information which, as in most social surveys, was not available.

Whether or not the responses are valid for the sample depends in part on the extent and nature of non-response. Maximizing response rates is an important objective of the survey design, and techniques available for achieving this are covered extensively by Scott (1961); Dillman (1978); and Kanuk and Berenson (1975). A number of these techniques were incorporated into the Miners' Survey including, preliminary notification from the National Union of Mineworkers, professionally printed questionnaires, display of the logo of the sponsoring body, use of stamps as opposed to pre-paid postage, inclusion of a covering letter explaining the purpose of the survey, assurance of confidentiality and details of access to and dissemination of the results for the survey participants.

Without a control group, one cannot judge how effective such techniques were in ensuring a high quality and quantity of response. However, the survey achieved a response rate of 52 per cent which is relatively high for a mail survey of manual workers. Even where a high response is achieved it is advisable to identify important differences between respondents and non-respondents in order to estimate, and possibly correct for, bias due to non-response. A variety of techniques which enable the researcher to do this are discussed under section 4 below.

3. Sampling and establishing the representativeness of the sample

Population sampling involves selecting, in a systematic way, part of a population for observation in order that inferences can be drawn from the observations on the sample about the whole population. Kish (1965) outlines the main sampling procedures and a set of criteria for choosing between them.

The sampling method chosen here was cluster sampling and involved selecting a sampling unit, a single colliery, from the set of sampling units which comprise the sampling frame of 32 collieries. The advantages of cluster sampling are practical ones. A complete sampling frame, that is the names and addresses of the workforces of each colliery which closed in 1985, would have been difficult to compile and would have necessitated seperate access negotiations for each mining area and each individual colliery. The sampling unit of the single colliery provides a natural grouping of members of the population and the concentration on a single unit is efficient in terms of resources. However, there are statistical disadvantages of cluster sampling. A cluster sample is not a random sample and therefore the error due to sampling is not minimized. Sampling error occurs when the characteristics of the sample are different from those of the population from which they are drawn. When the sample is selected by cluster sampling, the potential for sampling error depends critically upon the extent of variation between collieries. Only where inter-colliery variability is low, can the results be extended beyond the sample with any degree of confidence.[2]

The criteria used to select Markham colliery as the sampling unit cannot be described as scientific. The original population of 32 colliery closures was narrowed to the 11 collieries of South Wales on the basis of local knowledge and proximity. The criteria used to select the final colliery were size of and access to the workforce. Markham colliery employed a sufficiently large workforce to cope with the possibility of high non-response. Additionally, access to the workforce was established through union co-operation at the local level. The following discussion explains the procedure used to establish whether or not some degree of confidence might be placed on the claim that the chosen sample was representative of the wider population of redundant miners and thus establish the generalizability, or external validity, of the sample results.

Primarily, the survey results describe the reactions of a sample of miners to a local event which occurred in 1985. For the information generated by the Markham survey to be of more than local and historical significance, that is to be of relevance to the functioning of labour markets in other coal fields in response to mass redundancy, two criteria must be satisfied. First, the labour market under study must be similar to those of the wider coal fields; secondly, the characteristics, circumstances and experiences of the sample must closely match those of redundant miners in the wider labour market; and thirdly, there must be nothing peculiar about having worked at Markham colliery, or living in the Markham area, that would lead to different results. Tests which indicate that the first two criteria are satisfied are outlined below.

Using Department of Employment data, local labour markets with similar characteristics to the Markham labour market are identified. The 'peripheral' coal fields in Assisted Areas are virtually defined in terms of having similar employment distributions. The legacy of an early development in coal mining is high levels of structural unemployment and an under-representation of growth industries in overall employment. Table 4.2 records unemployment rates by Travel-to-work Area (TTWA) in four coal fields where redundancies from the National Coal Board (NCB) in 1985 exceeded 3000. In each of these local labour markets, coal mining accounted for over 10 per cent of employment and the local unemployment rate exceeded 20 per cent.

The data reported in Tables 4.3 and 4.4 enable the researcher to infer that the Markham sample was representative of the population of miners who lost their jobs in 1985, at least in terms of age and occupation. On the basis of the age (Table 4.3) and occupation (Table 4.4) distributions, the Markham sample compares favourably with the wider population of redundant miners. The major difference in the age distributions is accounted for by the over-representation of older redundant miners in North Yorkshire, Nottinghamshire and North Derbyshire and younger redundant miners in Scotland. It must be noted that, even if the sample is judged to be satisfactory on the above demographic characteristics, it may be unrepresentative in other ways. Without conducting the survey at

Table 4.2
Local unemployment rates in the coal fields in 1986

	Unemployment Rate	Redundancies
Scotland		3304
Alloa	20.1	
Bathgate	21.5	
North East		3616
South Tyneside	25.0	
Sunderland	22.0	
South Yorkshire		6796
Rotherham & Mexborough	22.8	
Barnsley	20.4	
Doncaster	20.6	
South Wales		5184
Blaenau Gwent and Abergavenny	20.9	
Merthyr & Rhymney	20.9	
Aberdare	21.6	

Source: Figures are taken from Monk (1986).

Notes: Only TTWAs where coal mining accounts for over 10 per cent of employment, where the unemployment rate exceeds 20 per cent and where redundancies from the NCB in 1985 exceeded 3000 have been reported.

alternative sampling units, the third criteria for generalization, which discounts the possibility of a Markham specific effect, cannot be established. However, in this case the demographic information which was available concerned two variables which were relevant to the objectives of the research; both age and occupation were related to specific skill acquisition and therefore, according to the research

Table 4.3

Redundancies in 1985/86, percentages by age group

Age Group Area	Under 40	40-49	50-55	over 55	Total
National (GB)	17.0	16.1	34.6	32.3	30095
Scotland	27.3	30.1	28.3	14.3	3304
N. East	21.5	20.0	39.3	19.2	3616
N. York	8.0	10.0	41.5	40.5	5431
S. Yorks	16.7	12.9	38.6	31.8	6796
N. Derbys	0.5	3.5	26.4	69.5	765
Notts	-	0.5	48.3	51.2	1467
S. Mids	15.1	10.6	46.7	27.6	1000
Kent	20.9	19.7	25.1	34.3	741
West	16.5	16.2	19.0	48.3	1791
S. Wales	24.2	22.1	24.7	29.1	5184
Markham (sample)	21.3	20.0	27.5	31.2	305

Source: Figures calculated from data reported by Monk (1986).

Table 4.4

Redundancies in 1985/86, percentages by occupation

Occupation Area	Manager/ Deputy	Craft	Underground	Surface
National GB)	12.6	18.8	53.0	15.5
Scotland	12.8	15.3	61.1	10.4
N. East	10.9	24.3	50.2	14.5
N. Yorks	11.0	19.2	53.9	15.8
S. Yorks	14.0	18.5	50.4	17.1
N. Derbys	12.7	18.8	52.6	16.2
Notts	19.0	14.9	48.5	17.5
S. Mids	14.9	21.1	49.0	14.9
Kent	14.0	17.9	51.7	16.2
West	12.6	15.5	58.6	13.2
S. Wales	11.1	19.0	52.5	17.3
Markham (sample)	14.3	15.6	57.2	12.9

Source: Figures calculated from data reported by Monk (1986).

hypothesis, key determinants of redundancy and post-redundancy labour mobility.

Therefore, and with the above caution in mind, it may be concluded that this study, although a purely local survey, may well be relevant to the labour market experiences of redundant miners throughout the coal fields.

Where inferences about a population are to be made on the basis of a sample, the sample data should be scaled-up to the population proportions using weights equal to the reciprocal of the ratio of the sample proportion to the population proportion. For example, using the information reported in Table 4.3, in order to generalize the survey results to South Wales, the data should be adjusted according to the following weights for each age group: 1.14 if under 40 years; 1.11 if 40-49 years; 0.90 if 50-55 years; and 0.93 if over 55 years. Comparing the occupational distribution of the survey sample to the wider GB population of redundant miners indicates that redundancies among craft and surface workers were under represented at Markham while deputies and underground workers over represented (Table 4.4). The former should be weighted by 1.22 and 1.34 respectively and the latter by 0.78 and 0.92 respectively bringing each group into line with the occupational distribution of the population of redundant miners.

4. Non-response and establishing the representativeness of respondents to the sample

Non-response is a particular difficulty associated with mail surveys and this may explain its prominence in the literature. The sample design breaks down in the presence of non-response and the selection probabilities are changed in an unknown way. The problem of non-response is critical where respondents differ from non-respondents and studies indicate that non-response is indeed non-random (see Rauta, 1985 for study of non-response in the General Household Survey; and Norris, 1987, for a study of non-response in the Labour Force Survey). Three types of check on questionnaire non-response are distinguished in the literature. The first assesses the extent and nature of non-response bias from data about the response mechanism. For example, early respondents and late respondents are compared across a series of relevant characteristics and responses on the basis that non-respondents are more like late respondents than early respondents (see Ferber, 1948; Lehman, 1963; Oppenheim, 1966; and Filion 1975). Alternatively, the number of follow-ups needed before a response is extracted can be used to identify a group of respondents who can proxy for non-respondents (see Holt and Elliot, 1991). Hence, a comparison between early (or first time) respondents and late (or follow-up) respondents provides an indication of the likely difference between respondents and non-respondents. Where data are available on relevant characteristics of the intended respondents, the sample, (and therefore non-respondents), a second check seeks to establish consistency between respondents and non-respondents in terms of these characteristics. A third check for the presence of non-response bias involves collecting information from a group of non-respondents and comparing this with data collected from respondents (Hansen and Hurwitz, 1946; Larson and Catton, 1959; and Donald, 1960). In all three comparisons, it must be noted that homogeneity between groups across a set of characteristics or responses does not imply homogeneity across all characteristics, 'the problem is to determine whether the sample [of respondents] is biased with respect to the characteristics most relevant to the subject of the study' (Ferber, 1949).

It is possible to estimate the extent of non-response error in the distribution of a variable across respondents using information on the distribution of this variable across non-respondents (or late respondents). The use of the response mean $\overline{X}_r$ to estimate the sample mean $\overline{X}$ causes a relative bias given by:

$$B = (\overline{X}_r - \overline{X}) / \overline{X} \qquad (1)$$

where $\overline{X}$ is the sample mean of characteristic X and $\overline{X}_r$ is the mean of this characteristic among the sample of respondents. Where the sample mean is unknown it may be estimated by:

$$\overline{X} = r\overline{X}_r + (1-r)\overline{X}_{nr} \qquad (2)$$

where r is the response rate and $\overline{X}_{nr}$ is the mean of X among non-respondents (or late-respondents). Substituting (2) into (1) gives:

$$B = (\overline{X}_r\text{-r}\overline{X}_r\text{-}(1\text{-r})\overline{X}_{nr})/\overline{X} \qquad (3)$$

$$B = (1\text{-r})[(\overline{X}_r\text{-}\overline{X}_{nr})/\overline{X}] \qquad (4)$$

Thus the magnitude of bias due to non-response depends on the response rate, r, and the difference between respondents and non-respondents as indicated by $\overline{X}_r\text{-}\overline{X}_{nr}$. If r is high or $\overline{X}_r\text{-}\overline{X}_{nr}$ is low then the bias will be low. However, where a significant proportion of non-response coincides with a significant difference between respondents and non-respondents, and empirical evidence suggests that it does (Holt and Elliot, 1991, p. 334), non-response bias will be important. In these circumstances, it is essential to estimate the potential for non-response bias in order to assess the reliability of results at the stage of inference.

In the Markham survey 505 questionnaires were sent out, 285 were returned after two reminders. This represents a response rate of 56.4 per cent. However, 23 of the questionnaires were unusable and only 262 (51.9 per cent) were used. The main group of unusable replies were those returned marked 'gone away'. A response rate of just over 50 per cent generates considerable potential for bias - up to 50 per cent if non-respondents are at the extremes of the sample distribution. It is therefore essential to make use of some of the above procedures as an indication of the representativeness of respondents to the survey sample.

The results from the first of the above comparisons are reported in Table 4.5 below. In the first test respondents' profiles for the first 20 questionnaires received were compared with the profiles of the last 20, the latter received after two follow-up letters. Comparing the extremes of the distribution of response times provides a more rigorous test of homogeneity between early and late respondents than previously reported comparisons; Ford and Zeisel (1949); Donald (1960); and Filion (1975) for example compare respondents over continuous waves of questionnaire returns. Early and late respondents were compared over six variables - age, occupation, location of residence, redundancy outcome, labour market outcome and lump sum redundancy payment. These variables were highly relevant to the purpose of the research (see Ferber, 1949). Differences in the distribution of characteristics across these two groups

Table 4.5

Distribution of characteristics across late and early respondents

	Early Respondents	Late Respondents
Age		
Under 35 years	6	4
35-45 years	5	4
45-55 years	6	8
over 55 years	3	4
calculated χ^2 value 2.9 is less than critical value of 7.8 (3 degrees freedom)[a]		
Occupation		
Underground and Surface	13	15
Deputy and Craft	7	5
calculated χ^2 value 0.2 is less than critical value of 3.8 (1 degree of freedom)[bc]		
Address		
Bargoed	4	6
Blackwood	2	6
New Tredegar	4	2
Tredegar	7	8
Markham and Hollybush	3	3
calculated χ^2 value 2.1 is less than crtical value of 9.5 (4 degrees of freedom)		
Redundant	15	19
Relocating	5	1
calculated χ^2 value 1.8 is less than the critical value of 3.8 (1 degree of freedom)[c]		
(Redundants only)		
Continuous unemployment	6	6
Employment/retraining	9	13
calculated χ^2 value 0.02 is less than critical value of 3.8 (1 degree of freedom)[c]		
Lump sum redundancy payment		
Under £10,000	5	5
£10,000-£20,000	3	8
Over £20,000	7	6
calculated χ^2 value 2.0 is less than critical value of 6.0 (2 degrees of freedom)		

a χ^2 values for $\alpha = 0.05$ and (r-1) (c-1) degrees of freedom.

b It was necessary to collapse occupation categories into two groups, skilled and less skilled, in order to achieve expected cell frequencies ≥ 3 for use with the χ^2 test.

c includes Yate's correction for 2×2 contingency table.

are reported in Table 4.5 and tested by means of the χ^2 test which showed, at the 5 per cent level of significance, the distribution of these characteristics and outcomes are independent of response period and therefore, under the assumption that late respondents are like non-respondents, response.

However, doubts have been expressed concerning the assumption that late respondents represent non-respondents (Campbell, 1949; and Ford and Zeisel, 1949). Nevertheless, where independent records from the sample or data concerning non-respondents are not available, this method would appear to offer 'a very promising line of approach' (Ferber, 1949).

An independent source of data on the sample was available in this study and a second test compared the profile of respondents with that of non-respondents across four variables - age, occupation, location of residence and outcome of redundancy.[3] The results of this comparison are reported in Table 4.6 and suggest that respondents were not significantly different from non-respondents in terms of three of the characteristics tested but that redundant miners were under-represented among respondents.

These tests are a useful guide to the extent and nature of non-response error. However, as illustrated here in the case of redundancy outcome, they may not yield consistent results. In addition, such tests can establish only that respondents are similar to non-respondents in terms of the characteristics tested. Even if respondents are judged to be satisfactory on the above demographic characteristics they may be unrepresentative in other unmeasured and possibly important ways (Lehman, 1963). As long as there is any non-response, it is not possible to eliminate non-response as a source of bias (Moser and Kalton, 1985). If, as a result of these comparisons, a consistent pattern of non-response is apparent, it is possible, as with differences between the sample and the population, to adjust the responses to take account of this bias through the application of appropriate weights. The data gathered from respondents are scaled-up or -down to the magnitude of the sample using information gained from late respondents, the sample or non-respondents. In this example, data relating to over- and under-represented groups were adjusted to account for their disproportionate representation in the sample, the data relating to each group being weighted by the reciprocal of respondents'

Table 4.6
Distribution of characteristics across respondents and non-respondents

Category	Respondents	Non-respondents	Weight
Age			
Under 35 years	84	88	1.06
35 - 39 years	33	30	0.99
40 - 44 years	24	28	1.12
45 - 49 years	37	46	1.16
50 - 55 years	40	30	0.91
Over 55 years	44	21	0.77

calculated χ^2 value 10.4 is less than critical value of 11.1 (5 degrees of freedom)[a]

Occupation			
Underground and Surface	194	181	1.00
Craft	36	38	1.07
Deputy	32	24	0.91

calculated χ^2 value 1.0 is less than critical value of 7.8 (3 degrees of freedom)

Location of residence			
Bargoed	30	30	1.04
Blackwood	48	38	0.93
Ebbw Vale	3	4	1.22
New Tredegar	41	27	0.86
Rhymney	18	7	0.73
Tredegar	61	75	1.16
Markham and Hollybush	61	62	1.05

calculated χ^2 value 7.6 is less than critical value of 12.6 (5 degrees of freedom)

Redundant[b]	147	179	1.15
Relocating	115	64	0.81

calculated χ^2 value 16.2 is greater than critical value of 3.8 (1 degree of freedom)[b]

[a] χ^2 values for $\alpha=0.05$ and $(r-1)(c-1)$ degrees of freedom.

[b] includes Yate's continuity correction for 2×2 contingency table.

Source: Information concerning the Markham workforce was supplied by British Coal.

represented and relocating miners over represented among respondents. The final column of Table 4.6 reports the weights used to adjust for non-response.

Responses from redundants were weighted by 1.15 to account for their under representation and responses from relocating miners were weighted by 0.81 to account for their over representation. Statistical analyses were representation in the sample. For example, redundant miners were under conducted, and reported, both with and without adjustments for non-response.

Another form of non-response, item non-response, has not been considered here because its incidence among returned questionnaires in this survey was very low; possibly because the questions were factual, were of considerable personal interest to the participants and had been thoroughly pilot tested. However, where item non-response is significant, similar procedures to those outlined above can be adopted to detect for the presence of non-response bias. Item non-response may also provide clues as to the reason for questionnaire non-response.

5. *Statistical techniques in relation to the data and the research objectives*

In order to produce the most accurate results and valid inferences from the survey responses, the method of statistical analysis must be appropriate to both the purpose of the research and the nature of the data collected. First, there is the descriptive function for the results of individual questions including measurement of distributional aspects of the responses such as central tendancy, dispersion and skewness. The measures used depend on the scales of measurement, as is the case with others statistical tehniques (see Silver, 1992). Secondly, we are concerned with association. Initially, bivariate analysis compares, over a variety of personal characteristics and circumstances, groups who experienced different labour market outcomes - retraining, unemployment, re-employment, self-employment and early-retirement. Since, these variables are measured on a nominal scale, the χ^2 test is used to establish whether personal characteristics are independent of labour market outcomes. In these ways, the data are summarized and possible determinants of outcome are identified. This bivariate approach is useful as a first stage analysis and also where the sample size of the groups involved is too small to facilitate more sophisticated techniques.

A multiple regression analysis is used to estimate the independent effects of personal characteristics and circumstances (independent variables), the direction of influence and relative importance of each on determining the outcome (dependent variable). Where the dependent variable is a categorical variable, that is it takes on only discrete values, as with the outcome of the redundancy process, a probabilistic regression, as opposed to an ordinary least squares (OLS) regression, is the appropriate econometric estimator. In this case, a non-linear logit regression was adopted from which it was possible to estimate the effects of each explanatory variable on the probability of experiencing a given outcome, in particular to estimate the impact of specific skills on the likelihood of redundancy. Details of the logit specification are given in the technical appendix to this chapter.

The adequacy of data in relation to the research objectives was raised in section 1. In this section, two examples of the use of statistical techniques to compensate for data which are incomplete in relation to research questions are described. The analysis of post-redundancy labour market outcomes encountered two problems which were solved using econometric techniques. The first source of bias was in the analysis of unemployment duration and was caused by censorship of the unemployme nt data. The second source of bias in the data was caused by sample selection and affected the estimate of the effect of retraining on unemployment duration.

The first form of bias arises because the respondents' labour market careers are followed for only two years and a number will not have completed their spell of unemployment at this cut-off date. This generates a bunching of observations at 24 months, the limiting value of the dependent variable. OLS regression cannot be used where the dependent variable, months of unemployment, is censored, i.e., contains uncompleted spells of unemployment, because the assumption of homoscedasticity of the error term is violated. Survival analysis, a technique developed in biological sciences, provides an alternative specification to OLS. The dependent variable is redefined as a hazard rate, in this instance a Cox proportional hazard function was estimated. The hazard rate, h_t, is defined as the probability of leaving unemployment at any given time conditional on being unemployed prior to this time,

$$h_t = \frac{\text{probability of leaving unemployment at time } t}{\text{probability of leaving unemployment after time } t}$$

The hazard rate is shifted around an arbitrary base line hazard rate by the impact of the explanatory variables. The coefficient estimates measure the impact of the explanatory variables. Further details concerning the technique of survival analysis are given in the technical appendix to this chapter.

Selectivity bias arises in the analysis of the effect of retraining on post redundancy unemployment because men who retrained are unlikely to be a random sample of all job seekers. Men who undertook retraining will be different, in terms of employment characteristics, from men who did not undertake retraining; the former are likely to be advantaged in the labour market relative to the latter group. If no account is taken of non-random selection into retraining then the estimated effect of retraining on the likelihood of re-employment will be biased and inconsistent: in this case too much importance will be placed on retraining in gaining employment.

A number of statistical procedures are available which seek to correct for bias caused by sample selection. Where there is access to data on the selection process, in this case an additional explanatory variable which affects the probability of participation in retraining but has no direct relationship with the probability of leaving unemployment, then it is possible, using a two stage procedure, developed by Heckman (1979), to correct for the problem of selectivity bias. However, it will only be able to do this to the extent that the selectivity variable captures the selection process. Details of the Heckman two-stage procedure are given in the technical appendix. Briefly, the first stage of this correction procedure estimates the probability of being selected into the sample of men who retrained. A variable, λ, the inverse mills ratio, derived from the residuals generated by this equation, is a measure of the unexplained difference between the selected sample, the men who retrained, and the entire sample of job seekers. In stage two, λ is included as a regressor in the analysis of re-employment probabilities. With the inclusion of λ, the parameters of the re-employment function and in particular the effect of retraining, which will be less affected by selectivity bias, can be estimated.

Whilst it is true that the results of statistical analysis can only be as good as the data upon which it is performed, as illustrated above, econometric techniques are often able to bridge the gap between the research hypothesis and data, where the latter are incomplete.

6. Interpretation in relation to identified sources of potential bias

The process of inference seeks to generate conclusions or inferences about the predictions of theory on the basis of the research findings. However, when interpreting the results of the statistical analysis it is important to reconsider the potential sources of bias identified in each of the previous phases of the research process.

In the example used here, the method of data collection was not entirely consistent with the research purpose. In particular, data were collected retrospectively rather than contemporaneously and respondents' recall of events may not be unaffected by their subsequent experience. Given the data, self-justification bias cannot be corrected for at the analysis stage, it can only be acknowledged at the inference stage and conclusions qualified according to the likelihood that such bias is present and, if it is, its likely effect on the results. The data are incomplete in other ways which also cannot be compensated for during analysis. For example, labour market destinations are the outcome of processes on the supply and demand side of the labour market and there is information only about the behaviour of labour suppliers. Neither was there quantifiable information about the social environment within which individual behaviour took place. Therefore the researcher is left to speculate about the possible influences such factors have on the results of the statistical analysis.

In a study which involves sampling and non-response, interpretation must be set within the context of sampling error and non-response error. Although it was established that respondents were not markedly dissimilar to the Markham workforce (see Tables 4.5 and 4.6) and that the Markham workforce shared similar broad demographic characteristics with the wider population of displaced miners in the peripheral coal fields (see Tables 4.2, 4.3 and 4.4), this does not rule out the potential for bias.[4]

Conclusion

In this chapter the choice of a sample survey conducted by postal questionnaire has been explained in relation to a particular theoretical understanding of the subject of study, and a particular set of epistemological assumptions about how this subject can be revealed. Redundancy and post-redundancy labour mobility are explained in terms of human capital accumulation and a set of positivist assumptions determined that this relationship could be revealed through a nomothetic methodology. The second part of the chapter dealt with the implementation of the chosen research methodology with the focus primarily on bias in the data: the control for bias being seen as a critical determinant of the quality of the findings.

Unlike the science laboratory, conditions in the field are not under the control of the researcher which generates potential sources of bias. Statistical techniques are used to re-establish control. A variety of statistical techniques which are useful in identifying and controlling for sources of bias have been illustrated with reference to a particular research project. The research design was subdivided into six constituent stages and the potential for bias analysed during each stage. The subdivision was seen to be an artificial one in that the stages overlapped but also because bias in any one of these stages undermines the overall quality of the research findings. For example, accurate responses generated by a well designed questionnaire will not result in valid inference if they are received from a proportion of the sample who are not representative of the sample as a whole or if statistical techniques, which are inappropriate to the nature of the data collected, are used to analyse the data.

The sample survey was an appropriate research methodology given the objectives of the research. It was, however, not perfect. Although, the research methodology was implemented with care and thought, it was not completely successful. As a result, the potential for bias was not, and can never be, eliminated and therefore inference must always be made with caution.

Notes

1.   Questions requesting precise data on wages and redundancy compensation were dropped because the pilotees indicated a disinclination to respond on account of the personal nature of this information. However, they were prepared to respond to a request for less precise information, e.g. questions which asked respondents to indicate an appropriate wage or compensation range.
2.   Conversely, if inter-colliery variability is high, the sampling error is potentially high, much higher than for a random sample, and the results will extend only to the selected sample.
3.   The NCB supplied information about the age, occupation and location distribution of the colliery workforce.
4.   In fact, it establishes only that there is no obvious difference between the respondents and the sample and the sample and the wider population.

Technical Appendix

1. Estimating a model with a dichotomous dependent variable

The redundancy outcome occurs when the net benefit for the individual, B_i, is positive. Individual attributes not observed in B_i, e_i, may also affect the probability of accepting redundancy. The probability that miner i accepts redundancy is given by:

$$P_i = \text{prob}(B_i + e_i > 0)$$
$$P_i = \text{prob}(e_i > -B_i)$$
$$P_i = \text{prob}(e_i > -X_i a)$$
$$P_i = 1 - F(X_i a)$$

By symmetry

$$P_i = F(X_i a)$$

where i denotes the individual; X_i is a vector containing j explanatory variables which affect B_i; a is a vector of j coefficients corresponding to X_i; and F is the logistic distribution function for e_i.

The probability of redundancy for an individual can be estimated using

$$P_i = 1/[1 + \exp(-X_i a)]$$

Given observations on the redundancy outcome and j explanatory variables in X for each i, the Maximum Likelihood Estimate (MLE) of the vector a is that which makes the likelihood of having observed the individuals' actual outcome as great as possible.

The coefficient estimates are not partial derivatives as in OLS but, for observations close to the mean of the dependent variable, the partial derivative for variable j is given by:

$$\delta P_i / \delta X_{ji} = a_j [\bar{P}(1-\bar{P})]$$

2. Survival analysis

In mathematical terms, the Cox's proportional hazard model defines the hazard rate for individual i at time t as:

$$h_i(t) = h_{i0}(t) \exp(X_{it} a)$$

where $h_{i0}(t)$ is the base line hazard rate, X_{it} is a vector of j individual characteristics, some of which may vary with time, and vector a contains the corresponding parameter estimates. The model assumes that the relative hazard across individuals and time is independent of elapsed time (see Keifer, 1988, for alternative specifications). The model is estimated using maximum likelihood techniques. The coefficient estimates measure the sign and size of the deviation of the hazard rate from the base line hazard when the explanatory variables, X_{it}, change.

3. Sample selection

Selectivity bias arises in the analysis of the effect of retraining on the chances of re-employment. Redundant miners who retrain are likely to be different, in terms of employment characteristics, from non-trainees, even in the absence of retraining. If this group are a non-random sample of job seekers, then their chances of re-employment will be different from non-trainees, even in the absence of retraining. In these circumstances, simply estimating coefficients based on the equation for the hazard rate, $h_i(t)$, above where X_i includes retraining, is not appropriate. The retraining outcome is not a random variable and will be correlated with the error term, e_i. Maximum likelihood estimates of the retraining coefficient will be biased and inconsistent. A two stage procedure, developed by Heckman (1979) will, under certain conditions, correct for bias.

Stage 1 Where there is access to data on the selection process, in particular an additional regressor which affects the probability of retraining but does not directly affect the employment outcome, then the probability of being selected into the sample of trainees, P_i, on the basis of X_i, is estimated. A probit transformation is used, where F is the cumulative normal distribution function for e_i, and the probability of retraining is given by:

$$P_i = \int_{-\infty}^{-X_i a} 1/(2\pi)^{1/2} \exp(-e_i^2/2) de_i$$

A variable, λ_i, the inverse mills ratio, is derived from the residuals generated by this equation:

$$\lambda_i = f(Z_i)/1 - F(Z_i)$$

where $Z_i = -X_i a/(\sigma_i)^{1/2}$ for the selected group; f and F are respectively the density and cummulative distribution function of the standard normal distribution; X_i is the vector of explanatory variables described above and σ_i is the vector of covariance for the individual. λ_i measures the unexplained difference between the selected sample, the retrainees in this case, and the entire sample.

Stage 2 In stage 2, λ_i is included as an additional regressor in the analysis of unemployment duration. The coefficient estimates are free from selectivity bias to the extent that the additional regressor used in stage 1 determines retraining but not re-employment.

References

Becker, G. (1975), *Human Capital*, 2nd edition, National Bureau of Economic Research, New York.

Campbell, D. (1949), 'Bias in mail surveys - a letter to the editor', *Public Opinion Quarterly*, Vol. 13, p. 562.

Dex, S. (1991), 'The reliability of recall data: a literature review', Working Paper of the ESRC Research Centre on Micro-social change, No. 11.

Dillman, D. (1978), *Mail and Telephone Surveys: The Total Design Method*, John Wiley & Son.

Donald, M. (1960), 'Implications of non-response for the interpretation of mail questionnaire data', *Public Opinion Quarterly*, Vol. 24, pp. 99-114.

Ferber, R. (1948), 'The problem of bias in mail returns: A solution', *Public Opinion Quarterly*, Vol. 12, pp. 669-76.

Ferber, R. (1949), A rejoinder to Campbell's letter to the editor, *Public Opinion Quarterly*, Vol. 13, pp. 562-63.

Filion, F. (1975), 'Estimating bias due to non-response in mail surveys', *Public Opinion Quarterly*, Vol. 39, pp. 482-92.

Ford, R. and H. Zeisel (1949), 'Bias in mail surveys cannot be controlled by one mailing', *Public Opinion Quarterly*, Vol. 13, pp. 495-501.

Hanson, M. and W. Hurwitz (1946), 'The problem of non-response in sample surveys', *Journal of the American Statistical Association*, Vol. 41, pp. 517-29.

Heckman, J. (1979), 'Sample selection bias as a specification error', *Econometrica*, Vol. 47,1, pp. 153-61.

Holt, D. and D. Elliot (1991), 'Methods of weighting for unit non-response', *The Statistician*, Vol. 40, p. 333-42.

Kahn, H. (1964), *Repercussions of Redundancy*, Allen and Unwin, London.

Kalton, G. and H. Schuman (1981), 'The effect of the question on survey response: A review', *Journal of the Royal Statistical Society A*, Vol. 145, Part 1, pp. 42-73.

Kanuk, L. and C. Berenson (1975), 'Mail surveys and response rates: A literature review', *Journal of Marketing Research*, Vol. 12, pp. 440-53.

Kiefer, N. (1988), 'Economic duration data and hazard functions', *Journal of Economic Literature*, Vol. 26, pp. 646-79.

Kish, L. (1965), *Survey Sampling*, John Wiley & Sons, New York.

Larson and Catton (1959), 'Can mailback bias contribute to a study's validity?' *American Sociological Review*, Vol. 24, pp. 243-45.

Lehman, E. (1963), 'Tests of significance and partial returns to mail questionnaires', *Rural Sociology*, Vol. 28, pp 284-89.

Monk, S. (1986), *Re-training Opportunities for Miners made Redundant*, Coalfield Communities Campaign, Barnsley.

Morris, L. (1987), 'The household in the labour market' in C. Harris (ed.), *Redundancy and Recession*, Blackwell, Oxford, pp. 127-40.

Moser, C. and G. Kalton (1985), *Survey Methods in Social Investigation*, Heinemann, London.

Norris, P. (1987), 'The Labour Force Survey: A study of differential response according to demographic and socio-economic characteristics', *Statistical News*, Vol. 79, pp. 20-23.

Oppenheim, A. (1966), *Questionnaire and Attitude Measurement*, Heinemann, London.

Rauta, I. (1985), 'A comparison of the census characteristics of respondents and non-respondents in the General Household Survey', *Statistical News*, Vol. 71, pp. 12-5.

Scott, C. (1961), 'Research in mail surveys', *Journal of the Royal Statistical Society*, Series A, Vol. 124, pp. 143-205.

Silver, M. (1992), *Business Statistics*, McGraw-Hill.

Part 2

Research in Organizations

5 Interviewing Techniques in Business and Management Research

MICHAEL HEALEY AND MIKE RAWLINSON

Introduction

This chapter is concerned with reviewing the use of standard and non-standardized techniques for face-to-face interviewing. Interviews with the owners and managers of business organizations are a valuable source of primary research material on the activities of businesses whether the purpose is to understand the organizational structure or spatial behaviour of business organizations or as a means of analysing the economic structure of a particular sector or area.

Business interviews range from asking the same list of questions in an identical form to all respondents to discussions of a series of topics in which the questions asked vary from respondent to respondent. The choice of standardized or non-standardized interviews is linked to the research design and philosophical framework adopted. However, the relationship between philosophy and technique is not exact as different philosophical approaches, such as Positivist or Realist, can lead to the use of similar methods of interviewing forming part of their respective research designs. There has been some focus specifically on interviewing (e.g., Briggs, 1988; and Gorden, 1975), however, most of the literature is concerned with social surveys rather than investigations of businesses. Although the general advice in these texts is relevant to business researchers, for the most part it lacks examples of business interviews and discussion of the specific problems involved. Some useful hints are contained in the literature on elite interviewing (e.g., Dexter, 1970; and Moyser and Wagstaffe, 1987), but, with the exception of Kincaid and Bright (1957a and b), little involves economic elites. Discussions by business researchers of interviewing business managers tend to be restricted to the methodology sections of research theses and monographs.

The traditional approach to interviewing has involved the generation of a questionnaire, often with pre-coded answers. The questions would then be systematically read out to the interviewee by a researcher, who would then record the responses or tick the boxes. With the continual development of the philosophy of research and a greater understanding of the utility and limitations of the knowledge that can be gained from such an approach (see Sayer, 1984; Keat and Urry, 1975; and Johnston, 1986), there is a trend for greater use of non-standardized interviewing.

This trend is not only a result of philosophical and theoretical considerations but also related to the more practical aspects of research. One such consideration is to make the process of interviewing interesting and stimulating for the interviewee who is giving valuable time to the researcher. Many people deliberately try to avoid the gaze of the market researchers in shopping precincts that are armed with large folders of pre-coded responses to questionnaire schedules. Such action may not just stem from an unwillingness to help the researchers but perhaps also avoid what can be a tedious and annoying process of trying to fit answers into someone else's categories that do not appear to coincide with their own. Furthermore, to engage in conversation (mostly for no reward) with someone who is constantly showing a series of cards with a range of responses in front of their face, whilst they are searching for the next question on their schedule sheet, cannot really be considered an engaging and lively experience for an interviewee. It is our belief that when interviewing owners and managers of businesses, academic researchers who often will have little tangible to offer as incentive to the interviewee for their time, should endeavour to make the process as interesting and stimulating as possible. Also the chances of a repeat visit, if needed, may well be increased.

This chapter outlines the major principles and practices of interviewing in business and management research. It focuses on when to interview and offers advice on obtaining, conducting and recording interviews. It examines the use of traditional standardized interviews and the increasingly popular non-standardized interviews. This review of successful practices should be useful as a guide to researchers unfamiliar with undertaking interviews of business owners and managers, and can also help more experienced researchers to reflect on the strengths and weaknesses of a widely used technique. It is important to appreciate the problems and potentials of interviewing if the findings of research using the method are to be understood fully. To supplement the limited number of published examples, 20 colleagues in the UK, North America and Australasia were invited to give us illustrations of their experiences of interviewing business owners and managers. These contacts provided many useful examples and emphasised the need to identify successful practices and to improve the standard of interviewing. The debate on the nature of the links between the methods used in practice and the underlying philosophy, epistemilogy and ontology will be discussed only briefly in this chapter as this topic is discussed elsewhere (Massey and Meegan, 1985; McDowell, 1992; and Schoenberger, 1992). In this paper the emphasis is on interviewing as a method or technique of gathering information once it has been chosen by researchers.

When to interview

Obtaining information direct from business owners and managers is a time-consuming and labour-intensive method of collecting information, and it is therefore usually sensible first to examine other sources. Much general information exists, at least about large businesses and the industries in which firms operate, and this should be examined before interviews are undertaken. Interviews are rarely used as the only source of information and are employed to complement other data sources, such as company accounts and aggregate industry statistics. Unfortunately, the quality of the information about businesses available to researchers is limited. Much published information 'tends towards either superficiality, as in company reports, or towards self-congratulatory rhetoric, as with glossy promotional publications' (Crewe, 1989, p. 70). However, when combined with other sources, such as local and national newspaper reports, trade journals and in-house company journals and newsletters, a useful overview can be built up. In many situations, however, the information and insights that researchers are seeking may only be obtained direct from people in the businesses being examined. A number of options remain for obtaining information; namely, a self-administered questionnaire, a telephone interview, or a face-to-face interview. However, in the absence of a skilled interviewer in a face-to-face situation, there is no control over the order in which the questions are completed or exactly who answers the questions. Furthermore, some questions may be missed by the respondent and there is no opportunity to probe vague answers (De Chernatony, 1988; Swain, 1978) or to probe answers that are too brief, and query discrepancies in the replies. It is also easier for a respondent to terminate a telephone interview.

Interviews are generally essential when there are a large number of questions, or the subject of the survey involves an investigation into the reasons for decisions or the perception of the owner or manager. Standardized interviews are often used as an alternative to self-administered questionnaires sent through the post. Although more expensive in terms of time and cost, they usually achieve a higher response rate. One review of 43 local and regional surveys of economic activity in the UK found that, although response rates varied widely, the average response rate for postal surveys was 50 per cent, while for face-to-face interview surveys it was 75 per cent (Healey, 1991).

In many instances an interview-survey of businesses is the only way to obtain the answers to the questions that researchers pose. For example, Fothergill and Guy (1990, p. 44), in examining the closure of factories state that 'The interview-based approach means that we can find out directly about the reasons for managers' decisions rather than merely infer causation from statistics. In our view, this is by far the most fruitful and illuminating way to understand branch closures.' Direct quotations from interviews can give useful insights into the way businesses respond to various situations and can provide anecdotes to illustrate other material (e.g., Markusen, 1991).

Interview techniques and research design

The reliability and usefulness of research findings and their interpretation are closely linked with the nature and quality of the survey methods used and reflect the underlying philosophy adopted. Interview techniques may be categorized into standardized and non-standardized. The main characteristics of these two types of interview are summarised in Table 5.1. With standardized interviews, each business owner or manager in the survey is asked an identical set of questions in a fixed order. They are most suitable for collecting information, which is largely factual, quantitative or non-emotive, from businesses with several features in common. They are particularly appropriate when the aim is to quantify the relative importance of different responses to questions about a set of well-defined topics. In contrast, a non-standardized interview is much less structured and the questions asked and the phrasing of the questions vary from interview to interview. However, non-standardized interviews are not 'unstructured rambles'. Interviews of this kind are most helpful when exploring new topics, sensitive or emotive issues, and when the businesses are highly variable in their characteristics. They are particularly suitable for detailed examination of topics and when the nature of the experience of respondents is likely to vary widely, such as when examining the sometimes conflicting logic that can underlie corporate decisions (Schoenberger, 1991), or where the issues are ill-defined, ill-understood or conceptually complex (Hedges and Ritchie, 1987).

Researchers need to be familiar with the strengths and weaknesses of both standardized and non-standardized interview techniques, and to know in what circumstances each is most appropriate. There are many examples where the design of standardized interview schedules is inappropriate, because insufficient thought is given beforehand as to why the information is being collected and the use to which it is to be put.

Table 5.1

Outline of the main characteristics of standardized
and non-standardized interviews

Characteristic	Standardized	Non-standardized
Research design	Usually extensive and quantitative, examines taxonomic groups	Usually intensive and qualitative, examines causally related groups
Philosophical approach	Commonly used in Positivist approaches	Commonly used in Structuralist and Realist approaches
Sample	Representative or whole population	Selected to cover a range of issues and a phenomena of interest. May be chosen as research progresses
Interview schedule	Identical questions in a fixed order	List of topics. Flexible, form and wording of questions vary with knowledge of respondents and interviewer, and direction of the interview
Interview style	Minimization of interviewer-related error	Interactive, following issues raised in the interview
Questions	Factual and pre-coded questions common	Nearly all questions open-ended
Suitability	For summarizing answers for sample, comparing responses to the same questions, generalizing, testing hypotheses, inferring causality	In-depth studies investigating causally related mechanisms. Exploring new research areas, seeking explanation and understanding
Interviewer skills	Ability to interview non-directively and consistently	Thorough understanding of research topic, ability to converse intelligently and with sympathetic understanding

Based in part on Table 6.1 in Sayer and Morgan (1985).
Note: Summaries of this kind tend to emphasize the differences between the two types of interview (see the text for a more balanced review).

Consequently, although some standardized surveys are technically very efficient, the findings may be of limited value (Bloom, 1988). On the other hand, there is the possibility that the findings from some non-standardized interviews may be vague and anecdotal because of lack of prior preparation and/or insufficient skill in obtaining information during the interview. It is apparent that researchers are making greater use of non-standardized interviewing techniques, particularly as they become more concerned with examining processes, relationships and interactions, rather than simply identifying patterns and outcomes (e.g., Cooke and Wells, 1990; Gibbs, personal communication 1991; and Le Heron, personal communication 1991). There is an increasing focus on causality rather than statistical inference.

The predominant type of interview used depends in part on the philosophy and research design adopted. Standardized interviews are most common in extensive research projects concerned to identify general patterns and outcomes. Such projects are typically associated with surveys of representative samples or populations and quantitative analyses in which taxonomic groups, such as 'branch plants' or 'plant closures' are used (e.g., Stafford and Watts, 1990; and Fothergill and Gudgin, 1982). Extensive research is the dominant research design used in positivist approaches to social research. In contrast, non-standardized interviews are associated more with intensive research designs in which the main questions involve how the observed behaviour of a business is related to its own history and circumstances, or how some causal processes work out in particular cases. These differences are elaborated in Table 5.1.

Intensive research typically uses mainly qualitative forms of analysis. It is the dominant research design associated with for example structuralist and realist philosophical approaches in the social sciences, which examine groups whose members are causally related (i.e., are connected in a relationship) to one another, such as firms which are related 'vertically' through linkages (e.g., Rawlinson, 1991) or 'horizontally' through competition (i.e., operate in the same market sector). The businesses selected may not be typical and may be selected one by one as the research proceeds and as an understanding of the membership of a causal group is being developed. Often businesses are chosen to encompass the variability in the situations they face as in Crewe (1989). The stress placed on identifying the context in which businesses operate in case study research means that sometimes lengthy interviews are required. Hayter (personal communication, 1991), refers to interviews with four large Japanese companies undertaken by a doctoral student extending in one case to between 16 and 18 hours in total.

Although associated with particular research designs, standardized and non-standardized interviews are not exclusive to extensive and intensive research designs, respectively. For example, non-standardized interviews may be used in the early stages of designing a standardized interview schedule. Moreover, the boundary between standardized and non-standardized interviews is indistinct (Burton and Cherry, 1970). In some interviews a mixture of interview styles is often used in the same investigation. Thus one section of an interview may ask a common set of factual questions of all respondents, while in another section a semi-structured qualitative approach may be used to explore an aspect of the behaviour of the business (e.g., Rawlinson, 1990).

One of the aims of standardized interviews is to minimize interviewer-related errors (Fowler and Mangione, 1990). This applies particularly where several interviewers are involved in the same project, though consistency of approach by a single interviewer is also important. With non-standardized interviewing the interaction between interviewer and interviewee is emphasized rather than minimized (Healey, 1991). Sayer (personal communication, 1986) suggests that, as non-standardized interviewing is a social process, which involves both the interviewer and the interviewee, it is important to give the interviewee an *active* role and try to be as flexible as possible e.g., regarding the form and order of questions so as to accommodate for this. This view is confirmed by Dexter (1970, p. 5) who states that 'the investigator is willing, and often eager to let the interviewee teach him what the problem, the question, the situation, is', within the limits of the research topic. It is important that the interviewer should also be actively involved in the process and 'the interview format should capitalize on the strengths of open-endedness ... In particular, it should allow for discussion and dialogue-even debate over controversial points' (Schoenberger, 1991, p. 187). With this method, the researcher is able to refer to and build upon knowledge gained beforehand about the specific characteristics of the business, 'instead of having to affect ignorance ... in order to ensure uniformity or 'controlled conditions' and avoid what might be taken as 'observer-induced bias' (Sayer, 1984, p. 223).

In non-standardized interviews the questions posed vary from one interview to the next, according to how the interview develops, the knowledge of the respondent and the level of understanding of the interviewer at the time of the interview. Consequently, a different form of analysis is required for quantitative and qualitative information (Silverman, 1985).

Gorden (1975, p. 61) notes, with respect to material collected in non-standardized interviews, that the resulting information cannot be statistically summarized to reflect the aggregate response of the group. However, analytical generalizations relevant to theoretical positions can be made (Sayer, 1986; and Keat and Urry, 1975). This does not, however, preclude the gathering of statistical information in non-standardized interviews, as long as some similar questions are asked of all respondents. Milne (1991), for instance, employed an unstructured discussion technique in an examination of small firms in the UK hi-fi industry. By asking a set of similar questions to the sample, a basic statistical analysis could be produced which helped to give an understanding of recent competitive pressures and reorganization in the sector.

The difficulty of generalizing about the responses to non-standardized interviews raised the debate about the validity and reliability of the findings of intensive qualitative research. Much has been written on this important issue (see Eyles, 1988; Kirk and Miller, 1986; and Sykes, 1990 and 1991). Here validity is taken to refer to the meaning and meaningfulness of the data, whereas reliability is taken to refer to the consistency of the results.

Validity may be assessed in terms of both the inferences which may be made from the findings and the kind and accuracy of the information obtained from individual sample units (Sykes, 1991). Some researchers emphasize the theoretical inferences which may be made from qualitative research. For example, Crewe (1989) argues that the goal of intensive research is to explain and promote theoretical inferences, not to enumerate frequencies. This view is also used to justify case studies (Mitchell, 1983), which 'like experiments, are generalisable to theoretical propositions and not to populations or universes' (Yin, 1984, p. 21). The second meaning of validity refers to the 'goodness' of the data. Here the strengths of qualitative research are clearest. As Sykes (1991, p. 8) notes 'the main reason for the potential superiority of qualitative approaches for obtaining information is that the flexible and responsive interaction which is possible between interviewer and respondent(s) allows meanings to be probed, topics to be covered from a variety of angles and questions made clear to respondents'.

Even if qualitative research is accepted as capable of producing 'valid' results, there may still be doubts about whether they are 'reliable'. These doubts are often expressed in terms of a question along the lines: would the same study carried out by two different researchers using the same techniques produce the same findings? The answer to this is perhaps not. However, this illustrates that the process of research and the interpretation of the research findings are as much determined and shaped by the philosophical background of the researcher as the subject matter. Qualitative researchers often point out the fallacy of assuming that theory neutral observation in social science is possible. In fact the meanings of action and the understanding of causality are bounded up in the mindset of the observer (e.g., Sayer, 1984; and Keat and Urry, 1975). It is questionable however, whether reliability and validity are entirely compatible goals (Briggs, 1986). Schoenberger (1991, p. 11) suggests that the standardized interview is undoubtedly more reliable than the non-standardized interview. 'But the latter, when carefully administered, may offer greater accuracy and validity because it allows a more comprehensive and detailed elucidation of the interplay among strategy, history, and circumstances. By contrast, the standardized survey instrument must necessarily standardize and simplify a complex reality'.

Identifying respondents and obtaining interviews

Whichever interviewing technique is used potential respondents have to be identified first. Talking to informed individuals and examining the business press are particularly useful when seeking case studies and when trying to maximize the range of experiences among the businesses chosen. Identifying the best person in a large company to approach for an interview can itself be a major problem, especially in a general survey. For example, the concept of business owners and managers is anathema in the case of worker co-operatives (Lowe, 1989).

In a specific study, for example of purchasing linkages, the section of the firm to approach can be much clearer. For many enquiries the most suitable person to contact may be someone at the head office or divisional office rather than at a branch. Sometimes the range of information required may make it desirable to interview more than one individual from a respondent company. Generally, when one good senior contact has been made it is easier to make others within the same organization. Introductions to managers in other firms in the same industry may also be generated as a survey progresses. For example, in a study analysing buyer-supplier relationships in the motor industry, many of the names of buyers were obtained from the supplying firm respondents (Wells and Rawlinson, 1992).

The best strategy for obtaining an interview seems to vary with the size of the business and the nature of the investigation. A short interview at a small firm can often be obtained by simply 'knocking on the door', although Clark (personal communication, 1991) suggests that it is now more important than ever to arrange interviews in advance for all types of businesses.

A request for an interview may be made either by letter or telephone. The latter often obtains an immediate reply, but may not achieve a higher response (Forsythe, 1977). Telephoning and 'fishing' for a named person who can best handle the enquiry before posting an introductory letter can work well (Peck, personal communication, 1991), as can obtaining an introduction by an appropriate intermediary (Linge, personal communication, 1991). Another possibility, when needing to contact people with broad overviews of their companies, is to write to the chief executives or managing directors requesting an interview with them or the person they think most appropriate (e.g., Crewe, 1989). It can be helpful to enclose with the letter a short outline of the nature and purpose of the research project, and how the findings may be useful to the respondent. A letter from the sponsor of the survey (where relevant) or another influential party may also be helpful in persuading business managers and owners to participate in the research.

It is often useful to follow up an introductory letter with a telephone call a few days later. It is more difficult for owners and managers to refuse an interview when speaking to the researcher over the telephone. It also provides an opportunity for the researcher to deal with any queries that may exist (North, personal communication, 1991). Polite persistence is important in obtaining an interview. A series of rejections can be dispiriting for the researcher; however, it is almost always worth querying an initial refusal to find out the reason. The approach or emphasis may then be modified to enhance the success rate of the survey.

Given the number of requests that busy executives receive, any 'opening' in the correspondence requesting assistance that gives them an excuse for refusal may be exploited. Although it is important to outline clearly the kind of information being asked for, refusal to cooperate is likely if the amount and level of detail of information requested is unreasonable. Kincaid and Bright (1957a) advise against multiple requests in the same letter. They report that, when they asked not only for an interview but also for any literature pertinent to the study, several companies refused cooperation on the ground that since they had no pertinent literature there would be no point in conducting an interview. Few researchers are prepared to risk marring their success by deliberately sending out shoddy work, but a well-designed and presented letter, typed on headed notepaper, which is personally addressed with a hand written signature, would seem to be a sensible way to trying to persuade the owners and managers of businesses to cooperate.

Preparation for interviews and obtaining accurate answers

Before contacting potential respondents considerable effort needs to be put into preparing and planning interviews so that the information collected is useful in meeting the aims of the research. The nature of the responses obtained in standardized surveys depends on the quality of the interview schedule design and the way the questions are phrased. In non-standardized surveys the quality of the answers is affected as much by the ability of the interviewer to engage the respondents in relevant discourse as by the phrasing of the questions. It is especially important in non-standardized interviews that the interviewer has a thorough understanding of the research subject so as to be able to make sense of the interview and to know when clarification or further probing is necessary. A pilot survey is essential to test a standardized interview schedule and is highly desirable for developing the skills and knowledge of the researcher undertaking a non-standardized interview.

It should be recognized that answers given to questions may differ when the respondent is not alone in the interview. For example, if a senior colleague is present, more critical comments about the organization may be withheld. Some understanding of the internal politics of an organization are essential so that more 'tactful' responses can be recognized. There is also the problem of inferring the motives of a company from the responses given by a single representative of an organization. It is important to establish whether the responses are a personal point of view or a statement about company policy. North (personal communication, 1991) also advises that interview data are treated with some scepticism, because for some owners/managers the interview provides an opportunity for an ego trip so that the successes may become exaggerated and the failures minimized. The material gleaned from interviews needs, of course, to be interpreted in the context of the conditions apparent at the time the interviews took place (Massey and Meegan, 1985).

Several researchers advise against accepting the view of one interviewee. For instance, at the conclusion of each interview, Stafford (1974) made a subjective attempt to corroborate the testimony of the respondent through a brief discussion with another senior manager involved in the location decision. Sayer and Morgan (1985) recommend interviewing 'both sides' of industry in order to learn about their different interests, perceptions and responses, so as to reveal the structural positions of capital and labour. Fothergill and Guy (1990, p. 106) also emphasize the dangers of accepting only one viewpoint in their study of the reasons for closures. They state that 'where management blamed the local trade union we therefore did not take their view as the gospel truth.

But equally, where the union blamed the management we did not necessarily accept their view either'. Perceptions may also vary between establishment and higher-level managers. In managing reductions in the workforce and the introduction of new technology Edwards and Marginson (1988), for example, found that the local managers perceived less involvement from above than their higher-level counterparts.

The responses given to the researcher can be influenced by the nature of the relationship established. Respondents, in attempting to be helpful, may give answers which they think will please the questioner, or they may try to justify their actions (the problem of *post-facto* rationalization). Moreover, the interviewer cannot safely assume that the particular words used in a question are in fact the stimulus to which the interviewee responds (Dexter, 1970). As much, if not more, skill and thought is needed in undertaking the non-standardized interviews used in intensive research as is required in constructing the standardized surveys used in extensive research. Not only does the interviewer need a thorough understanding of the research topic, but he or she should also have a sound knowledge of the industrial sector of the business and background information on the business itself, particularly where it is a large concern. Where the interviewer is well informed about the firm and the business it is engaged in, the respondent is likely to be more open and more detailed (Schoenberger, 1991). A well-informed interviewer has a basis for assessing the accuracy of some of the information offered. This may be illustrated by the experience of two researchers undertaking a study of strategic alliances (Cooke and Wells, 1990). In one interview they were given the impression that the joint ventures the company was involved in were going smoothly. However, when one of the researchers mentioned that he knew of one which had run into problems, the respondent opened up and a frank discussion of the advantages and disadvantages of joint ventures followed. The knowledge level required by the interviewer to carry out non-standardized interviews means that they should be undertaken by the principal researchers and should not be delegated to a team of interviewers.

Conducting and recording interviews

The most important factors contributing to a 'successful' interview are trust and rapport (Moyser and Wagstaffe, 1985). Dexter (1970, p. 25) recommends that 'sympathetic understanding' is the attitude most likely to promote such an atmosphere and hence yield the best response. The social skills of the interviewer are thus a key factor.

In most business research investigations it is appropriate to emphasise that no commercial secrets are being sought. Stafford (personal communication, 1991) recommends starting interviews by telling the respondents that no confidential information is being sought and that they should feel free to ignore any questions they wish. This, he suggests, allows the respondents to feel that they control the interview and as a result they are more relaxed and usually more forthcoming. Furthermore, commercially sensitive material tends to be too 'near the market' and of limited academic use. A promise of confidentiality is reassuring to respondents and is likely to make them more cooperative and open. However, it is not always possible to hide the identity of the businesses being examined, particularly when examining industries or local economies dominated by a few large enterprises. Where anonymity has been promised, the problem becomes one of how to guarantee it. This may require a degree of judicious vagueness. Some detail may have to be suppressed in order not to provide a set of clues that, taken together, would lead someone else to be able to identify the firm. Similarly, if direct quotations from interviews are to be used in the final report these should be non-attributable, unless permission has been given from the respondent.

Starting an interview on the right note is important. Initially, it is polite to explain who you are, the purpose of the study and its sponsorship. An open question is useful in starting a rapport with the interviwee. Dexter (1970) advises that a question which sharply defines a particular area for discussion. Some researchers (e.g., Hague, 1978b), favour using pre-coded responses because they save respondents having to think of possible replies and avoid having to make difficult coding judgements at the analysis stage. Other investigators choose to use open questions so as not to restrict the range of responses. Many elite interviewees prefer to give their own interpretations rather than be forced to choose between categories of responses which often do not seem to give an adequate summary of the situation as they perceive it.

Asking questions about sensitive issues can be a problem. It is usually best to leave sensitive questions until near the end of an interview because this allows a greater time for the respondent to build up trust and confidence in the researchers. In a six-country study of the automotive industry, which dealt with many commercially sensitive issues, such as future corporate strategies, the researchers noticed that the first part of the interviews were used by the respondents to assess the interviewers and how much they could safely be told (Wells and Rawlinson, 1992). Once this early period of probing by the respondents had taken place and they were satisfied that they had confidence in the researchers, the interviews were more relaxed and the respondents were more prepared to answer the sensitive questions. This view is supported by Peck (personal communication, 1991) who has found that once a degree of rapport is established many managers are prepared to be surprisingly open about potentially sensitive issues, such as attitudes to unions, labour relations, closures and redundancies. He has found that managers appear to be prepared to say quite a lot of things which might be considered self-critical, or at least critical of the methods used by their firms.

It can also be useful for researchers to summarize their understanding of complex issues to check that they have understood the issues correctly. The interviewee can then evaluate the adequacy of the interpretation and correct where necessary. In a standardized interview a useful check on the completeness of the information provided is to end the interview with an open-ended discussion. This technique was used in a case study of defence-based industries in Chicago where the researchers closed each interview by eliciting from their informants their views on why Chicago has not fared better as a centre for defence production and research (Markusen and McCurdy, 1989).

In many interview situations the interviewer needs to be flexible as to where and when interviews take place and to be prepared for frequent interruptions as the respondent continues to 'run the business'. This is particularly true for small businesses where interviews may take place on 'the shop floor'. Clark (personal communication, 1991) recommends that the interviewer is suitably dressed for the likely location of the interview so that he or she blends in. Sensible attire for the farm is clearly different from that for the head office of a large corporation. Inappropriate clothes may have a quite disproportionately negative effect (Bulmer, 1988).

Obtaining an accurate record of an interview is an important skill. There is a wide variety of ways of taking notes. However, one thing on which all researchers agree is the importance of writing up the notes as soon as possible after the completion of the interview. Some researchers favour interviewing in pairs as a way of eliminating interviewer bias and providing a check on what is said during the interview (e.g., Kincaid and Bright 1957b; and North et al. 1983). In one study of the competitive performance of small firms one interviewer used a schedule to structure the interviews, while a second engaged the respondents at appropriate points in a more discursive dialogue about their knowledge base, competitive strategy and flexibility (Horne et al., 1987). Interviewing in pairs is also useful when the interviews tend to be long and the subject matter dense or complex. If the concentration of one of the researchers slips then the other researcher can take the lead in the discussions.

An alternative to taking notes is to tape-record the interviews. This is common practice in North America (e.g., Gorden, 1975; and Stafford, 1974) and has been used successfully in Britain (e.g., Crewe, 1989; and Pratt, 1989). It provides an accurate record of the interview and enables the finished report to be enlivened with extended direct quotes. The acceptability of taping an interview may, however, depend on the approach the interviewer takes. Gorden (1975) advises *explaining* why it is used rather that *asking* for permission. By taping interviews it enables the interviewer to concentrate on the phrasing and order of questions rather than on note taking. On the other hand, the act of taping may inhibit the responses and transcribing and analysing the interviews can take a considerable time. Several commentators (e.g., Bulmer, 1988) have noted that some of the most interesting insights are obtained when the tape recorder is turned off.

Conclusions

Face-to-face interviewing is an important method of obtaining information in business and management research. However, surprisingly little has been written about this method. Although the issues involved in business surveys are not unique, several issues concerning the interview as a reseach method are highlighted when undertaking business interviews, including the link between interview techniques and more fundamental characteristics of the research process such as the adopted philosophical understanding of social science. This in turn determines the adopted ontology and epistemology which then influence the entire research design and the more practical considerations therein, such as, identifying respondents and obtaining access, preparing for interviews and obtaining 'accurate' answers, and ways of conducting and recording interviews. This paper has drawn upon both published sources and a survey of British, American and Australasian researchers in an attempt to identify some of the successful methods of interviewing. A number of general conclusions arise from this review of interview methods and techniques.

Done properly business surveys take considerable time and effort and should only be contemplated after all other sources of information have been exhausted. It is also desirable to examine the interviewing process from the point of view of the respondents. To encourage their continued cooperation in survey work it is important to maintain good relations with the business community, not least because of the value of resurveying the same businesses at a later date (e.g., Munton et al, 1988 and North et al, 1983). Too often researchers neglect to send a short thank you letter following an interview or forget to send interviewees the promised summary of the results of their projects. Surveys which attempt, within the limits of the research topic, to make the experience as interesting and stimulating as possible for the participants are also likely to make business owners and managers more favourably disposed to participate in future surveys (Healey, 1991). This may be easier with the increased use of qualitative non-standardized interviews which give a more active role to respondents.

There is no one 'best' way of interviewing business owners and managers. Methods vary for different situations, depending on a range of factors, including the research design, the kind and amount of information required, the resources available, and the size, organizational structure, sector and location of the business to be approached. Although the philosophy of the researcher may provide a guide to the methods used and different interview methods have associated characteristics (as illustrated in Table 5.1), the reality of undertaking research shows that the fit between theory and method is not nearly so neat as is sometimes supposed. As Bryman (1984, p. 89) notes 'there is no necessary 1:1 relationship between methodology and technique'. Different philosophical assumptions do not simply imply different approaches but also imply the different usage of similar approaches, and different interpretations of meaning derived from the information collected in interviews.

The lack of clear accessible guidance in the literature means that most researchers have little choice in designing their surveys than to rely on a combination of common sense and previous experience. Little progress will be made with improving the quality of information obtained from interviewing business owners and managers until researchers are prepared to experiment with different methods to try to increase response rates, hasten replies, obtain clearer answers, improve the flow of interviews and so on. Equally it is important that researchers disseminate these findings so that a reasonable guidence to other researchers can be developed.

* For a more detailed elaboration of the points made in this chapter see Healey, M.J. and M.B. Rawlinson (1993), Interviewing Business Owners and Managers: a Review of Methods and Techniques, *Geoforum,* 24, pp. 399-55. The authors are grateful to Pergamon Press for Permission to reproduce material from this article.

References

Bloom, N. (1988), 'The limitations of unqualitative research', *Industrial Marketing Digest*, Vol. 13, pp. 49-56.

Briggs, C.L. (1988), *Learning How to Ask: a Socio-linguistic Appraisal of the Role of the Interview in Social Science Research*, Cambridge University Press, Cambridge.

Bryman, A. (1984), 'The debate about quantitative and qualitative research: a question of method or epistemology?', *British Journal of Sociology*, Vol. 35, pp. 75-92.

Bryman, A. (1988), *Doing Research in Organisations,* Routledge, London.

Bulmer, M. (1988), 'Some reflections upon research in organisations', in A. Bryman (ed.), *Doing Research in Organisations,* Routledge, London.

Burton, T.L. and G.E. Cherry (1970), *Social Research Techniques for planners*. George Allen & Unwin, London.

Cooke, P. and P. Wells, (1990), *Strategic Alliances in ICT: Learning by Interaction*. Regional Industrial Research Report 4, University of Wales College of Cardiff.

Crewe, L. (1989), 'Industrial restructuring in West Yorkshire: some empirical and theoretical developments with particular reference to the textiles-clothing-retail distribution system', Unpublished Ph.D thesis, University of Leeds.

De Chernatony, L (1988), *Getting the Most from Postal Research*, Occasional Paper No. 3, Industrial Marketing Research Association, Lichfield.

Dexter, L.A. (1970), *Elite and Specialised Interviewing*, Northwestern University Press, Evanston, Il.

Edwards, P.K. and P. Marginson (1988), 'Differences in perception between establishment and higher level managers', in P. Marginson (ed.), *Beyond the Workplace: Managing Industrial Relations in the Multi-establishment Enterprise*, Basil Blackwell, Oxford.

Eyles, J. (1988), Interpreting the geographical world: qualitative approaches in geographical research, in J. Eyles and D.M. Smith (eds), *Qualitative Methods in Human Geography*, Polity Press, Cambridge.

Forsythe, J.B. (1977), Obtaining cooperation in a survey of business executives, *Journal of Marketing Research*, Vol. 14, pp. 370-73.

Fothergill, S. and G. Gudgin (1982), *Unequal Growth: Urban and Regional Employment Change in the UK,* Heinemann Educational, London.

Fothergill, S. and N. Guy (1990), *Retreat from the Regions: Corporate Change and the Closure of Factories,* Regional Policy and Development Series 1, Jessica Kingsley and Regional Studies Association, London.

Fowler, F.J. and T.W. Mangione (1990), *Standardised Survey Interviewing: Minimising Interview-related Error*, Applied Social Research Methods Series 18, Sage, London.

Gorden, R.L. (1975), *Interviewing: Strategy, Techniques and Tactics*, Dorsey Press, Homewood, Il.

Hague, P. (1978b), Good and bad in questionnaire design, *Industrial Marketing Digest*, Vol. 12, pp. 161-70.

Healey, M.J. (1991), 'Obtaining information from businesses', in M.J. Healey (ed.), *Economic Activity and Land Use: the Changing Information Base for Local and Regional Studies*, Longman, Harlow.

Hedges, B. and J. Ritchie (1987), *Research and Policy: the Choice of Appropriate Research Methods*, SCPR, London.

Horne, M.R., P.E. Lloyd, J.L. Pay, and P. Roe, (1987), *Structuring Knowledge of the Small Firm: a Framework for Informing Local Authority Intervention within the Private Sector*, Working Paper Series 20, School of Geography, North West Industry Research Unit, University of Manchester.

Johnston, R. (1986), *Philosophy and Human Geography*, Edward Arnold, London.

Keat, R. and J. Urry (1975), *Social Theory as Science*, Routledge and Kegan Paul, London.

Kincaid, H.W. and M. Bright (1957a), Interviewing the business elite, *American Journal of Sociology,* Vol. 63, pp. 304-11.

Kincaid, H.V. and Bright, M. (1957b), The tandem interviews: a trial of the two-interviews team, *Opinion Quarterly,* Vol. 21, pp. 304-12.

Kirk, J. and M. Miller (1986), *Reliability and Validity in Qualitative Research*, Sage, London.

Lowe, M. (1989), Worker co-operatives - panacea or radical enterprise?, *Environment and Planning D,* Vol. 7, pp. 31-48.

Markusen, A. (1991), *The Rise of the Gunbelt*, Oxford University Press, Oxford.

Markusen, A. and K. McCurdy (1989), 'Chicago's defense based high technology: a case study of the seedbeds of innovation hypothesis'. *Economic Development Quarterly,* Vol. 3, pp. 15-31.

Massey, D. and R. Meegan (eds), (1985), *Politics and Method: Contrasting Studies in Industrial Geography,* Methuen, London.

McDowell, L. (1992), 'Valid games? A response to Erica Schoenberger', *Professional Geographer,* Vol. 44, pp. 121-15.

Milne, S. (1991), 'Small firms, industrial reorganisation, and space: the case of the UK high-fidelity audio sector', *Environment and Planning D,* Vol. 23, pp. 833-52.

Mitchell, J.C. (1983), 'Case and situational analysis', *Sociological Review,* Vol. 31, pp. 187-211.

Moyser, G. and M. Wagstaffe (1985), *The Methodology of Elite Interviewing,* Report to the Economic and Social Research Council, Grant H00250003, London.

Moyser, G. and M. Wagstaffe (eds), (1987), *Research Methods for Elite Studies*, Allen & Unwin, London.

Munton, R., S. Whatmore, and T. Marsden (1988), 'Reconsidering urban-fringe agriculture: a longitudinal analysis of capital restructuring on farms in the Metropolitan Green Belt', *Transactions of the Institute of British Geographers, New series,* Vol. 13, pp. 324-36.

North, D.J., R. Leigh, and J. Gough (1983), 'Monitoring industrial change at the local level: some comments on methods and data sources', M.J. Healey (ed.), *Urban and Regional Industrial Research: the Changing UK Data Base,* Geo Books, Norwich.

Pratt, A. (1989), Towards an explanation of the form and location of industrial estates in Cornwall 1984: a critical realist approach, Unpublished Ph.D thesis, University of Exeter.

Rawlinson, M.B. (1990), Subcontracting relationship between small engineering firms and large motor vehicle firms in the Coventry area, Unpublished Ph.D thesis, Coventry Polytechnic.

Rawlinson, M.B. (1991), Subcontracting in the motor industry: a case study in Coventry, C. Law (ed.), *Restructuring the Global Automotive Industry*, Routledge, London.

Sayer, A. (1984), *Method in Social Science*, Hutchinson, London.

Sayer, A. and K. Morgan (1985), 'A modern industry in a declining region: links between method, theory and policy', in D. Massey and R. Meegan (eds), *Politics and Method: Contrasting Studies in Industrial Geography,* Methuen, London.

Schoenberger, E. (1991), 'The corporate interview as a research method in economic geography', *Professional Geographer*, Vol. 43, pp.180-89.

Schoenberger, E. (1992), 'Self-criticism and self-awareness in research: a reply to Linda McDowell', *Professional Geographer,* Vol. 44, pp. 215-18.

Silverman, D. (1985), *Qualitative Methodology and Sociology*, Gower, Aldershot.

Stafford, H.A. (1974), The anatomy of the location decision: content analysis of case studies, in F.E.I. Hamilton (ed.), *Spatial Perspectives on Industrial Organisation and Decision making*, John Wiley, London.

Stafford, H.A. and H.D. Watts (1990), 'Abandoned products, abandoned places: plant closures by multi-product multi-locational firms in urban areas', *Tijdschrift econ. soc. Geogr,* Vol. 10, pp. 206-27.

Swain, W. (1978), The postal questionnaire, in A. Rawnsley (ed.), *Manual of Industrial Marketing Research*, John Wiley, Chichester.

Sykes, W. (1990), 'Validity and reliability in qualitative market research: a review of the literature', *Journal of Market Research Society*, Vol. 32, pp. 282-89.

Sykes, W. (1991), 'Taking stock: issues from the literature on validity and reliability in qualitative research', *Journal of Market Research Society*, Vol. 33, pp. 3-12.

Wells, P. and M. Rawlinson, (1992), 'Technology procurement practices, and structural change in the automotive presswork sector', in B. Shirvani and D. Briggs (eds), *Sheet Metal,* Institute of Physics, Bristol.

Yin, R.K. (1984), *Case Study Research: Design and Methods*, Applied Social Research Methods Series 5, Sage, Beverly Hills, Ca.

6 Strategic Organizational Analysis in Four Dimensions

DAVID STILES

Introduction

Devising and implementing workable business strategies for organizations has been a genuine concern of management for many years. Some academics, too, have sensed the need to develop detailed understanding about social processes in specific micro environments, rather than just seek generalizable laws concerning the macro business world. This chapter is about conducting research with needs such as these in mind.

Indeed, the methodology presented here recognizes that when managers are faced with the task of matching organizational capabilities with internal and external environmental forces, the overriding concern is often 'How do I develop and implement a successful strategy for my organization?' Generalizations, although useful in providing guiding principles, become less important than specifics concerning one's own situation.

This chapter draws from a study of two business schools: one in the UK and one in Canada. With recent fundamental changes in higher

147

education, there is a pressing need for strategy research that is practically useful to those managing universities. Conventional strategy models developed in the world of private big business often seem irrelevant in the rarefied academic environment, where even the nature of the product, the teaching process, is far from straightforward. Current dilemmas faced by managers of academic institutions include defining, measuring and evaluating learning inputs and outputs; determining whether process or outcome is to be focussed upon; deciding how the often conflicting goals of stakeholders, such as students and faculty, are to be balanced; and even what actually constitutes the 'teaching' or 'learning' product for actors. For the educational administrator, there also remains the tricky problem of actually implementing any quality teaching strategy devised. A substantial part of this issue revolves around the identification of internal organizational processes phenomena like culture and politics, and then deciding what to do about them. These are much neglected topics in conventional marketing strategy literature.

This chapter sketches a methodology which recognizes such difficulties. It was chosen as a means of exploring organizational structures, constructs and processes. The methodology has actually been applied in practice to two business school settings, testing the strengths and weaknesses of the analytical tools in reality. However, the methodology is not restricted to use in business schools. Rather, it has been designed to be transferable across to other organizational settings in the public and private sectors, with necessary modifications. The framework described here rests upon the premise that no one research perspective is adequate by itself in explaining how organizations work. Many research projects draw either explicitly or implicitly upon a single, though not necessarily pure, epistemological perspective, be it positivist, realist or interpretivist. However, the methodology outlined here is best viewed as multi-faceted, with the quantitative aspects fitting more into the positivist perspective mould; and the qualitative discourse analysis following more readily an interpretive approach. This is because, as Feyerabend (1978) argues, using a combination of techniques from both perspectives helps uncover different sorts of data, which can then be compared and contrasted. This is done by feeding back the results to discussion, or 'focus' groups of organizational members, to determine which data correspond with their own perceptions of organizational reality.

In addition, the use of change analysis and an exploration of perceptual constructs and processes draw upon neo-structuralist notions of social reality. This is in keeping with an underlying model of the organization as a multi-layered phenomenon, rather than a discreet, bounded entity. In fact the methodology can be justifiably regarded as integrative, combining conceptual developments in strategy implementation, organizational behaviour, social psychology and political sociology. In exploring the complex nature of organization, innovative techniques have been applied combining quantitative methods, projective exercises, ethnography and discourse analysis in a case study situation.

Participant observation, secondary data analysis, face-to-face interviews and focus groups provide a triangulated exploration of the issues and processes facing the quality-seeking academic institution. Specific instruments include a technique especially designed for investigating academics' value systems; a cluster analysis of demographic data, attitudes and values; verbal discourse analysis; and pictorial representation. A time-oriented approach is used to enhance understanding of organizational change processes in a university environment.

Ultimately, as well as providing an holistic analytical tool for examining intra-organizational structures, constructs and processes, the methodology aims to assist in the formulation and introduction of workable strategies. Higher education institutions have been used as illustrations here, and in many ways represent an unique form of organizational setting; but versions of these analytical instruments could be used anywhere. By undertaking a highly-detailed examination of organizational phenomena in two business schools, lessons are drawn concerning the successful implementation of strategy in complex and often frustrating organizational cultures.

The challenge to rational models of strategic planning

The methodology outlined in this chapter has developed from a critique of mainstream strategic management literature. Since the 1960s, organizational strategy has mutated into a variety of forms - including long-range planning, corporate planning, business policy and strategic management. An emphasis has been placed upon rational frameworks for strategy formulation, including Strengths Weaknesses Opportunities and Threats (SWOT) Analysis, Management By Objectives, Boston Consultancy Group matrices and Porter's Structural Industry Analysis. (Kotler, 1986 and 1988; Johnson and Scholes, 1988). These derive from inherent positivistic assumptions about the primacy of 'Rational Man'. (Handy, 1985). However, as Etzioni (1961), March and Simon (1967), Pfeffer (1981) and others have argued, organizations in reality often function in a way that at best uses only an incremental, modified rationality: perhaps revealing pluralistic or other non-unitary tendencies. Some models of humanity contest the rational-economic world-view even more strongly. Schein's (1980) 'Complex Man' and Levinson's (1972) 'Psychological Man' are amongst contrasting frameworks which challenge the fundamental assumption that collections of individuals can be managed, planned and controlled in a mechanistic manner. Various challenges to the rationalist orthodoxy have also come from the 'Excellence' movement, initiated by Peters and Waterman (1982); and strategic contingencies theorists, such as Hickson (1971).

However, despite these efforts, the rationalistic paradigm in marketing strategy has proven difficult to modify. Witness the status still conferred upon Kotler whose marketing and strategy textbooks remain amongst the most influential in the field (Kotler, 1986 and 1988). The result is the tendency to present strategic management as the largely linear process represented in Figure 1 - beginning with a definition of organizational principles, vision, and operating domain (Mission); before formulating strategy goals and detailed functional plans from a systematic review of the environments inside and outside the organization. At best, there is lip-service towards the end of the process concerning how to implement such grandiose schemes. More often, it is assumed that somehow things will take care of themselves.

There is some evidence that a challenge to rationalistic strategic management is taking shape, if rather embryonically at present. One observer has recently chronicled the emergence in the UK of two distinct groupings of strategy academics: one adhering to traditional mechanistic

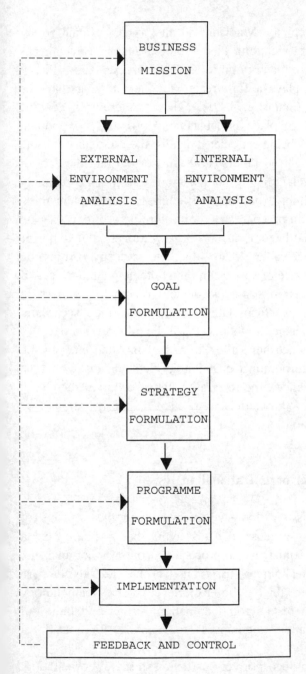

Figure 6.1   The rational view of strategic planning

marketing planning, such as MacDonald; the other around more politically-oriented writers, including Piercy, who argues that planning is not linear but can begin from any point in Kotler's representation. Piercy also argues that politics plays a far greater role in planning than the rationalists would allow (Stainsby, 1991). Whether there is a genuine paradigmatic struggle taking place is debatable. However, it is evident that some dissatisfaction is being articulated against the rationalist school.

One reason for this might be Peters' (1989) assertion that the rate of change in markets is accelerating faster than rational strategic planning can cope with. More simply, perhaps, difficulties with implementing elaborately-devised plans in practice seem to be forcing a refocussing on 'softer' intra-organizational factors, such as organizational culture, power and politics. It is conceivable, then, that the strategy profession hasunderstated the importance of soft factors in strategic planning. Yet, if strategic management fails to focus adequately on such realities, in implementing as well as formulating strategies, the successful introduction and maintenance of any strategy will be infinitely harder.

The methodology explained here aims to go beyond such mechanistic constraints. Although incorporating quantitative elements that could be ascribed to positivist influences, the integrative nature of the methodology helps circumvent many of the criticisms levelled at purely rationalistic views of human organization.

An holistic framework for organizational analysis

The epistemological basis for this study draws upon the writings of Feyerabend (1978), who argues that, to avoid being bound by a paradigmatic view, the scientist should proceed by contrast, not analysis. One should use different techniques, based on rival theories - to compare ideas with ideas, rather than with experience. The methodology developed for this study rests upon this notion: using a 'bundle' of quantitative and qualitative techniques to explore organizational phenomena.

The methodology also incorporates an action research orientation. Lewin argues that causal inferences about the behaviour of human beings are more likely to be valid and enactable when the human beings in question participate in building and testing them (Lewin, 1948). In keeping with Whyte's (1991) definition of 'Participant Action Research' (P.A.R.), the study design accepts the rationale that only by immersing oneself in the social processes of an organization as a participant - and also involving organizational members in developing one's research - can one possibly hope to obtain an adequate interpretation of that organization. As well as aiming to achieve an increase in academic knowledge and testing or replicating existing theory, it also serves a third aim of involving and promoting a decision on action by organizational members. The stance taken in this project incorporates elements from all of Gold's (1968) field roles typology (see Delbridge and Kirkpatrick in this volume), but falls most readily into the 'participant-as-observer' category. In other words, the researcher participates and observes by developing relationships with informants, making no secret of the research.

However, participant observation is only one part of the overall framework. In fact, the concept of organizational culture provides a conceptual lynchpin for the methodology. Much has been written about organizational culture. So much so, that a prospective researcher could justifiably feel confused as to what 'culture' actually is. So, before embarking on a cultural investigation, the researcher must be clear about what he or she is looking for. Schall (1983, p. 557) argues that cultural analysts share common ground in generally regarding organizational culture as 'a relatively enduring, interdependent symbolic system of values, beliefs, and assumptions evolving from and imperfectly shared by interacting organizational members'. In other words, there seems to be an understanding that organizations contain deeper levels, or 'layers', of embedded phenomena underlying people's activities. It is this 'layer' idea that is used to develop a comprehensive analytical framework here. In fact, Schein (1985) and Morgan (1986) both suggest viewing the organization as a complex multi-layered phenomenon, rather than a simple unitary entity. Schein argues that an holistic understanding of intra-organizational processes should involve the penetration of successive layers of organizational culture; whilst Morgan (1989, p. 157) urges the analyst to penetrate beneath visible rituals, ceremonies and symbolic routines to discover 'innermost values and assumptions that lend meaning to the outward aspects of the culture'. This multi-layered metaphor provides the basis for an holistic organizational model. By examining and penetrating each layer in turn, greater understanding of the organization is developed. Strategies can subsequently be developed to address the issues raised in each dimension.

A conceptual way of distinguishing between these layers is provided by Lukes (1974), who develops a multi-layered metaphor about power. Lukes (1974) proposes that power can exist in three 'dimensions', or layers: overt (observable, behavioural, authority-based), covert (hidden exercises of interest involving mobilization of bias) and latent (the contextual influence of inexplicit assumptions). Put more simply, overt power is visible and often formal; covert power is invisible and can involve political acts; and latent power is unconscious, conferred on someone by their environment or by unchallenged assumptions. The issuing of a formal instruction, or a sanction such as a sacking, are examples of overt power; forming a secret coalition with other parties to unseat a board member is an extreme example of covert power; whilst seating arrangements in a lecture theatre often force students to focus on their lecturer - an example of latent power.

If we extend this power model to other organizational processes, such as culture, we are close to a framework that can distinguish between phenomenal layers: by characterising all organizational structures and processes as overt, covert or latent. However, two further elements need to be added: a more explicit notion of what exactly the 'values, beliefs and assumptions' are that comprise Schall's definition of culture; and how these things change over time as the organization develops.

Rokeach (1968) has developed a psychological model which helps categorize human values, beliefs and assumptions. It is based upon the idea that some of these characteristics are more fundamental to an individual's personality and motivations than others. For example, believing in family life may be more important to someone than a belief that blue is the best colour to paint a particular room. From this, Rokeach constructs a continuum between superficial, changeable beliefs (which he calls 'attitudes') and deeper-set, less transient beliefs or assumptions ('values'). He also devises a ranking technique for identifying basic values, which is used in a modified form in this methodology. Rokeach's continuum seems to fit in quite neatly to the layer metaphor, with changeable attitudes lying nearer to the surface of the organization than deep-set values.

Implicit here is the understanding that an organization contains a 'deeper' level of embedded phenomena. Epistemological support for this is given by the 'social constructionist' school, embodied in the work of Berger and Luckman (1965) and Weick (1979). These argue that individuals and groups can experience the same reality in different ways, forming their own 'social constructions' or 'enactments' - shared perceptions that serve to reconstruct the reality they have experienced. This is in contrast to the passive role positivists see human beings as adopting in the scientific process. Again, deeper-set human constructs are seen to reside towards the bottom of the organizational mind-set. The penetration of this deeper level seems significant to organizational theorists. If values, perceptions and other organizational processes can be examined in an integrated way, we might come significantly closer to understanding how particular organizations are culturally constructed; and thereby suggest which organizational change strategies are most likely to succeed. Integrating such ideas with cultural concepts, allows the analyst a more holistic organizational perspective than the culture metaphor alone provides. Combining the multi-layered metaphor with Lukes' power model, internal organizational processes - including power and culture - can be analysed in a systematic way.

The final challenge is to incorporate a time dynamic into the framework, since organizational change is of fundamental importance in developing long-term strategy. Including a temporal dimension in the model permits a dynamic interpretation of organizational structures and processes. Pettigrew (1979) provides a conceptual link between organizational culture and the temporal dimension; arguing that longitudinal studies, such as the identification and analysis of 'social dramas', are of fundamental importance. He later suggests that dynamic studies should try to identify 'embeddedness', 'inter-temporal connectedness', 'context' and 'action' (Pettigrew, 1990). Certainly, the concept of 'embeddedness' involves the implicit acceptance of several organizational layers. Similarly, Van de Ven (1987, p. 331) conceptualizes change as 'an empirical observation of differences in time on one or more dimensions of an entity'; whilst the process of change is described as 'an inference of a latent pattern of differences noted in time'. Such ideas are firmly grounded in a multi-layered metaphor. Others have argued that the identification of events, congruences, breakpoints, reoccurancies and continuities are vital in studying organizational change (Nadler and Tushman, 1982; Rosenfeld et al, 1989). As long as this occurs, an holistic perspective is easier to achieve - and organizational change strategies are more likely to be successful, because we know far more about the organization we are planning for, and are more likely to choose strategic options that are implementable.

The result, then, is an holistic, 'four-dimensional' framework, as depicted in Figure 6.2. This visual organizational metaphor is one way of representing the case study organization. As a theoretical model, it forms the basis for the subsequent research design. Assume that an organization's overt surface phenonema can be contained within a simple geometrical shape such as a circle, drawn on the top left of the diagram. If we then extend those boundaries factionally downwards, we can then examine those hidden covert manifestations just below the surface. Deeper still into this now three-dimensional cylindrical shape are the organization's latent phenomena, underlying and supporting all those phenomena. Now, assume that we can view this cylinder shifting along a time dimension, represented by the repeat images to the right of the original shape. It is this dynamism that we are attempting to capture in our temporal analysis. Of course, this is only a visual metaphor, but it does help to emphasise the distinctive categories of data we are trying to capture. The methodology thus becomes an exploration of organizational processes descending through the overt dimension (observable behaviour, readily quantifiable organizational characteristics), via the covert layer (attitudes, hidden political and social interaction) to the latent dimension (unchallenged contextual and personal assumptions and perceptions) - over time.

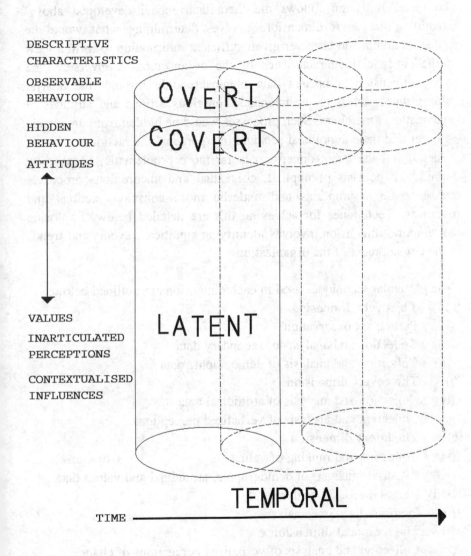

Figure 6.2   Organizational phenomena in four dimensions

The research design

The research design follows the theoretical model developed above. Examining the overt dimension involves determining what would be evident to an outside observer given sufficient information to form a view of the superficial characteristics of the organization. Conversely, the covert dimension comprises data obtainable only through the analyst being granted access to the intended, conscious actions and attitudes of organizational members. Such processes would be hidden from an outside observer and include political acts and interpersonal interactions.

Identifying the latent dimension is far more problematic, because by definition it consists of implicit, contextual and unconscious processes that generate assumptions and underlie more conscious actions and processes. Techniques for achieving this are detailed below. Exploring the temporal dimension involves identifying significant events and trends in the development of the organization.

The particular techniques used in each dimension are outlined below.

(a)   The overt dimension
  (i)   Participant observation
 (ii)   Collection and analysis of secondary data
 (iii)   Collection and analysis of demographic data
(b)   The covert dimension
 (iv)   Collection and analysis of attitudinal data
  (v)   Collection and analysis of verbalized perceptions
(c)   The latent dimension
 (vi)   Collection and ranking of values
 (vii)   Cluster analysis of demographic, attitudinal and values data
 (viii) Verbal discourse analysis
 (ix)   Pictorial discourse analysis
(d)   The temporal dimension
  (x)   Collection and analysis of verbalized perceptions of change
 (xi)   Chronology of significant past events
 (xii)   Collection and analysis of future expectations

Data collection and analysis occur in two distinct phases: Phase one incorporates the majority of face-to-face interviews concerning individuals' cultural perceptions of the organization. Phase two uses discussion groups to focus and aggregate these data into commonly-shared perceptions; as well as exploring change processes in more depth. Note, however, that the methodology is not linear. In the tradition of Glaser and Strauss (1967), data emerge in a grounded fashion, and iterations continue until further new information is judged by the researcher to be of insufficient added value. A more detailed explanation of these elements follows.

(a) The overt dimension

(i) Participant observation Using an interpretive stance for this part of the methodology allows one to analyse culture from an insider's perspective. Such participant observation involves personal observations in diary form of reactions to, and interpretations of, each business school culture. It also includes observing and recording the process of strategy formulation within internal working parties, to provide greater insight into the aims, assumptions and group dynamics of the strategists themselves. Diaries are also kept by selected new entrants to the organization concerning their initial experiences and perceptions of the organizations. This phase provides greater depth to other project data and is run simultaneously with other phases. In practical terms, this has meant two research placements with the Canadian institution in successive years; whilst the UK case is based on three years' continuous work. This difference in time spent at the respective organizations highlights a major problem with longitudinal case study research where extreme distance limits access to data. This can be compensated for, to some extent, by revisits and by maintaining contact by letter, telephone, fax and electronic mail. However, although the remaining research instruments used are identical for both cases; it must be accepted that the degree of insight obtained from briefer, if more intense, periods of participant observation is different than that from longer stays.

(ii) Collection and analysis of secondary data   To forge an early link with business strategy, it is important that existing strategic plans for each business school are analysed. This provides part of the overt aspect of the model. In addition, written documents relating to formal management mechanisms (committee minutes, personnel procedures, formal rules, organizational structure etc.) and publicity material in each school are assessed. Historical archives are examined in keeping with the temporal dimension of the study. Furthermore, any available data relating to strategy and policy derivision and implementation, staff turnover, research contracts, roles and any other information deemed relevant, is viewed. Documents reviewed or produced by the internal quality assurance working parties in each institution are also analysed. Background information on national and regional historical, political and cultural influences is sought from published sources.

(iii) Collection and analysis of demographic data   At this point, however, the methodology differs substantially from earlier work: combining both quantitative and qualitative approaches. Semi-structured face-to-face interviews are conducted with business school participants. Interviews last one-and-quarter hours on average, but have been known to take three hours for some particularly-enthusiastic interviewees! The instrument's first section records simple descriptive data relating to such variables as age, sex, grade and previous employment. Although such data is collected as part of the personnel function in many organizations, information is often unsystematic, incomprehensive and out-of-date. Consequently, it is important to obtain demographic data from as many organizational members as possible, to build an accurate view of the overt nature of the organization.

The emphasis in this chapter is upon technique, but it is useful to provide examples to illustrate the types of data generated. Such data, for example, reveals that one of the business schools is heavily male dominated, especially in the area of quantitative methods; has a very uneven grading structure, with an overrepresented full-Professorial grade; exhibits a distinct emphasis upon human resource management in terms of staff numbers; and is composed of a largely new faculty, with 24 per cent of staff in employment at the School for less than a year and 68 per cent of faculty less than five years. It is also a faculty with limited recent full-time industrial or commercial experience; one whose mean age is 34.7 years old; and whose members are drawn largely from outside its regional boundaries. In addition, 40 per cent have a Doctorate degree; there is a high median income, but a very skewed income distribution; and a large number of peripheral faculty (short-term or fixed-contract). Comparisons may be drawn with other organizations' profiles. However, even in the absence of comparative data, a demographic profile is a useful starting point for probing further into the case study organization itself.

(b) The covert dimension

(iv) Collection and analysis of attitudinal data. If attitudes are accepted as being more transient than values, the use of Likert scales at this point will reflect part of the second dimension - the covert side of the model. Within the formal research instrument's second section, three-point Likert scales are used to assess attitudes towards the official, stated objectives of the Business School. Analysis of these data can be very revealing - at least as a second-dimensional 'staging-post' on the way to third dimensional values and perceptions. Simple association tests, such as χ^2, also help to illuminate findings.

Illustration of the use of such data can be made by referring to attitudinal information from one of the organizations studied. For example, recall of the official strategy of the Business School was fairly limited. Initially, 57 per cent claimed to be aware of the strategy document, and 52 per cent claimed to have read it. However, unprompted recall of more than two or three specific major goals in the document was low. Although 60 per cent knew or guessed that growth in student numbers was a main goal, 57 per cent thought that being research-led was a priority, and 41 per cent stated teaching quality as an objective; no other goal was mentioned by more than a fifth of respondents. No one recalled all ten goals without prompting. χ^2 revealed that those who had read the strategy tended to be male permanent staff, active on committees and had been employed at the institution for at least five years. This helped identify organizational personnel to target when communicating existing and future strategies.

(v)   Collection and analysis of verbalized perceptions   Recording more qualitative comments in relation to the organization's strategy objectives provides additional insightful data. These are useful in determining organizational constructs, before deciding upon appropriate strategies. As an example, in one of the schools there appeared to be a widespread lack of belief in the real importance of teaching or research quality to organizational strategy-makers. Comments made include a belief that organizational leaders are only interested in:

> Achieving certain perceived minimal quality standards in teaching delivery. I don't believe that the Business School has serious research or quality objectives, although it purports to do so.

Attitudinal analysis also helps identify particular areas where strategy implementation may be more problematic because of disagreement over particular goals. For example, when a Likert scale analysis of attitudes towards the specific goals of one of the business schools was conducted, four out of ten goals were broadly accepted by interviewees, but the remainder were not as well supported. On a three-point scale, there was almost universal agreement (89 per cent +) with the goals of improving teaching quality, expanding post experience teaching, becoming more international, and the provision of more buildings. However, although 65 per cent agreed with the goals of being research-led and of increasing the scale of the institution, 30 per cent and 22 per cent respectively voiced strong disagreement with these two goals. From cross-tabulation data, academics in accountancy and marketing departments were particularly concerned about the research-led goal, whilst those in economics and marketing departments were most concerned about the increasing scale goal. A further 22 per cent disagreed with the school's aim to lead regional business education. In addition, only 57 per cent agreed with the existing undergraduate degree scheme split, 54 per cent with a concentration upon postgraduate schemes, and 46 per cent with the major goal of growth. These data assisted in the revision of strategic objectives and in the formulation of internal communication exercises concerning less-supported goals.

(c)   The latent dimension

(v) Values ranking This is the first of the techniques used for examining the more latent aspects of organizational processes. It involves applying the Rokeach (1968) value analysis methodology to two original lists of academic values (Instrumental values, or means-to-achieve-work-goals; and Terminal values, or end-goals in themselves) rearranged by each respondent in order of centrality to his/her own working life. These values are listed in the appendix and were generated from a search of the literature on academic culture. Thus, whilst 'achieving excellence in teaching' might be an end-goal; one might prefer to 'use case studies' or 'use large group lectures' as means to achieve this. Both value lists were subsequently tested during a pilot study of 10 academics in the UK institution. It had already been hypothesized that at least 27 different primary and hybrid subcultures associated with these values may exist: including 'teachers', 'researchers', 'administrators' and 'consultants'. Cluster analysis using SPSS help determine whether any of these types actually exist, whether others appear, or whether no patterns are evident.

The modified Rokeach method involves scoring the values on each list between one and 18, depending on how the respondent ranks them relative to each other. The value ranked highest scores 18, the one ranked lowest scores only one on each list. Any considered 'Not at all important' by respondents are also given one. Where respondents articulated other values not on the list, these are examined separately. Median and mode scores for each value are then used to manually calculate an overall values ranking for the organization. This is the closest one will get to a statistical profile of the underlying value system of the respondents.

In the two business schools, for example, values analysis reveals that 'have a fulfilling personal life' is the highest-ranked terminal value (end-goal in working life) amongst academics, whilst 'completing an academic project' is the highest ranked instrumental value (means-to-end-goals). Academics also value research and teaching excellence highly, as they do learning from others' business experience. Having complete control over work seems less important than being able to choose work methods. Securing high financial reward is not a priority; and neither is getting to the top of organizations, nor competitiveness. Academics are highly discipline-oriented and value contact with the business world; but are neither particularly supportive of their local region nor of the ritualistic side of university life. Involvement in administration is least valued.

Data are also subject to the Mann-Whitney U Test to determine whether there were any significant associations between any of the values and the remaining variables, as a precursor to cluster analysis. In the UK case it was found, for example, that non-Professors tend to value T4 ('freedom of method') higher than Professors; whilst those aware of the institution's strategy document rank T4 higher than those who are not. Males tend to value 'theoretical concepts' (T6) higher than females; and older faculty (over 40 years old) seem to value theories more than younger faculty. Older faculty also seem to rank T7 - 'establishing an academic reputation' - significantly higher than younger members; and this is even more pronounced for Professors against non-Professors and also active committee members against those not active. Doctors value T7 higher than non-Doctors, whilst permanent staff also give this value higher regard than short-term faculty.

Amongst instrumental values in the UK school, full Professors and committee activists generally rank I1 ('accept the authority of academic experts') higher than non-Professors and non-activists; Professors, males and activists all rank I2 ('assess evidence using established methods') significantly higher than their counterparts; non-Professors generally value 'using case studies' (I12) more than Professors; and those under 40, non-Professors and non-Activists prefer small group tutorials - I14 .

(vi) Cluster analysis This is as far as quantitative analysis is able to go in terms of defining clusters - akin to homogeneous groups or even subcultures - from the descriptive data. In fact, this is a prime example of a quantitative technique using non-parametric statistics (Aldenderfer and Blashfield, 1984). Dummy variables are created from the original categorical data and clustered with the attitudinal variables, the Rokeach Values data, and the straightforward interval data. Squared euclidean

distance and average linkage proved superior to other alternatives. The resulting dendograms, agglomeration schedules and icicle plots are then used to determine the number and composition of clusters in the organization. Internal and external validation procedures are followed to ensure clusters are meaningful: for the researcher must be aware of the dangers of 'naive empiricism' with this technique. This arises from the ability of the software to generate many possible 'solutions'. The researcher must be capable of selecting a valid one. In other words, to decide whether an observed pattern is truly a pattern. Only knowledge of the organization and experience of using this technique can help in this.

In illustration, for one of the institutions, three distinct academic clusters have been identified, whose members shared reasonably similar characteristics in terms of demographics, attitudes and values. One cluster comprises mainly permanent staff, another short-term faculty, and a third students. In the other, two clusters are evident; with a separation of faculty into 'teachers' and researchers. Such clusters may be used as the basis for a segmented organizational strategy, but care should be taken in deriving them.

(vii) Verbal discourse analysis More fundamental discourse analysis starts here, with any rigid pre-imposed structures rejected in favour of a grounded approach. However, in keeping with Potter and Wetherell's (1987) suggestions, the following broad principles are followed using interviews transcribed in the form of a conversation between the participants:

(a) Patterns are sought in the data relating to (i) variability, and (ii) consistency between the answers given by respondents to the same question. Variability relates to differences in either the form or content of answers.
(b) Hypotheses are then drawn concerning the functions and effects of verbal responses and perceptions.

Unlike content analysis, which assumes that verbal accounts reflect underlying attitudes and dispositions, discourse analysis pays as much attention to the language itself: how it is organized and what it is doing.

This is why very detailed transcripts have been made, which include length of pauses, hesitances, word emphasis, overlap between speakers, mannerisms, and verbatim comment by both interviewer and interviewee.

All transcripts are recorded on computer file, which allows an integrated wordprocessing/graphics/spreadsheet package enormous flexibility in cutting, pasting, annotating and rearranging passages during the analysis. The transcription process used rules based on a modified version of Gail Jefferson's (1985) discourse notation system.

Amongst major consistencies identified at one school is the desire to see the institution achieve recognition as a major centre of excellence in research - the main emphasis of the strategy document. Gaining a strong research reputation is often seen as the precondition for other goals to be achieved, such as differentiation from non-university institutions, attracting outside funding and achieving a high public profile for the recruitment of faculty and students. However some evidence also emerges that a growth in student numbers is seen as detrimental to achieving excellence in research and in teaching. Growth is largely seen as a means to an end, rather than an end in itself, with the ultimate goal being 'to prosper' or even just 'to survive'.

Teaching is also emphasized by eight of the respondents as central to the school's strategic objectives; but of a developmental rather than a training-based variety. For example, respondents speak of, 'well qualified students who are not just well qualified in terms of degrees'; and 'something not necessarily training, but more developmental, that will enrich analytical skills - the ability to think'.

The second phase of the research involves feeding-back the draft findings of the face-to-face interviews into discussion, or 'focus', groups consisting of members of each business school for their evaluation and suggestion. Hedges (1985), and Robson and Foster (1989) discuss various uses for focus groups. Sometimes they are used independently, sometimes as exploratory vehicles prior to detailed quantitative or qualitative analysis. In this context, however, focus groups are used to refine or 'focus' face-to-face interview data already obtained. This is similar to delphi-type techniques, which also use iteration stages to refine original data (Paliwoda, 1983). It is the aim to develop a consensus concerning the validity of the data obtained from the first phase of the project. The groups also serve the purpose of 'building-up' from individuals' perceptions up to commonly-shared group perceptions, grounding group stimulae in original face-to-face data.

(ix) Pictorial discourse analysis This is perhaps the most original part of the methodology, since it explores the use of image in perceptions. Precedents for pictorial representation originate from four sources: psychotherapy, neurophysiology, art theory and qualitative marketing research. Clinical psychotherapy bases its use of drawing on Freudian theories of repression, which hold that human beings tend to suppress unpalatable thoughts and emotions in a way that internalizes tension. Such internalized latent fears and anxieties can, however, be 'projected' onto external objects, animals and people - and this is what projective techniques aim to reveal. Tests such as the Rorschach inkblot, Thematic Apperception Tests, Szondi, and 'World' Techniques have been specifically designed to permit subjects to reveal fears and anxieties, which can then be identified and treated (Semeonoff, 1976; Branthwaite and Lunn, 1985). Neurophysiological research on brain functioning and consciousness indicates that visual, spatial, arational thought processes are localized in specific areas of the brain - the right cerebral hemisphere - whereas verbal, logical, rational processes are localized in the left hemisphere. To ensure complementarity in thinking, both parts of the brain need to be activated, which necessitates using images in addition to words when researching people's perceptions (Ornstein, 1977; Mintzberg, 1988).

A large part of art theory is, of course, based on pictorial representation. In addition, Edwards (1981) links neurophysiological research with drawing techniques in an effort to teach drawing skills in an holistic manner. Some of Edwards' suggestions for drawing 'warm-ups' are used in this methodology.

Although little is published on the use of pictorial representation in qualitative market research, the author has been personally involved with one major exercise for a UK building society and is aware of two others, which allow consumers to represent their perceptions of the company. Such exercises tend to be conducted in the pre-testing stage of television advertisements, where the imaging of existing perceptions of companies and brands and the exploration of alternative visual treatments is important.

Two pictorial techniques are included in the methodology: a free drawing exercise based on depicting the organization as a personality metaphor; and card-selection, incorporating representations of animal characteristics.

The emphasis in this chapter is on the techniques used. However, case study findings do help in providing examples of the practical use of pictorial representation. For example, the free-drawing personality metaphor exercise reveals some fascinating perceptions. Discourse analysis reveals common themes that emerge across images, derived from respondents' verbal explanations. Such themes equate with perceived organizational strengths and problems. These are then refined and explored in subsequent focus groups, to form the basis of an internal strategic audit, from which more precise strategic solutions are sought. Amongst positive consistencies, the British business school personality is often drawn with baseball shoes, representing a feeling that it is a young institution. In addition, the figure is often drawn holding a coffee cup, symbolising a generally relaxed environment. However, a further element is also commonly introduced, represented by either speed or a shirt rolled-down to the waist and a shovel; showing a periodically-intense pace of work. The character is also consistently shown with a scientific prop - such as a white laboratory coat, or a briefcase marked 'research-led growth'; indicating that research is felt to be a clear, major goal of the institution. On the negative side, this is also felt to be too much of a preoccupation, with students disregarded - either 'dropped' in favour of books (research), or unable to reach the academic hidden behind a transparent door. Also negatively, the UK school character is overwhelmingly depicted as male; reflecting a male-dominated faculty that many feel to be an imbalance. Most interviewees also draw a mouth that appears either downturned or as a straight line. In fact in none of the drawings is the personality smiling. This is explained to be due to a sense of disenfranchisement, in that the Head of the school was felt to be omnipotent as far as resource and policy decisions were concerned. In one drawing this is emphasized by the distance between the Head (depicted as an actual head on a long neck) and the remainder of the staff (the faraway body). In others, a character preoccupied with money emerged - as shown by pound signs in its eyes. Respondents mostly clothe their figure in a business suit, which is verbalized as a form of conventionality or respectability. However, it is also suggested several times that there is a hidden, mismatched side to this apparel: that the suit is either ill-fitting or fairly scruffy, showing a general disbelief in the externally-projected professionalism of the school.

The free drawing exercise at the Canadian school generally reveals a fairly young, medium-sized, reasonably intellectual, fairly conservative character. Although maleness is the most popular gender characteristic, it is not perceived to be a great organizational problem. However, the figure is also depicted as unsmiling - which verbal explanations indicate is due to perceptions of relatively weak organizational performance, especially in research terms. In addition, there is a very strong perceived difference in the treatment of contractual and non-contractual faculty, with the former group seen as receiving unfavourable teaching and research terms; and denied resource and other requests by the Head of the school in return. Some of these have, in consequence, packed their cases ready to leave when the opportunity arises. A tension also emerges over formality versus informality, with some faculty perceived as being unapproachable - perhaps clothed in barbed wire. Also arising as a perceived problem is a sense of organizational directionless; portrayed as fuzziness, a boat being rowed in different directions, or as a person suffering from role conflict. Many faculty feel there are no real strategic objectives for the business school.

The animal metaphor cards were chosen, following a pilot exercise, both for their universal familiarity and for their ability to be readily linked to a wide range of specific adjectives. They were also selected to correspond with the major organizational cultural types found in the culture literature. For example, the change-oriented chameleon card corresponds with elements of both Miles and Snow's (1978) 'prospector' organization and Handy's (1985) 'task culture', being adaptable/fluid and a fast reactor. Similarly, the wise/logical owl card exhibits facets of Miles and Snow's 'analyzer' organization, Handy's 'role culture', and Deal and Kennedy's (1988) 'process culture'. A full list of the characteristics found to be commonly attributed to each animal card is given in the appendix.

Card selections for each organization are ranked in order of most popular choice, to derive metaphorical profiles for each school. Discourse analysis then reveals the reasons why each animal is chosen. The chameleon, fox and owl cards appear joint first for the British business school. The chameleon card is selected because its external image of efficiency contradicts the perceived internal reality of inefficient systems and procedures. The fox, like the snake, is deemed to portray some cunning or astute element in relation to its establishment. The owl is largely chosen for wisdom, although some feel that this is still embryonic. At the Canadian school, the dog is the most popular selection because obedience, faithfulness, honesty and reliability are perceived to characterize members. However, the school is also seen as being relatively ordinary compared to other organizations and subject to inaction - certainly less positive attributes. The cat, whilst exhibiting affectionate leanings, is likened to the school by respondents because of its unpredictable or opportunistic nature. This is considered to be representative of one or more individuals currently associated with or attempting to gain positions of formal power. The dolphin is picked because it is seen, like the school, to exhibit a degree of intelligence and playfulness; but it is also felt to represent some degree of insularity.

Interestingly, these findings also seem consistent with academic studies of the prevailing societal cultures of the two countries. Hofstede's seminal (1980) work suggests that the British are less risk-averse, and display more individualistic and masculine characteristics than their Canadian counterparts. In this study, British academics appear as changeable, cunning and astute; whilst Canadian scholars seem faithful, good-natured, feminine, warm and playful! Certainly one would expect some degree of each institution's respective external culture to be reflected, since type of organization has been 'controlled for', but societal setting 'varied'. However, sufficient data emerge in the free-drawing exercise to suggest particular internal organizational strengths and weaknesses. Further analysis is, of course, possible, based on correlating characteristics expressed through both drawings and cards with variables such as age, sex, academic discipline, and so on. However, even at this level, problems and strengths identified with the aid of pictures have helped in both institutions to build a more comprehensive internal strategic audit.

Respondents in both schools also articulate their ideal organizational images: useful in contrasting with perceptual realities during subsequent focus groups. In the British case, the dolphin appears popular because of its grace, intelligence and associations with quality. The lion also emerges, due to its perceived astuteness, ferociousness in the market and its internal strength/cohesiveness. In the Canadian school, the eagle is easily the most popular ideal image. This represents a bird of vision; a powerful and respected monarch of all that it surveys, scanning its environment and making rapid decisions. It is also felt to look after its young and build its own nest, representing an additional, caring side.

The second phase of the project also includes an attempt to encourage each group to compose a single personality metaphor drawing which encompasses the perceptions of all group members, so that no one individual's input dominates. Thus, we get closer to Schall's (1983) definition of a shared organizational culture, rather than simply an agglomeration of individuals' views. It is still, of course, possible that focus groups will not reach a consensus as to their school's cultural descriptions, strengths and weaknesses and strategic options. However, this was found not to be the case in the two institutions studied.

(d) The Temporal Dimension

(x) Verbalized perceptions of change Special face-to-face interviews during phase two with key internal and external actors from representative grades, disciplines and employment durations are discourse analyzed. This helps to add perceptual data on organizational change. It is important to obtain perspectives on significant events as determined by the actors themselves - since the importance attributed to specific happenings may vary considerably from one person to another. Ultimately, as Nadler and Tushman (1982) emphasise, the aim is to seek patterns of continuity and discontinuity, reoccurrence and turning-points in events that in some way have shaped the organization and may help to explain why it now exhibits some of the cultural characteristics it does.

(xi) Chronology of significant past events   As a result of the discourse analysis of change perceptions, a simple sequence of major events and turning-points in the organization's history is constructed. Further evidence is obtained by consulting secondary data produced by the entity or its actors, such as archive material, publicity documents and internal memoranda. Where possible, this is cross-checked for accuracy. Following Whipp et al's (1989) suggestions, links are also explored between change at the levels of organization, sector and economy. In the cases explored during the study, these levels were represented by the business school, the higher education sector, and the macro socio-economic environment respectively.

(xii) Future expectations   Forecasting is, of course, a science in itself and could easily consume the entire efforts of the researcher. In this context, the focus is again on seeking perceptions of change. This is achieved during phase two interviews by asking participants to project five to ten years into the future and verbalize scenarios they believe will exist for the organization at that time. These are again discourse analysed. Focus groups are also used to determine whether shared visions of the future exist; and thereby which strategic options are likely to be regarded as feasible or not.

Conclusions: Towards a four-dimensional understanding of organizations

Naturally, the potential amount of data generated by such a detailed organizational analysis is vast. The methodology was selected to uncover organizational constructs, structures and processes in four-dimensions. The researcher must be able to use the data collected and adhere to any timetable or other resource constraints - which may themselves impose arbitrary cut-off points. In the cases outlined here, consultancy-type documents were eventually produced for each institution containing (a) a full analysis of the business school in four-dimensions; (b) the strategic implications of the project findings for the business school concerned;

and (c) any wider implications for strategic planning in university business schools derived from aggregate project data.

To date, the methodology has been successfully piloted and applied in two 'live' situations. The breadth and richness of data obtained has proven extremely useful in understanding organizational perceptions and processes in both institutions - and in how to deal with them in strategy formulation and implementation. The methodology also provides a good example of how a systematic analytical framework can be derived using grounded theory principles and applied to different organizations. Although conceptually grounded, it is essentially a practical tool to inform the strategic analyst how to better implement internal organizational strategies.

Although there is an inherent danger in applying several diverse techniques to the same situation - for example, triangulation may not always reveal common data - a carefully chosen 'bundle' of analytical tools does generate rich insights. Discourse analysis, both verbal and image-based, is particularly effective in analysing those processes and perceptions that purely quantitative tools would be unable to do. In any case, as Feyerabend's (1978) argument suggests, generating different types of data is useful, because it reveals alternative explanations of 'reality'. These can then be checked with organizational members in focus groups to determine which explanations most closely correspond with their perceptions of reality. Alternative explanations can also be presented, to challenge such perceptions and uncover new ways of looking at the organization.

It would, of course, be unwise not to recognise shortcomings in this type of framework. It is intra-organizational, so one pursues richness in the depth of data, rather than in its breadth. In this way, insights prove invaluable both for case-study and consultancy work. However, the approach sacrifices data about a large number of organizations in favour of detailed data about a very small number. Thus, the ability to generalize from data is limited - unless you have an army of researchers, each able to examine two or three organizations over time. Yet, even without such assistance, the study may reveal hypotheses one might test on a larger sample afterwards.

The nature of the methodology does mean that results take a long time to emerge. In this project, data collection and analysis is so detailed that the draft report from phase one was provided approximately six months after a cut-off point was decided. On this note also, accepting Glaser and Strauss' (1967) grounded theory principle inevitably creates ambiguity in deciding cut-off points for data collection. However, the defence here, as in any grounded research project, is that the researcher continues to add data until he or she judges that further data is likely to be of insufficient added value to justify its inclusion. Although in theory this is likely to be problematic, in practice, at least for this project, the case for particular logical cut-off points was not difficult to make. However, transcription did prove very time consuming.

Ensuring the fourth dimension is adequately covered means that (depending on the organization and its sector) several years may be required before longitudinal results are obtained. It is not, therefore, easy to pursue within the traditional Ph.D time constraint. Even if outsiders are brought in to help in the transcription part of data processing, this brings its own problems. It may involve expense in hiring a transcriber. It may be difficult to obtain sufficiently skilled transcribers, who must not only be trained audio-typists but must also be familiar with discourse analysis techniques. Training them to required skill levels takes precious time; whilst the coordination difficulties of managing others must also be bourne in mind. More fundamentally, even with the most-skilled transcriber, that person will not have been there at the time of the interview, so he or she may not understand the context, people mentioned, specific words, and so on. All transcripts therefore need to be reviewed by the researcher to check accuracy. For focus groups, this may mean using videotapes to determine who said what, and for additional 'body language' visual data.

Even using computer software can't solve many of these problems at present. Packages like 'Ethnograph' have not been designed for the level of detail needed in full discourse analysis - and certainly not for pictorial representation. The arrival of voice activated computer transcription software and improved pictorial devices will revolutionize things; but unfortunately these aren't here yet!

With any form of action research there are, of course, dangers of bias. The researcher must make his/her own personal assumptions and agendas explicit, and be wary of a typical interviewees' perceptions creating distortions through an outlier effect. The normal access/relationship management problems also apply here. After initial entry to the organization is obtained, keeping good relations with organizational personnel to ensure long-term access is essential. Reliance is placed upon interviewees' cooperation and frankness, and must be reciprocated with assured confidentiality. Two-way confidentiality is vital, not only in the reporting phase, to ensure contributors cannot be identified; but in the data collection phase, when neither interviewer nor interviewee should leak data gathered during interviews, for fear of compromising a party, or of contaminating others' 'virgin' perceptions before they can be recorded. Of course, some leaks are inevitable, because cultures are all about informal communication channels. Careful minimization of these is a true test of a well-managed project.

Certainly, the acceptability of this approach depends, as in any other piece of reputable research, upon making the assumptions of the underlying theoretical model explicit. This model must be communicated to target audiences such as sponsors, organizational participants and the wider academic and business worlds, to enable a proper understanding of the research to be gained. One might also need to 'sell' radical ideas about pictorial representation to sceptical positivists: a strategy many advertising researchers have become very skilled at.

Generally, however, the merits of this approach lie very much in its adaptability and its holistic nature. The integration of both research perspectives and analytical techniques allows the researcher a powerful means of intra-organizational analysis - and the opportunity to examine organizations in no less than four dimensions.

Appendix

1. Academic values ranked alphabetically

TERMINAL VALUES		INSTRUMENTAL VALUES	
T1	Achieve excellence in RESEARCH	I1	Accept the authority of ACADEMIC EXPERTS
T2	Achieve excellence in TEACHING	I2	Assess evidence using ESTABLISHED METHODS
T3	Be COMPETITIVE	I3	Be involved in ADMINISTRATION
T4	Be free to choose my METHODS	I4	Be involved with GENERAL BUSINESS STUDIES
T5	Emphasise PRACTICAL TECHNIQUES	I5	Be involved with non-academic PROFESSIONAL BODIES
T6	Emphasise THEORETICAL CONCEPTS	I6	Be paid by MY PERFORMANCE
T7	Establish an ACADEMIC REPUTATION	I7	Complete an ACADEMIC PROJECT
T8	Express my OPINION	I8	Learn from others' BUSINESS EXPERIENCE
T9	Follow a rational SCIENTIFIC APPROACH	I9	MAINTAIN INDEPENDENCE from the Business World
T10	GET TO THE TOP of an organisation	I10	Support the community of (REGION)
T11	Have a CALLING NOT A JOB	I11	Support UNIVERSITY TRADITIONS
T12	Have a fulfilling PERSONAL LIFE	I12	Use CASE STUDIES
T13	Have COMPLETE CONTROL over what I do at work	I13	Use large-group LECTURES
T14	Promote my INTELLECTUAL GROWTH	I14	Use small-group TUTORIALS
T15	Provide intellectual HELP FOR ALL	I15	Use the LATEST TECHNOLOGY
T16	Secure high FINANCIAL REWARD	I16	View students as CUSTOMERS
T17	Take part in DECISION MAKING	I17	Work in a BUSINESS ENVIRONMENT
T18	Work with COLLEAGUES	I18	Work within my OWN DISCIPLINE

2. Animal metaphor cards used

CARD NUMBER	ANIMAL CHARACTERISTICS
1. MOUSE	Small, timid, scurrying
2. ELEPHANT	Large, powerful, lumbering
3. GAZELLE	Fast, agile, slim
4. SNAIL	Slow, self-protecting, slimy
5. SHARK	Vicious, dangerous, cold, sleek
6. DOLPHIN	Friendly, intelligent, warm, playful
7. OWL	Wise, all-seeing, old
8. MULE	Foolish, stubborn, cantankerous
9. FOX	Cunning, devious, wily
10. DOG	Faithful, loyal, obedient, good-natured
11. SNAKE	Treacherous, underhand, poisonous
12. LION	Proud, strong, magnificent, regal, feline
13. EAGLE	Soaring, independent, sharp-eyed, taloned
14. OSTRICH	Short-sighted, awkward, flightless
15. CHAMELEON	Changeable, strange
16. CAT	Affectionate, telepathic, feminine

References

Aldenderfer, M.S. and R.K. Blashfield, (1984), *Cluster Analysis*, Series: Quantitative Applications in the Social Sciences, Sage University Paper, Beverley Hills, Ca.

Berger, P.L. and T. Luckmann (1965), *The Social Construction of Reality: A Treatise in the Sociology of Knowledge*, Pelican, Harmondsworth, Middlesex.

Branthwaite, A. and T. Lunn (1985), 'Projective Techniques in Social and Market Research', in Walker, R. (ed.), *Applied Qualitative Research*, Gower, Aldershot.

Deal, T. and A. Kennedy (1988), *Corporate Cultures: The Rites and Rituals of Corporate Life*, Penguin, London.

Edwards, B.R. (1981), *Drawing on the Right Side of the Brain: How to unlock your hidden artistic talent*, Souvenir Press, London.

Etzioni, A. (1961), *A Comparative Analysis of Complex Organisations*, Free Press, New York.

Feyerabend, P. (1978), *Against Method: Outline of an Anarchistic Theory of Knowledge*, Verso, London.

Glaser, B.G. and A.S. Strauss (1967), *The Discovery of Grounded Theory*, Aldine, Chicago.

Gold, R. (1958), 'Roles in Sociological Field Observation', *Social Forces*, Vol. 36, No. 3, pp. 217-23.

Handy, C.B. (1985), *Understanding Organisations*, (3rd edition), Penguin, Harmondsworth.

Hedges, A. (1985), 'Group Interviewing', in Walker, Robert (ed.), *Applied Qualitative Research*, Gower, Aldershot.

Hickson, D.G. (1971), 'A strategic contingency theory of intraorganisational power', *Administrative Science Quarterly*, Vol. 16, No. 2, pp. 314-40.

Hofstede, G. (1980), *Culture's Consequences: International Differences in Work-Related Values*, Sage, Beverly Hills, Ca.

Jefferson, G. (1985), 'An Exercise in the Transcription and Analysis of Laughter', in Van Dijk (ed.), *Handbook of Discourse Analysis*, Vol. 3, Academic Press, London.

Johnson, G. and K. Scholes (1988), *Exploring Corporate Strategy*, (2nd edition), Prentice Hall International, Hemel Hempstead, Herts.

Kotler, P. (1986), *Principles of Marketing*, (3rd edition), Prentice Hall, New Jersey.

Kotler P. (1988), *Marketing Management: Analysis, Planning, Implementation, and Control*, (6th edition), Prentice Hall, New Jersey.

Lewin, K. (1948), *Resolving Social Conflicts*, Harper, New York.

Levinson, H. (1972), 'An Effort Towards Understanding Man at Work', *European Business*, Spring.

Lukes, S. (1974), *Power: A Radical View*, Macmillan, London.

March, J.D., and H.A. Simon (1976), *Organisations*, John Wiley, London.

Miles, R.E. and C.C. Snow (1978), *Organisational Strategy, Structure, and Process*, McGraw-Hill, New York.

Mintzberg, H. (1988), 'Planning on the left side and managing on the right', in J.B. Quinn, H. Mintzberg and R.M. James, *The Strategy Process: Concepts, Contexts, and Cases*, Prentice Hall International, Englewood Cliffs, NJ.

Morgan, G. (1986), *Images of Organization*, Sage, Newbury Park, Ca.

Morgan, G. (1989), *Creative Organization Theory*, Sage, Newbury Park, Ca.

Nadler, D.A. and M.L. Tushman (1982), 'A Model for Diagnosing Organizational Behaviour', in Tushman, Michael L. and Moore, William, L., *Readings in the Management of Innovation*, Pitman, Marshfield, Mass.

Ornstein, R. (1977), *The Psychology of Consciousness*, (2nd ed.), Harcourt Brace Jovanovich, San Diego.

Paliwoda, S., (1983) 'Predicting the Future Using Delphi', *Management Decision*, Vol. 21, No. 1, pp. 31-7.

Peters, T.J. and R.H. Waterman (1982), *In Search of Excellence*, Harper & Row, New York.

Peters, T. (1989), *Thriving on Chaos*, Pan Books, London.

Pettigrew, A.M. (1979), 'On Studying Organizational Cultures', *Administrative Science Quarterly*, Vol. 24, pp. 570-81.

Pettigrew, A.M. (1990), 'Longitudinal Field Research on Change: Theory and Practice' *Organization Science*, Vol. 1, No. 3, August, pp. 225-47.

Pfeffer, J. (1981), *Power in Organisations*, Pitman, London.

Potter, J. and M. Wetherall (1987), *Discourse and Social Psychology: Beyond Attitudes and Behaviour*, Sage, London.

Robson, S. and A. Foster (1989), *Qualitative Research in Action*, Edward Arnold, London.

Rokeach, M. (1986), *Beliefs, Attitudes, and Values: A Theory of Organization and Change*, Jossey-Bass Publishers, San Francisco.

Rosenfeld, R., R. Whipp, and A.M. Pettigrew (1989), 'Processes of Internationalisation: Regeneration and Competitiveness', *Economia Aziendale*, 7, 1, April, pp. 21-47.

Schall, M.S. (1983), 'A Communication-Rules Approach to Organizational Culture', *Administrative Science Quarterly*, Vol. 28, pp. 557-81.

Schein, E. (1980), *Organizational Psychology*, Prentice Hall, Hemel Hempstead, Herts.

Schein, E. (1985), *Organizational Culture and Leadership: A Dynamic View*, Jossey Bass, San Fransisco.

Semeonoff, B. (1976), *Projective Techniques*, John Wiley & Sons, London.

Stainsby, L. (1991), 'Marketing Planning: A Qualitative Review', *Paper presented at the Marketing Education Group Annual Conference*, Cardiff Business School.

Van de Ven (1987), 'Review Essay: Four Requirements for Processual Analysis', in Pettigrew, Andrew H. (ed.), *The Management of Strategic Change*, Basil Blackwell, Oxford.

Weick, K.E. (1979), *The Social Psychology of Organising*, (2nd edition), Addison-Wesley, Reading, Mass.

Whipp, R., R. Rosenfeld, and A.M. Pettigrew (1989), 'Culture and Competitiveness: evidence from mature UK industries', *Journal of Management Studies*, Vol. 26, No. 6, November, pp. 561-86.

Whyte, W. Foote (1991), 'Participatory Action Research: Through Practice to Science as Social Research', in Whyte, W. Foote (ed.), *Participatory Action Research*, Sage, Newbury Park, Ca.

7 From 'Man-in-the-Middle' to Front Line Manager: Investigating the Changing Role of the Supervisor

JAMES LOWE

Introduction

This research looks at the nature of the supervisory role under conditions of 'just in time' (JIT), total quality management (TQM), and so called 'lean production' (Womack, Jones and Roos, 1990). The supervisor has been termed the 'man-in-the-middle' (Roethlisberger, 1945) because, although formally the first level of management, the supervisor is often excluded from participating and influencing the management decision making process (Wray, 1949). At the same time, the supervisor is frequently promoted from the shop floor, yet faces opposition from sub-ordinates. The author has argued elsewhere that this is an outcome of the conditions of mass production which encourage 'functional foremanship', de-skilling of supervisory jobs, and the centralization of authority (see Lowe, 1993). It is argued that these conditions have opened up a social and educational gap between the supervisor and other levels of management (Child and Partridge, 1982). In addition, supervisors under these conditions have been found to experience conflicting job demands, role strain and lack effective authority to deal with their many responsibilities. The position lacks the pay and status of a managerial position and is frequently held by an unskilled worker. These factors have combined to weaken the link between the strategic and operational levels of the management control system with detrimental consequences for overall organizational performance.

Under lean and total quality production the integration of strategic and operational levels is heightened because of the need to produce 'right first time'. Furthermore, any disruption to production has a more pervasive effect on production because of the absence of inventory (Oliver and Wilkinson, 1988). Noting that these high performance production systems require 'integrated production', i.e. responsibility for quality, maintenance, materials handling, and cost control to be handled in discrete areas (sometimes referred to as 'cells') at shop floor level, the main hypothesis addresses in this research is that the supervisor's integrative role is transformed. Specifically, the supervisor's role in the management control system is heightened. Thus, the position enjoys greater discretion, authority and influence over technical and people decisions (Wickens, 1987). Accordingly, the supervisor's pay and status are more clearly aligned with that of a management position. The relative positions of the supervisor under lean and mass production are summarized in Tables 7.1 and 7.2.

Table 7.1

Mass production and lean production: Two contrasting 'ideal' production systems

	Mass production	Lean production
Production system characteristics	standard product quality inspected high specialization assembly line pdn. fragmented responsibility	variable products quality built-in low specialization cellular pdn. local responsibility
Role of the supervisor	'man-in-the-middle'	front line manager

Table 7.2

The role of the supervisor: Two models of practice

Role	'Man-in-the-middle'	Front line manager
Authority and influence over decision making	low	high
Nature of relations with specialist departments	subordinate	dominant
Pay differential with nearest subordinate	low	high
Skill levels required	low	high
Educational profile	unskilled worker	graduate
Status	low	high
Time horizon	short term	long term
Action	reactive	strategic

In order to test the models described in the tables above, a methodology which would collect information on each of the model's dimensions was required. To achieve this the research methodology drew on a range of techniques. The choice of research techniques which together comprise the research design are outlined in the following section.

Research design

The methodological approach adopted sought to ensure that the research design was appropriate to the research subject, that is 'derives from the nature of the social phenomena to be explored' (Morgan and Smircich, 1980) and the results of an initial exploratory survey of supervisors formed the basis for the subsequent research design. Each part of the model (see Table 7.2) was investigated by a principal method and these were supported by other methods as part of a triangulation approach. For example, authority, influence and work priorities were measured by a questionnaire, and this allowed triangulation with data collected from interviews with supervisors and with the researcher's own observations of supervisors during the participant observation of their activities.

The structured questionnaire of supervisors sought to explore the issues of authority and influence, adapting approaches used by Lennerlof (1966) and Child and Partridge (1982). Factual information, such as service history and qualifications, were also gathered in the questionnaire. Where model elements relied more on the values, views, and perceptions of supervisors, such as their status and their relationship with higher management specialists, the research relied on more qualitative methods of interviewing and shadowing. In-depth interviews with supervisors, supported by participant observation, were used to ameliorate some of the weaknesses associated with questionnaire techniques (see Easterby-Smith, 1991, for a critique). This approach gave the respondents the ability to articulate to the researcher first hand their views on the changing role of the supervisor as well as offering the researcher the opportunity to probe, clarify and question further. The use of self-completion questionnaires afforded the advantage of being low-cost in terms of data collection effort, which enabled the researcher to concentrate on the more time-consuming qualitative collection techniques.

A second set of data collected through a questionnaire survey and interviews with senior management sought to locate the study within the wider literature on lean production by adopting the methodology employed by Krafcik and MacDuffie (1989).

Two main constraints guided the choice of methods: resources and access. The researcher's access to the case study plant was restricted to two periods of two weeks each. Furthermore, the case plant was some distance from the University where the researcher was based. On a limited budget it was, therefore, necessary to maximize the data collected given the finite access time of these two time periods. In the event, the researcher decided to use the first two-week period as an opportunity to leave a questionnaire (and freepost envelope) for self-completion. Interviewing the sample first also provided a means of meeting the supervisors, and for learning more about them and the company. This was useful for gaining background information and selecting members for 'shadowing' during the second two-week period (see p. 195).

An exploratory survey and the subsequent development of a research design

Forty semi-structured interviews were initially conducted at a UK automobile manufacturer. Supervisors were questioned about how their jobs had changed in the context of moves by their company towards lean production. These changes involved the creation of integrated production areas, with maintenance, quality and production the sole responsibility of the supervisor. A flexible research design was pursued because at this exploratory stage the researcher was interested in eliciting from the supervisors their perceptions of the extent and nature of the changes. Also, it was hoped that this approach would uncover the maximum in terms of diversity and breadth of responses. In this way, the researcher believed that the supervisors' themselves would help to pin-point areas of interest not previously considered by the researcher or the existing literature. Pursuing this 'open' research design allowed the supervisors themselves to drive the agenda of debate as well as help to formalize the subsequent research design used in the main part of the research.

The initial findings of the pilot study were that supervisors' jobs had changed (detailed findings are reported in Lowe, 1993). The supervisors' operational responsibilities had increased significantly. However, their authority, status, skills, and pay remained largely unchanged. In particular, supervisors felt unable to take decisions or tackle problems because of a managerial system which relied heavily on motivating by fear. For this reason they felt isolated and removed from the managers above them. In terms of job content, many still saw themselves as operating in a 'fire-fighting' and troubleshooting capacity. Furthermore, many supervisors felt that they did not have the ability or skills to perform the role expected of them. With the creation of integrated production areas there was a degree of disagreement amongst supervisors about the extent to which relationships had been redefined. All these issues were important in considering how the role of the supervisor was changing and hence required a methodology which measured the extent and nature of those changes. In practice, no one method was felt to be suitable, rather a range of approaches seemed to offer the best prospect of analysing the research problem. In each case, the method or methods used were shaped by the particular research question being addressed and the practical constraints imposed on the project.

A summary of the main research questions which arose from this initial study and the implication for the subsequent research design are outlined below:

(1) The need for a precise measure of the extent to which movement towards a total quality or lean production had been made, so that the changes in the supervisor's role could be located more effectively in the context of the organization's overall restructuring

(2) The need to find a quantitative method which would measure the extent of the supervisor's perception of their authority and influence over decisions, so making cross-company comparisons possible

(3) The need to find a quantitative method which would measure the extent of the supervisor's perception of how their priorities had changed as a result of the introduction of new manufacturing techniques (e.g., quality vs. output)

(4) The need to assess the changing nature and operation of the whole supervisory/management control system in order to reveal how restructuring affected the connection between strategic and operational levels. Areas of particular focus were: (i) the relationship between higher management and supervisors (ii) the relationship between the supervisor and specialist departments

(5) The need to get behind formal job labels, official organizational pronouncements, etc. in order to examine 'real' and 'effective' authority, influence, skills, priorities, and status of the supervisors.

Elements of the research design

Questionnaire survey and interviews with senior management

This method addresses item 1 above. In order to locate the supervisor in the context of mass/lean production a survey methodology developed by Krafcik and MacDuffie (1989) was used. This approach provided a more precise measure of just how far the case study plant had moved towards a 'lean' manufacturing production system. It also provided a set of structural measures which enabled the researcher to cross-reference and contextualize the supervisors' own experiences and perceptions of change at the shop-floor level.

A measure for mass/lean production was based on an index of management practices and involved studying three broad areas of production system management: factory practice, work systems and human resource management policy.

Factory practice measures a set of 'production practices which are indicative of overall production practice' (MacDuffie 1989, p. 3). Variables are scored so that low values reflect 'lean' practice. The variables are:

(i)   The percentage of assembly space allocated to final repair, adjusted by relative space efficiency of plants, scored between $1 =$ smallest repair area and $4 =$ largest repair area.
(ii) The capacity of in-process buffer between paint and assembly areas, adjusted for overall plant capacity, where $1 =$ smallest buffer capacity and $4 =$ largest buffer capacity.
(iii) A measure of inventory policy that measures the level of inventory stocks (days of stock on hand for 8 parts, weighted by their estimated costs) and the frequency of parts delivery parts to the line (how many deliveries per hour, shift, or day for the same 8 parts). Plants are

scored 1 = lowest inventory stocks and most frequent deliveries and 4 = highest stocks and least frequent deliveries.

Work systems measures three key aspects of shop floor policies and practices: how direct tasks are organized (the extent to which work teams and job rotation are used); how indirect tasks traditionally handled by functional specialists are handled (the extent to which quality inspection, SPC, and the programming of robots is assigned to production workers); and the level of worker participation in problem solving activity (the percentage of the workforce in employee involvement groups and the number of production related suggestions received and implemented). A low score was given to variables indicating a work system which is 'multiskilling' in orientation while a high score indicates a 'specializing' orientation. As with the above parts of the index, a scale of one to four was used.

The human resource management (HRM) policy variable measures a set of policies which contribute significantly to the development of a workforce that is skilled, flexible, and motivated. Its components include the recruiting methods and hiring criteria used in selecting the workforce, the extent to which pay is related to performance, the extent to which status barriers between management and workers are present or absent, and the level of ongoing training offered to experienced production workers, supervisors, and engineers. A low score for this variable indicates a 'high commitment' set of HRM policies and a high score indicates 'low commitment' policies. Because the scales of these measures differ they are standardized before being combined into a HRM policy measure.

When the variables making up work system and HRM policy are combined, their scales are reversed to facilitate the construction of the management index. This measure proved to be a powerful predictor of differences in productivity, quality, and overall manufacturing performance. MacDuffie (1989) found a great deal of interdependence between the three sets of variables: Factory practice with work system, r = .55, factory practice with HRM policy, r = .54, work systems with HRM policy, r = .50.

Structured questionnaire of supervisors

A structured questionnaire of supervisors was used to address items two and three above. The questionnaire contained three sections. The first asked for some personal details about the supervisor's work experience, area of responsibilities, age, etc. The second part asked a series of questions about the extent to which supervisors believed they exercised authority over certain decisions, i.e. what they believed to be their formally designated and socially accepted discretion over certain decisions. Measuring the supervisor's perceived discretion over certain decisions offered a number of design advantages. A modified version of Child and Partridge's (1982) questionnaire was used. One can concentrate on supervisory authority by looking at the formal right to make a decision (Lennerlof, 1966). However,

> a supervisor's authority is only partly laid down in written form in job descriptions, procedures, and the like. Supervisors also have to rely on verbal statements from superiors and sometimes have to infer their authority from their superior's behaviour. These cues are not without their contradictions and are open to different interpretations (Child and Partridge, 1982, p. 39).

As a result, decisions in practice are often a complicated, continuing interaction process, even when the formal system denotes one individual as the decision maker on a given question. Therefore, a broader conception of authority was required which captured the complexity of the concept and made allowances for the supervisor's ability to affect others' decisions, and more importantly to influence the decision making of others. For instance, the supervisor may have no formal authority for a decision but may well be able to shape its outcome through the influence they are able to bring to bear on others, e.g., workers, shop stewards, other supervisors and managers.

The methodology used was adapted from (Lennerlof, 1966) and (Child and Partridge, 1982) and attempts to capture the dynamic nature of the authority/influence process. Supervisors were asked to complete a questionnaire which asked them the degree to which they shared authority for 24 decisions. For every decision, authority was coded on a five-point scale indicating whether the supervisor had sole or full authority (coded 5), whether he had no authority at all (coded 1), or whether he shared authority with others: shared with one other (coded 4), shared with two others (coded 3), or shared with more than two others (coded 2). Supervisors were also asked to rate their influence over each decision along a 21-point scale, even where they perceived that they had no authority for that decision.

The range of decisions were taken from (Lennerlof, 1966) and (Child and Partridge, 1982). Lennerlof (1966) started with 76 decisions grouped under 14 headings. Using factor analysis, Lennerlof constructed three authority indices, which he labelled production, technical, and personnel. Most supervisory jobs contain: (1) elements which are administrative, concerning planning, organization, the interpretation of rules and regulations; (2) elements which are technical, relying on specialized knowledge, skills and experience; and (3) elements which are mainly concerned with people. While supervisory decisions are relatively easy to separate conceptually, in practice it is recognized by the researcher that many will be interdependent (Child and Partridge, 1982, p. 41).

The advantage of this research design was that it enabled some contrasts to be made with Child and Partridge's research, thus allowing some limited longitudinal comparisons to be made with their research which was conducted over ten years ago.

The third section sought information on how supervisors prioritized their tasks. Many of the early completed questionnaires demonstrated that supervisors responded to the questions in the priorities section by marking almost everything as a top priority. While this was, nevertheless, a revealing result in itself, the researcher was also interested in the relative importance of the various priorities in relation to each other. After all, much of the supervisor's job involves juggling these priorities and deciding between various courses of action, the classic one being quality vs. output. In order to elicit this additional information the researcher told supervisors to fill out the questionnaire as indicated but then to return to the priorities section and to ask themselves out of the 17 priorities which was the most (first) important, second most important, third, fourth and so on. This allowed for a more precise relative breakdown of supervisory work priorities.

Another issue which emerged was that many supervisors pointed out that their priorities vary depending on circumstances. To compensate for this, the researcher asked them during the questionnaire briefing session to try to average out these variations and also add any comments or points of clarification if they felt uncomfortable about circling a particular response. Many supervisors were quite happy to do this.

A number of advantages were derived from designing the questionnaire in this way. First, it allowed supervisors' jobs to be assessed as a whole system of tasks and relationships in which they may be exercising discretion, and not just the supervision of subordinates. Secondly, it moved away from formally designated authority. Supervisory discretion could also reflect informal accommodations and custom and practice. Thirdly, it allowed comparisons across areas of the plant and between different types of supervisors, i.e. production, maintenance, materials handling and quality control.

Superintendents were also asked to fill in the questionnaire from a 'third party' perspective, i.e. they were asked to rate what discretion they believed their supervisors had over those decisions. Again, this was done so that the supervisors' responses could be located in context. Furthermore, the data produced from this also allowed contrasts of authority perceptions between supervisors' and their immediate bosses to emerge. This would in turn reveal information about the relationships between supervisors and higher levels of management (issue 4(i)), and particularly about the so-called organizational and social gap that exists between supervisors and their immediate superiors. For similar reasons, the third part of the questionnaire asked supervisors and superintendents about the relative importance they attached to certain work priorities.

In-depth interviews with supervisors and participant observation

Two criticisms of questionnaire survey techniques, outlined by Easterby-Smith et al. (1991), are that they often do not explain *why* relationships exist and, furthermore, there is commonly a difficulty in eliminating all the factors which could possibly have caused observed correlations. The research focus required an approach which could explore the role of the supervisor in a changing context. There was a need to examine complex social relationships between supervisors, higher management and specialist departments, assessing supervisors' pay and status and attempting to get a 'real' as opposed to reported insight into supervisors' informal authority, priorities, skills, and work experience (see items 4 and 5 above). As Pettigrew (1985) suggests, a longitudinal method using case studies and a variety of qualitative approaches allows a focus on the broader economic and political context surrounding the organization, while the gathering of time series data over periods of time significantly longer than the immediate focus allows explanations to emerge from examining patterns in the process of change. Starkey (1990) has also demonstrated the superiority of qualitative methods over quantitative methods in capturing the dynamics and essence of organizations undergoing change and transition.

Pursuing the logic of using a qualitative approach, the researcher returned to the original pilot case study plant (exactly two years later) to conduct structured interviews. The clear advantage of this approach was that it:

> presents the opportunity for the researcher to probe deeply to uncover new clues, open up new dimensions of a problem and to secure vivid, accurate inclusive accounts that are based on personal experience, (Burgess, 1982, p. 107).

Interviews were conducted with a sample of 65. The sample was drawn from a number of different areas of the plant and were selected on a random basis subject to availability, i.e. some were on holiday, off sick, etc. The final sample consisted of ten superintendents and 55 supervisors. These interviews averaged an hour in length. This represented over 90 per cent of the supervisors working in the case study plant. As a result the internal reliability of the data is high.

The supervisors were told that the researcher was conducting some independent Ph.D research, and that the information collected would remain confidential and was the 'personal property' of the researcher. As the researcher had been employed on a part-time basis with the company three years previously, it was important to reassure the supervisors that comments and remarks would not be fed back to management (although some said that this was a pity because they would have liked them to be heard by management. Others told the researcher that management were left in no doubt about their views as they had voiced them unreservedly). Supervisors were then given the option of having the interview recorded, which most agreed to. The researcher tried to minimize the initial insecurity of those supervisors who did not want to have the interview recorded by telling them 'It was no problem' and that the exercise was only carried out so that if anything important was said the researcher would not miss it.

The approach adopted aimed to put the supervisors at ease so as to minimize any 'contamination' of the data. For instance, if supervisors felt threatened or insecure, this would be reflected in their responses in the form of more glossy or pro-management answers. Supervisors were put at ease by beginning the interviews by asking technical questions about their responsibilities. For instance, what area of the plant did they cover? How many men did they supervise and how had this changed over the last five years? What type of mechanical breakdowns took place in their area? What frequency are parts delivered to the line, etc., etc. As well as serving the purpose of building a picture of the operational responsibilities of the supervisor as they perceived it, the use of uncontroversial, 'neutral' questions allowed the researcher to develop a rapport with supervisors. Thus, the interview systematically progressed into more controversial areas. Changing procedures and systems were explored, then relationships with specialist departments, the skills required by supervisors in their job, relationships with higher management and the status of the supervisor, and finally satisfaction with pay levels and union identification. Lastly, a period of about five minutes was spent at the end of the interview briefing the interviewee about the questionnaire. It was hoped that, at the end of the interview process, a reasonable relationship would be established between interviewer and interviewee so that the questionnaire response rate would be high.

The researcher encountered only one instance where a supervisor wished to discontinue the interview because he disliked its direction. Remembering that the researcher had at one time worked for the personnel department, the individual suspected that the researcher was a management mole. As a result, the researcher asked the interviewee if he wanted the interview schedule with some of his responses written down, ripped up. This was performed in front of the interviewee. The researcher later found out that the supervisor in question was a relief supervisor in an area which was being restructured and that his job would disappear. It was perhaps understandable that this supervisor felt extremely insecure about answering questions about how his job was changing!

This was an isolated response to the interviewer's approach and questions. On the whole, the rest of the sample were extremely co-operative, forthcoming and even candid about themselves and their organization. Indeed, sometimes they were overwhelmingly (and often disparagingly) frank about how their jobs, responsibilities, relationships with other groups had changed. Most, however, showed some initial reluctance at tearing themselves away from their on-going operational duties. After the interview, many supervisors told the researcher that they enjoyed the process of being talked and listened to. One said it was 'great to get it all off my chest ... I feel great!'. It was evident to the researcher from a number of comments like these that the interview process itself seemed to act as a kind of therapy for these supervisors. It provided a mechanism for these supervisors to 'let off steam'. This too was a result in itself, because it demonstrated to the researcher that many of the supervisors frequently lacked a means for expressing and voicing their concerns and problems. As a consequence, many had developed a coping strategy which led them to 'bottle up' their emotions, deal with their own frustrations and disguise their true feelings. Some of the interview questions seemed to dig below the surface of bravado and machismo projected by most supervisors to reveal frustrated, unhappy and isolated individuals alienated by what they felt to be a demanding and unrewarding work environment.

Silverman (1985) has argued that the validation of qualitative research can also be achieved by testing actor response (Silverman, pp. 43-5). This was initiated by circulating draft copies of a paper which reported findings of the initial study previously conducted. Supervisors were told that any comments or suggestions for improvements would be welcome. Their typical response to the paper was 'Yes, that's just what it is like in here [i.e., a mass production rather than lean production system]'. These comments were useful because they tacitly confirmed the construct validity of the research. A small number of supervisors also wrote additional notes or gave the researcher copies of relevant reports which helped to highlight issues which he had not initially been aware of. For instance, one supervisor had pointed out that he had been trained and prepared for a JIT 'mind set' only to unlearn everything by being dumped into a mass production environment.

Although the interview schedule was structured, the interview style adopted by the researcher attempted to project an open, interested and enthusiastic manner. This prevented the interview from being overly focused or restricted, to the extent that important issues were excluded or sidelined. Rather, this style prompted the supervisor to lead and generate the discussion, to take the researcher by the hand so to speak, and point out what was important. To prevent the interview from degenerating into irrelevant recitals of the supervisors' personal experiences, respondents were encouraged to back-up their assertions by providing concrete examples, or explain incidents at work which highlighted their arguments. Like Burgoyne and Hodgson (1983), the researcher found that the very act of discussing incidents with individuals actually facilitated the development of trust and made it easier as the interview went on for subjects to explain what had been going on in their minds. This approach produced a rich source of data and provided valuable insights about the supervisors' work experience which doubtless would not have been uncovered had the researcher stuck rigidly to the interview schedule.

To accommodate the research at the case study plant, the researcher was allowed to walk around the plant and interview supervisors when they became available. This often involved interviews which were conducted at the side of the line, and this allowed the researcher unique opportunity often to observe the supervisor in action and in their natural habitat. Several times an interview with a supervisor would be interrupted by a telephone call, or a subordinate or superior would require information or ask for advice or for a decision to be taken. These instances were extremely valuable because they provided a mix of occurrences where the supervisor was sometimes unaware of being observed. For instance, while the researcher was interviewing one superintendent he was telephoned by one of his supervisors, who reported that he could not get an important tool fixed or replaced and that as a result output was being affected. The superintendent asked several questions to explore the likelihood of repairing or replacing the tool. However, neither of these outcomes was a viable option. So, the superintendent asked whether the supervisor had considered borrowing a spare from an adjacent line. The supervisor had not considered this. On first analysis this might appear an ordinary and not particularly revealing observation. However, it showed the competence of the supervisor (not exercising common sense) in the context of losses to production and also how the superintendent got drawn into operational issues as a result. Furthermore, it raised issues about the effectiveness of delegating more responsibilities to the supervisor, a critical issue of the research. These types of observations would not have been possible if the interviews themselves had been scheduled and held in an office free from interruption.

In order to validate the data gained from these interviews, further interviews were also conducted with members of specialist departments and higher management. These interviews were conducted in order to increase the internal reliability of the study by exploring the relationships between the supervisor and other significant groups or individuals, so that different perspectives were presented and could be used to cross-reference with the supervisors' own responses.

Using interviews as a qualitative method would arguably present only a partial picture of supervisors' jobs, responsibilities, priorities, authority and status. Even the most frank and open interviewee projects a public front which often hides the reality of their real self and disguises their true feelings in certain situations (Goffman, 1963). Furthermore, attribution theory demonstrates that individuals tend to function as 'naive psychologists' by assigning causes to other peoples' behaviour (Heider, 1944; and 1958). Furthermore, individuals tend to accord an actor's behaviour to a personal disposition or characteristics rather than environmental factors, a phenomenon termed 'fundamental attribution error' (Ross et al., 1977). Moreover, even when individuals are questioned over the motives behind their responses they cannot always be trusted to give an honest answer because often they get their ideas from commonly accepted half truths (McClelland, 1965), while at other times they are not even aware of their motives (Mangham, 1986). As the researcher was exploring relationships between supervisors and other individuals and departments, these types of biases need to be addressed by the research design.

An appropriate methodology which the researcher believed would overcome some of the limitations and biases of the interview method was the use of participant observation or 'shadowing'. As the term suggests, 'shadowing' supervisors and Superintendents involved literally following the sample wherever events, problems and decisions took them. In Junkers's (1960) classification this can be referred to as mainly 'participation as observer' and it has been argued that:

> The participant as observer not only makes no secret of his investigation: he makes it known that research is his overriding interest. He is there to observe. The participant observer is not tied down; he is free to run around as research interest beckons, (Roy, 1970, p. 217).

Certainly, in this study, shadowing the sample meant a lot of walking at pace, sometimes over wide geographical distances. Apart from a few instances, there were no restraints placed on the researcher pursuing his subjects. As all the sample were male, fortunately the researcher was able to take 'toilet breaks' at the same time as his sample! Thus, shadowing the sample allowed 'activity analysis' to be conducted. This involved noting down all the observable actions as and when they occurred. Figure 7.1 describes one hour spent with a production supervisor.

A number of studies have highlighted the difficulties of observing managerial work through activity analysis. First, supervisory work is preoccupied with irregular tasks which can vary day-to-day in the time it takes to deal with them (Child and Partridge, 1982, p. 105), raising the issue of the representativeness of the data collected. Secondly, studies of managerial work have found that activities overlap and the nature of managerial work is characterized by fragmentation, brevity and variety

4.13   Line stops (due to stop on line 2, caused by failure of gas damper and tailgate falling on operator). Supervisor talks to operators on his line responsible for gas damper operation. Checks to see if operation has been stamped off as okay. It is.

4.20   Sees cleaning subcontractor and arranges pick up of litter.

4.22   (Superintendent arrives).

4.26   Checks other gas dampers on line 1.

4.30   Senior supervisor tells supervisor to check every gas damper.

4.31-34   Called over to fix the gas damper on line 2 car. Direct work.

4.35   Collects parts and fixes it.

4.37   Sheared off screw head (using inappropriate tool), (Manager arrives)

4.40   Senior supervisor helps out, fix in headlining.

4.45   Telephones line 5 to inform them of need to remove screw/rivet from tailgate

4.47   Tries to get rivet out.

4.51   Checks other gas dampers.

4.52   Operator informs supervisor that they may have dropped a key barrel in a vehicle (between body panels). Supervisor sticks his hand into a hole to see if it is there (covering his hands in sealant).

4.53   Washes hands.

4.56   Checks out repairs being made with repair man.

4.57   Operator asks for a scheduled day off.

5.03   Provides operator with air hose.

5.04   Attends transfer breakdown. Flicks switch to reset. Direct work.

5.06   Lost tool.

5.08   Superintendent asks what caused line to stop.

5.09   Transfer breakdown, Supervisor pushes car on skid (with Superintendent) Tries to work hand control panel for transfer.

5.11   Supervisor talks to operator with skin complaint on his hand.

5.12   Shop Steward talks with supervisor about use of glycerine.

5.14   Checks model mix and especially of a particular variant being produced with operator who keeps track of model mix.

Figure 7.1 An hour in the life of a production supervisor

(Mintzberg, 1973; Kotter, 1982) so that clearly 'pigeon-holing' certain activities into discrete categories is difficult. In the researcher's experience, supervisors often talked simultaneously with several different people about entirely different issues in the course of just one minute. Similarly, in walking up and down the line in pursuit of one activity quite often a supervisor would pass on a vital bit of information or issue a one sentence order to an operator. In other words, activity analysis on its own is limited in the extent to which it can explore the interrelationships between activities or even similar activity fragmented over time.

Despite the limitations of activity analysis for examining the complexity of the supervisor's work it was adopted because the researcher believed that it would provide an overview of the patterning of supervisory activities and allow major actions and communications to be monitored. It was anticipated that this would in turn provide additional data which would allow a triangulation of questionnaire data concerning supervisory planning horizons and work priorities. To cope with the difficulties of observing the complexity of supervisory activities the researcher adopted two approaches. The first focused on simplifying the nature of the observation phenomena being studied. This approach recognized that it would be impossible to collect and record all the interactions that took place and therefore some simplification was needed. Therefore, where possible, the researcher classified supervisory activities using a coding scheme which broadly reflected the activities highlighted as priorities in the questionnaire. In this case, the emphasis was on the amount of time spent engaged in a particular activity. This was measured by the time spent on a particular activity before the supervisor made an observable switch to deal with another priority. In this case the researcher was concerned to triangulate reported work priorities (given by the supervisors in the questionnaire data) with actual time spent engaged in dealing with those priorities (measured by the shadowing observations).

The second element of the shadowing abandoned passive observation in favour of a shadowing style which was interactive and continually questioning the sample about their motives, priorities and actions. In this way the sample were able to provide explanations about the nature of their tasks and the reason for undertaking a particular course of action.

The above example is illustrative of the approach. Here the researcher observed a stoppage caused by an incorrectly fixed gas damper, (a gas damper is a component which holds up the tailgate of the car; if it fails it can cause a serious injury to an operator working underneath it or to the final customer). This was a serious health and safety concern but at the time of the incident the supervisor's immediate action was to check the paperwork on the windscreen of the vehicle. The researcher asked the supervisor why he had done this and was told that the gas damper component was an item which was subject to a 'buy-off' quality check. In other words, because of the importance of failure for worker and ultimately customer safety, this item was stamped as being defect free by the operator responsible for assembling it. Without asking such questions the researcher would have been unaware of the purpose of the supervisors actions immediately following the event, which was to question his operators about the use of their quality 'stamps' and to systematically check for stamps on vehicles in-process. This approach was especially desirable when significant events or observations such as the gas damper failure occurred, events which clearly required further exploration.

This technique also provided 'access' to critical incidents in which the supervisor became involved. Shadowing allowed the researcher to view the events first hand rather than through the 'reconstructed' view of the supervisors themselves. The methodology relied on Flanaghan's (1954) original definition of an 'incident', which is that an incident is any observable human activity which is sufficiently complete in itself to permit inference or prediction to be made about the person performing the act. Furthermore, Flanaghan argues to be 'critical' the incident must occur in a situation where the purpose or intent of the act seems fairly clear to the observer and that its consequences should be sufficiently finite to leave little doubt concerning its effect.

Individuals were shadowed mostly for half a day at a time. One supervisor was shadowed for a whole day to see if any important differences existed between supervisory activities over the course of a day. For this reason some of the shadowing was done on the night shift. While the researcher aimed to shadow a representative sample of supervisors and superintendents those shadowed were younger and less experienced than the total supervisor/management population of the plant. This in part reflected certain critical research design constraints. First, access provision was only two weeks and thus the time taken to conduct the shadowing exercise restricted the breadth of the sample. Secondly, by its very nature shadowing is intrusive and the observation process is clearly overt. In order for the sample to feel comfortable and react as normally as possible under such conditions, it was necessary to focus on certain individuals where a good rapport had been developed between the subject and researcher during the interview stage of the research. Four of the 11 individuals observed actually invited the researcher to shadow them for a day. Thus, the research techniques employed implicitly restricted the sample to those who the researcher felt able to approach for the shadowing stage of the research.

Given the relatively short contact shadowing time, the researcher was particularly concerned about suffering from what Agar (1986) has termed, research 'breakdowns', where the researcher's previous knowledge or experience of what is being observed gives him/her little or no assistance in understanding what is going on. The researcher believed that a high degree of trust and rapport between subject and observer was necessary so that in the event of a 'breakdown' the sample would assist the researcher's understanding of complex events or situations would be observed. For instance, it was anticipated supervisors might have to interpret jargon and abbreviations used by the supervisors themselves in order to make its meaning clear to the researcher. The loud background noise of machinery in the plant also made it likely that the researcher would not be able to hear what was sometimes being said to and by the supervisor. Furthermore, to overcome the inherent weaknesses of activity analysis, the sample needed to explain the link between the fragmented activities in which they engaged. Thus, the researcher believed it would not have been sufficient to purely shadow and note down his 'objective' observations. Rather, it was necessary for the subjects to provide the researcher with almost a running commentary of what was going on, why they were doing certain activities, and how they were going to achieve certain objectives. Rather than being a passive observer, it was anticipated that the researcher would need to engage supervisors in an interactive process, clarifying points, asking for more information, and above all, for explanations for why and how things happened. This approach not only required its subjects to put up with being followed around, but also to be able and willing to answer persistent questioning. A legitimate concern of the reader might be the extent to which the researcher interfered with, got in the way of, or broke up the natural flow and activity of his subjects, thereby affecting the nature of the observations made. To minimize the disruption and guard against falling into, effectively an indepth interview situation with the subjects, interruptions and questions were mainly reserved for periods of time when the subjects were walking between areas (this withdrawal was especially important during critical incidents where the researcher needed to retain his objectivity). Indeed, in one case, the researcher had to abandon 'shadowing' one individual because he treated the exercise as an extended interview and the distraction of the researcher's presence stopped him from doing his job, thereby making observations of 'normal' activities impossible.

Above all the researcher attempted to use a 'reflexive' approach to the shadowing process (Hammersley and Atkinson, 1983). In other words, rather than eliminate the effects of the phenomenon under investigation, the researcher attempted to understand the way in which he affected the research setting. This approach highlights an important philosophical issue which underlay the researcher's methodology. For writers like Batstone, Boraston and Frenkel (1977) any form of overt participant observation is flawed because people act differently when they know they are being observed. Therefore, the degree of 'naturalism' is reduced and by implication the researcher must try to reduce or minimize the impact of their personal qualities and research techniques in order to get close to the phenomena under study. However, the researcher shares the view that:

> instead of treating reactivity as a source of bias we can exploit it. How people react to the author may be informative as to how they react to other situations (Hammersley and Atkinson, 1983, p. 15).

Furthermore:

Once we abandon the idea that the social character can be standardised out, or avoided by becoming a 'fly on the wall' or a 'full participant', the role of the researcher as an active participant in the research process becomes clear. He or she is the research instrument *par excellence*. The fact that behaviour and attitudes are often not stable across contexts, and that the researcher may play an important part in shaping the context become central to the analysis. Indeed, it is exploited for all its worth (Hammersley and Atkinson, 1983, p. 18).

Where possible then the researcher attempted to monitor the effect he had on his subjects at both the interviewing and participant observation stages. In some cases the best course in the researcher's view was to adopt a 'fly on the wall' approach. As will be shown there were a number of other instances where the overt presence of researcher caused reactions from the subjects which yielded additional insights that often had a direct bearing on the researcher's research hypotheses.

Another criticism of overt participation is that it leads the researcher to impose his/her own value system on the phenomena being observed. To further ensure that the activity analysis had been coded appropriately and that the conclusions about the nature of the sample's work activities were reasonably accurate (again especially important given the relatively small contact time between researcher and subject), subjects were sent a detailed breakdown of the observed activities made by the researcher. They were given the opportunity to comment on whether the day on which they were shadowed was representative of a typical working day and also whether they agreed with the researcher's conclusions. Of the six responses returned, there was largely agreement about the conclusions made by the researcher concerning his observations and confirmation that the day in which the subjects were shadowed was broadly typical. Unusual events (for example, the gas damper fault) were highlighted by the sample. Those shadowed also agreed with most of the researcher's conclusions about their activities although some specific differences were expressed.

A further important factor which reduced the extent to which the sample could alter their behaviour/activities under the gaze of the researcher was the extent to which their own actions were directed by the need to respond to unplanned situations, different people or events. The very fact that the supervisors were so dependent on others for achieving their objectives meant that it offered them very little scope for hiding their activities from the public domain. Thus, in contradistinction to Roy (1970), rather than running after research interest the very nature of the supervisor's activities tended to force research interest out into the open as the supervisor attempted to deal with unplanned situations and circumstances.

Conclusion

This paper reports the development of a research design which sought to reveal and explain the changing role of the supervisor in the context of changes in organizational structures, systems and philosophies, from mass to lean production. Following Smith (1975) and Todd (1979), the research design sought to explore the central hypothesis - that the role of supervisors had changed - by a combination or 'triangulation' of several distinct techniques which individually appeared appropriate for different aspects of the phenomena under investigation. The research design and constituent techniques enabled a high degree of flexibility in terms of data collection which was important given the exploratory nature of the study. The research design, by combining different methods, generated results which were characterized by internal and ecological validity and could also be generalized to a wider sample of organizations. In this respect, the researcher shares the view of Easterby-Smith et al. (1991) who argue that management research 'is largely about compromise, to pose the right questions, and to answer them in a way that satisfies the majority of interested parties.' (p. ix).

References

Agar, M.H. (1986), *Speaking of Ethnography*, Sage, California.
Batstone, E., I. Boraston and S. Frenkel (1977), *Shop Stewards in Action: The Organisation of Workplace Conflict and Accommodation*, Blackwell, Oxford.

Burgess, R.G. (1982), *Field Research: A Source Book and Field Manual*, Allen and Unwin, London.

Burgoyne, J. and V. Hodgson (1983), 'Natural Learning and Managerial Action: A Phenomenological Study in the Field Setting', *Journal of Management Studies*, Vol. 20, No. 3, pp. 387-9.

Child, J. and B. Partridge (1982), *Lost Managers*, Cambridge University Press, Cambridge.

Easterby-Smith, M., R. Thorpe, and A. Lowe (1991), *Management Research: An Introduction*, Sage, London.

Flanaghan, J.C. (1954), 'The critical incident technique', *Psychology Bulletin*, Vol. 51, pp. 327-58.

Goffman, E. (1963), *The Presentation of Self in Everyday Life*, University of Edinburgh, Social Sciences Research Centre, Monograph No. 2.

Hammersley, M. and P. Atkinson (1983), *Ethnography: Principles and Practice*, Tavistock, London.

Heider, F. (1944), 'Social Perception and Phenomenal Causality', *Psychological Review*, Vol. 51, pp. 359-74.

Heider, F. (1958), *The Psychology of Interpersonal Relationships*, John Wiley, New York.

Junkers, B.H. (1960), *Fieldwork: an Introduction to the Social Sciences*, Chicago University Press, Chicago.

Kotter, J. (1982), *The General Managers*, Free Press, Collier Macmillan, London.

Krafcik, J.F. and J.P. MacDuffie (1989), *'Explaining High Performance Manufacturing: The International Automotive Assembly Plant Study'*, IMVP Forum, May.

Lennerlof, L. (1966), *Dimensions of Supervision*, Stockholm, Swedish Council for Personnel Administration.

Lowe, J. (1993), 'Manufacturing reform and the changing role of the supervisor', *Journal of Management Studies*, Vol. 30, No. 5, pp. 739-58.

MacDuffie, J.P. (1989), *'Worldwide Trends in Production System Management: Work System, Factory Practice, and Human Resource Management'*, IMVP Forum, May.

McClelland, D.A. (1965), 'Achievement and Enterprise', *Journal of Personal Social Psychology*, Vol. 1, pp. 389-92.

Mangham, I.L. (1986), 'In Search of Competence', *Journal of General Management*, Vol. 12, No. 2, Winter, pp. 5-12.

Mintzberg, H. (1973), *The Nature of Managerial Work*, Harper & Row, New York.

Morgan G. and L. Smircich (1980), 'The case for qualitative research', *Academy of Management Review*, Vol. 5, pp. 491-506.

Oliver, N. and B. Wilkinson (1988), *The Japanisation of British Industry*, Basil Blackwell, Oxford.

Pettigrew, A.M. (1985), 'Contextualist Research: A Natural Way to Link Theory and Practice' in E.E. Lawler (ed.), *Doing Research that is Useful in Theory and Practice*, Jossey Bass, San Francisco.

Roethlisberger, F.J. (1945), *The Foreman: Master and Victim of Double Talk*, Harvard Business School, Vol. 23, pp. 283-98.

Ross, L.D., and T.M. Amabile and J.L. Steinmetz (1977), 'Social Roles, Social Control, and Bias in Social Perception Processes', *Journal of Personality and Social Psychology*, Vol. 35, pp. 485-94.

Roy, D. (1970), 'The Study of Southern Labour Union Organising Campaigns' in R. Haberstein (ed.), *Pathway To Data*, Aldine, New York.

Silverman, D. (1985), *Qualitative Methodology and Sociology*, Gower, Aldershot.

Smith, H.W. (1975), *Strategies of Social Research: The Methodological Imagination*, Prentice-Hall, London.

Starkey, K. (1990), 'Review Essay: Studies On Transitions: Meanings and Method', *Journal of Management Studies*, Vol. 27, No. 1, pp. 97-110.

Todd, D.J. (1979), 'Mixing Qualitative and Quantitative Methods: Triangulation in Action', *Administrative Science Quarterly*, Vol. 24, December, pp. 602-11.

Wickens, P. (1987), *The Road to Nissan*, Macmillan, London.

Womack, J.P., D.T. Jones and D. Roos (1990), *The Machine That Changed The World*, Rawson Associates, New York.

Wray, D.E. (1949), 'Marginal men of industry: the foremen', *American Journal of Sociology*, Vol. 54, pp. 298-301.

8 Investigating Marketing Change: A Comparative-Intensive Approach

MARTIN KITCHENER

Introduction

This paper describes the methodological approach that has structured a research project entitled, 'Managing Marketing Change: A Study of the NHS in Wales'. The project was primarily concerned with investigating hospitals' responses to the imposition of the health quasi-market as outlined in Working for Patients (HMSO, 1989). Using the study of organizational change as an illustration, this paper demonstrates how the 'comparative-intensive' case method (Whipp and Pettigrew, 1991), when used in conjunction with a selection of other data gathering tools, can represent a step beyond the prevailing questionnaire survey or incidental case study approaches. The primary aim was to provide a robust explanation of the way that hospitals handle the change process.

Based on Miles' (1979) pragmatic modification of the grounded theory approach (Glaser and Strauss, 1967), this method seeks to generate conceptual frameworks, built upon observations and complemented by a dialogue with the existing literature, rather than to test hypotheses which have been established a priori. To achieve this, over 100 interviews have been triangulated (Todd, 1979) with for example, documentary examination, observation and a series of structured comparisons with other units in England and Wales. Through the use of such multiple techniques and a longitudinal lens, considerable emphasis has been attached, to the often neglected, prior social influences on attitudes and behaviour and to the economic and social contexts in which the NHS operates.

This paper explores the processes of data collection, preparation and analysis which have often been given little consideration or treated as unproblematic (Read, 1989, p. 45). The paper is divided into three main sections. The first justifies the multiple research methods that have been adopted against the background and objectives of this largely interpretative research. Unusually, idiosyncratic features of the process, such as the development of an 'interactive' research relationship (Lincoln and Guba, 1985, p. 37), are explained in detail. The second section describes and illustrates the research experience. Particular attention is paid to practical considerations such as site selection, respondent sampling and access negotiation. Finally, section three examines the lengths that were taken to carefully manage issues of vital importance to interpretative research such as credibility, reactivity and transferability. The result is that this paper uses an investigation of NHS marketing change to explain and illustrate a systematic and pragmatic research methodology.

The selection of research design and methods

Objectives of the study

As a result of the Government's attempt to commercialize the NHS, hospitals' survival has become increasingly dependent upon gaining competitive success in an emerging market place (Sheaf, 1991). In response, the NHS is paying greater attention to the ideas and techniques of marketing (Scrivens, 1991). However, the implementation of marketing is considered to be problematic (Webb and Morgan, 1992), and neither the marketing nor the management of change literatures offer much help to puzzled NHS managers (McNulty et al., 1993). Much of the existing work in these areas suggests a limited conceptual understanding of change processes, offers few examples of failure and is not addressed to the unique context of the NHS.

This study sought a deeper, longitudinal understanding of the processes by which hospitals develop dynamic marketing responses over time within the broader context of NHS organizational change. The project, which was the first to investigate the implementation of marketing in the NHS in Wales, emphasised the development of a market-orientation as a process of organizational change and avoided the more usual deterministic approach to marketing. Indeed, the legitimacy of marketing was challenged and the whole process is viewed critically as something which is problematic, often irrational and bound up within the processes of social construction within organizations (Berger and Luckmann, 1971).

Methodological perspective

A naturalistic approach was adopted which involved an 'interactive' relationship between the researcher, a human instrument, and the people and phenomena being researched. This required that throughout the study, which often relied on tacit knowledge, both the researcher's own implicit and explicit assumptions be recognized, and that any idiosyncratic factors associated with the research design are acknowledged. The process by which the research methodology was selected is described below and emphasizes two important issues. First, it makes explicit how the researcher's epistemological and ontological outlook influenced the choice of methodology, towards the subjective rather than objective end of Burrell and Morgan's (1979, p. 22) methodological continuum. Second, it illustrates how the methodology was selected with both the nature and aims of the study as major determinants.

The researcher's epistemological and ontological lead to a choice of methodology located towards nominalism (the belief that social entities or abstract concepts do not have absolute meaning or reality) and voluntarism (that belief that man, is at least in part, the creator of his own environment). Consequently, the development of an interpretative approach, involving intuitive reflection, in-depth study and personal encounter, was explored.

The subject matter of the investigation was also considered when designing the research. As many of the key marketing and organizational change components are essentially socially and politically constructed (Hirschman, 1986) it was important to employ a largely qualitative perspective, permitting research questions to emerge from the research process, rather than be wholly predetermined from the start.

In developing the research design a number of other constraints and circumstances were influential. These included the problems associated with being the sole researcher on a project (such as the need to punctuate periods of observation with teaching and other commitments), and the opportunities offered by the researcher's previous experience of the NHS. The investigator's first involvement with the NHS occurred between October, 1989 and September, 1990, when employed as a Management Services Officer for Dinas Health Authority.

A preliminary literature review further strengthened the belief in the potential value of investigating the concept of market-orientation as part of a study concerned with NHS organizational change. This review involved an exploration and critique of published literature (including books, academic articles, journals and unpublished papers). It concentrated mainly on the following four areas; managing change, marketing, methodology and context - both external (NHS and public sector) and internal (the units under investigation).

Research methods

In attempting to understand the subjective meanings and definitions of participant's social worlds, this project utilised an array of interpretative techniques to describe, decode, translate and otherwise come to terms with the meaning of certain more or less naturally occurring phenomena, (Van Maanen, 1983). Responding to the call from leading change theorists such as Van de Ven (1987), this approach was adopted to emphasize interpretative research features such as, attention to context and a concern for process.

Pragmatic grounded theory Whilst the design was based on a grounded theory approach (Glaser and Strauss, 1967), a loose, early framework of issues was taken into the field. This offered a very broad control structure to the data collection and management process. In this respect, the approach reflected the position of Miles who contends that the risk of adopting 'pure' grounded theory is:

> that an incoherent, bulky, irrelevant, meaningless set of observations may be produced, which no one can (or even wants to) make sense of. (Miles, 1979, p. 119)

As with grounded theory, this pragmatic approach continually flowed between interviews and observations, analysis, tentative theorizing leading to further changes in design, and so more interviews and analysis (Emerson, 1983, p. 95). For example, the establishment of a marketing department at one unit required a new line of enquiry to be developed and incorporated into the topic schedule. As such, modified grounded theory has been used as a pragmatic and systematic guide to the generation of inductively 'discovered' concepts and explanatory frameworks.

Methodological triangulation This investigation used the complementary methods of data collection employed in methodological triangulation as an integrated way of increasing the amount and quality of data collected. This research tool was viewed as neither an end in itself, nor as being without its philosophical opponents (e.g. Easterby-Smith et al., 1991). Rather, triangulation was used to introduce variety into the research process and prevent the investigation from becoming method-bound. As Abrahamson states:

> the strength of almost every measure is flawed in some way or another and research designs and strategies can be offset by counterbalancing strengths from one to another. (Abrahamson, 1983, p. 12)

Triangulation has therefore been used to separate the logics of actions present within the situation being studied and to trace their evolution over time. Semi-structured interviews and observation have been applied to investigate how people construct their reality of the implementation of marketing change. In tandem, longitudinal archival data - such as long-term comparative performance indicators - have also been analysed (Zajac and Bowman, 1985), so facilitating a systematic comparison between qualitative interview data and quantitative statistical measures.

The Comparative-Intensive case approach   Case studies were considered to be a necessary starting point to this first investigation into NHS marketing development in Wales, as little information existed on which to base other forms of research methodology (Yin, 1984). Moreover, the adoption of a case study approach allowed the comparison of marketing and change theories with the reality of the NHS, while preserving the unitary character of the social processes under investigation (Mitchell, 1983, p. 191).

To mitigate against the traditional case study problems regarding the establishment of causality and the elimination of external factors, the 'comparative-intensive' case method was adopted to provide a contextual view of an emerging process. This involved the in-depth analysis of the NHS marketing change process in a relatively few hospitals over time, rather than the more superficial analyses of a larger number. The two major holistic studies, set in context, were strengthened by the collection of longitudinal archival data covering the history of the units and district studied.

As this investigation was concerned with generating information regarding the whole of Wales, considerable importance was attached to capturing data from structured comparisons with other units and districts in Wales and England. Despite their time-consuming nature and the complexity of data collected, the studies attempted to provide an unusual 'video-tape' analysis of the change processes over time as opposed to the traditional, 'snap-shot' view. The comparative-intensive approach produced extensive data regarding both the prior social influences of the change process and the economic and social contexts of the focal organizations. These data gave valuable insights into such dynamic issues as changing attitudes and power-relations.

Interviews During the study, in excess of 100 interviews were conducted and transcribed. For the purposes of this investigation, an interview was defined as a pre-arranged discussion with an individual (or sometimes a small group), which is recognized by the participant(s) as a contribution to the data collection process of the project. The decision to use conversation as a method of data collection was taken to provide an opportunity to uncover and discuss clues, assumptions and values and to secure accounts based on personal and group experience. In using interviews to uncover these vital elements of the change process, contextual information - behavioural as well as structural - also emerged. For example, a number of insights were obtained of the often obscure process by which consultants 'become' Clinical Directors.

Observation In conjunction with the decision to undertake interviews, this study included first-hand observation of organizational dynamics. The virtues of this technique are well developed and concisely articulated by Mintzberg:

> The researcher who never goes near the water, who collects quantitative data from a distance without anecdote to support them, will always have difficulty explaining interesting relationships. (Mintzberg, 1983, p. 113)

After considering the forms of observation available (Easterby-Smith, 1991), the particular characteristics of the research design indicated that observation took the form of overt, pseudo-participant observation (Delbridge and Kirkpatrick, Chapter Two). This approach involved a partial involvement in a number of projects - necessitated by the researcher's lack of specific accounting competence - in conjunction with periods of purer observation. Having negotiated the period of observation with the gatekeeper, the researcher overtly moved around, observed, interviewed and participated as appropriate, without incurring the ethical problems that deception entails. Following from the preceding discussion of the methodological perspective of the investigation, section two describes the practical issues that were encountered during the study.

The research experience

This second part of the paper provides a discussion of some of the main issues that were encountered as a result of adopting and combining the multiple methods that were outlined above.

The Sampling of research sites

The decision to adopt hospitals, rather than districts or regions, as the level of analysis was taken for two main reasons. First, the attention given to the hospitals in Working for Patients (HMSO, 1989), indicated that provider units would experience the greater, and more immediate challenge of bringing about organizational change. Second, it was decided that focusing on providers within a single District Health Authority (DHA) allowed the opportunity to obtain comparative data by comparing and contrasting providers within a single district.

The choice of Dinas DHA, satisfied Schatzman and Strauss, (1973) 'casing criteria'. The district contains three large hospital units with comparable attributes in terms of technology, size and diversity of professional and managerial workforce, but with contrasting historical and managerial backgrounds. The location of the district within the organizationally distinct Welsh situation and close proximity to the headquarters of this NHS division, allowed the study to be conducted in an area so far unresearched by a major academic study. Finally, the chosen District had considerable practical advantages in terms of proximity to the research base.

Two of the DHA's three groups of hospitals (units) were selected as major research sites. While the choice of units was in no way based on a search for typical units both share the general features of many hospitals (and public sector organizations) such as goal ambiguity, diffused authority, centralised accountability mechanisms and dominance by professionals. Both Tyfu and Marw are classed as district general hospitals (DGHs) and were chosen because they displayed both similar and contrasting features that could be compared in terms of their implementation of the same Government-imposed marketing change initiative. The common features included: the wide range of services provided, the common DHA, an early indication of marketing awareness, and their willingness to participate in the study. There were also obvious contrasts between the two units and these include the service-mix, age, management structure, district-planned future and location (Tyfu is a city centre hospital whereas, Marw is located on the edge of a conurbation). A broad comparison of the two units is made in the table below.

Table 8.1
The two major research sites compared

Factor	Tyfu	Marw
Age	170 years	60 years
Budget (1991-92)	£50m	£38m
No. beds	750	520
Status	DMU	NHS trust (1.4.93)
Staff	2300	2000
Major depts.	Trauma and orthopaeds., Accident and emergency, General surgery, Medicine	Maternity, Care of the elderly, General surgery, Medicine

Two major factors determined the choice of these particular research sites. First, the established network of ex-colleagues at district level was regarded as significant potential benefit to the study. Second, the hospital within the district of which the researcher had some working knowledge was not used as a major research site. Therefore, the investigation was carried out in settings that were anthropologically unfamiliar and in which there were no existing allegiances to individuals or groups. Great attention was paid not to let the researcher's administrative background adversely affect contact with clinical professionals and management or the interpretation of their social worlds. For example, similar length interviews were held with approximately the same number of all groups, using the same flexible topic schedule, all within the respondents' own work areas and utilizing a consistent language.

After access to both units had been agreed in 1990, Tyfu was chosen to be the first major site as a result of the relative uncertainty surrounding its future. Frequent contact was maintained with Marw, to keep the site 'warm' until major research at this second hospital began in 1992.

Access negotiation and gatekeeper-selection

During this interpretative study, the access negotiation process was regarded as an integral part of the data collection phase, because each meeting spawned topical and current information. Particular care was taken at this early stage of the research so as to avoid the problems caused by the inability to negotiate satisfactory access (Watson et al., 1991).

In terms of the strategy for gaining entry into the organisations, there were three key features of the initial approach for access that are important to note. First, purposefully maintained contacts with ex-DHA colleagues informed the selection of the Unit Management Accountant (UMA) of Tyfu and the Quality Manager of Marw as access-sanctioning gatekeepers. The UMA of Tyfu was chosen because of his position on the Management Board and his declared intention to raise the profile of marketing within the Unit. The Marw gatekeeper was chosen because of the early enthusiasm he had displayed for embracing marketing-type activities within his role as Quality Manager. Fortunately, when the occupant of this post left (for a marketing post in the chemicals industry) his replacement (the Marketing Officer), proved equally enthusiastic towards the project.

Second, it was decided to be relatively open about the key issues and problems of the investigation. Early in negotiations, the gatekeepers requested indications of the research's aims. This hurdle was overcome through discussions of the key issues of the research and the perceived level of access required. As such, an 'open' as opposed to 'secret' research role was adopted. Through this approach it was felt that all parties consented to the 'agenda' of the research and there was very little need for covert activity during the process.

Third, after initial contact was made at the units, the researcher was informed by ex-colleagues that his credibility and trustworthiness had been informally checked by the gatekeepers of both major sites. Accompanying what must have been favourable references, presentation and image management remained high amongst the researcher's priorities and involved the adoption of the research style outlined later in the paper.

After assurances regarding such issues as confidentiality and minimal disruption were given, the gatekeepers granted access. At Tyfu access was granted immediately, by the UMA, whereas at Marw the gatekeeper's less senior position required him to submit the proposition to the Board for approval. This process took around five months. If nothing else, a year's employment in the NHS had taught the researcher the virtue of patience. Both gatekeepers proved to be interested in aiding the investigation and offered help, advice and encouragement rather than attempting to alter the focus of the study in any way. Both eagerly accepted the offer of feedback sessions and the researcher was left in no doubt that even at that stage, they envisaged some practical returns from the project.

Early help from the gatekeepers, such as the use of rooms and telephones, was gratefully received but never abused or over-stated for fear of being viewed unsympathetically by other members of staff. Both organizations proved to be generous hosts and despite the many demands on managers' and medics' time, the research appeared to rate as quite a high priority in the minds of those involved (see Watson et al., 1991). Bearing in mind that the core interest of the project was the introduction of organizational change, the gaining of entry into the Units during the first few months of the reforms was regarded as vital to the theoretical interests of the investigation. During this first crucial fieldwork period it was anticipated that the disruption resulting from the changes was likely to be at its height. Therefore, whilst time was of the essence, sensitivity to context was maintained at this and all times.

In particular, the Marw gatekeeper, especially, provided legitimacy to the project as and when necessary. For example, the UMA's sponsorship of the investigation was emphasised when arranging interviews with clinicians' secretaries who were sometimes very protective over their medics' time. It transpired from subsequent conversations that the gatekeeper had once started a Ph.D but had been unable to complete it. Here then was a 'champion' of the cause (somebody with at least some affinity with doctoral research). So, due to a mixture of experience, careful manipulation of contacts and luck, access had been established to all parties' satisfaction.

Respondent sampling

Due to the vast number of stakeholders associated with the NHS hospitals, a range of non-probability sampling methods were used to reach the many disparate groups and to maintain a degree of structure and control over the research process. At the outset, purposive sampling occurred through the selection of the project-focus and the choice of hospitals as the sites of investigation. Early random sampling (Miles and Huberman, 1984) was superseded by judgement sampling (Honigmann, 1982, p. 80) based on occupational situation. The latter was facilitated by consulting organization charts which provided a 'map' to guide a route through the sampling process. Due to the nature of professional organisation within the NHS, integrated sampling was necessary in order to reach a group of individuals who were often key players but who as individuals occupied no formal managerial position. For example, an interview with a clinician (who it subsequently transpired was an informal adviser to the Marw UGM) occurred through a social contact. Perhaps the most productive sources of interviewees were the nominees of previous participants and volunteers who emerged as a result of the lively organizational grapevines.

Bearing in mind the research questions and the unit of analysis, a balance of occupations within the interview sample was needed i.e. 1/3 managers, 1/3 professionals and 1/3 others such as 'external stakeholders' and 'marketers'. The 'external stakeholders' included GPs and purchasers. By 'marketers', it was not meant simply those with formal functional responsibility, but also the emerging 'part-time' marketers (Gummesson, 1990) from a variety of backgrounds. By involving medics, managers and other staff, not only was it possible to compare the way different people view situations, but it also enabled better lines of enquiry to be developed and provided the opportunity to investigate emergent themes and patterns as the interviews progressed.

Interviews

Interview conduct While respecting the axioms of qualitative research, pragmatism dictated the use of a semi-structured interview schedule. This was so, partly because certain respondents, such as senior clinicians, were only able to guarantee an hour for interviews due to their other commitments. It was important to maximize the capacity to elicit descriptions and clarifications about issues of relevance to the project. Conscious attempts were made to pose all questions in a neutral manner, to avoid the infiltration of bias, and to encourage the respondent to reflect and think deeply about their feelings and attitudes. Prompts and probes were also as well-timed and as objective as possible. This edited excerpt from an interview with a sister at Tyfu Hospital gives a good indication of the interview style:

MK Has Working for Patients affected your day to day work?

S Yes, it means much more paperwork and long nights of administration work at home after shifts [...] now Sisters, or Ward Managers, that's what we have to call ourselves now, have to fill in training and sickness records for ward staff [...] once it was District Personnel's job and then this hospital's administration, now we have to do it.

MK What has been your colleagues' reaction to this change in job title?

S Most of the older ones don't like it but most have accepted it [...] we wouldn't mind that change if it didn't mean that we spent less and less time doing hands on nursing tasks.

To cope with this form of research it was vital to prepare well for every interview. Before each, key issues were reviewed, alternative perspectives were acknowledged, and appropriate terminology and tactics assessed. Much archival and contextual data was investigated to increase the chances of detecting continuities as well as change during the development of NHS change (Van de Ven, 1987). For example, documentary evidence was sought, especially internal literature, (mission statements, brochures, annual reports and planning documents). These data were also used to indicate shifts in 'representation', just as in interviews, and helped to provide another index of change. For example, variations in the way major investment proposals were justified were a key indicator of a shift towards marketing orientation. The availability of archival evidence including strategic plans, minutes from meetings, proposals for resource allocation and memoranda between key participants, varied greatly between departments and units. However, the quality of the access proved vital in securing almost all documentary evidence that was requested. As well as the use of archival data a regular and systematic scan was made of all health service related journals and a variety of national and local newspapers. For example, considerable use was made of a library newspaper scanning service which provided a regular flow of relevant cuttings from a number of selected publications including the *Financial Times*.

This preparation was rewarded in two ways. First, on numerous occasions participants referenced these sources, so knowledge of these materials maintained the credibility of the researcher. Second, it helped to foster trust and as a result all interviewees appeared to be interested in, and to enjoy, the interviews. Some stated that the process had helped them to think about issues that they had not considered or had time to consider. Others commented that they found great benefit in talking to an independent outsider about themselves and/or learning something about the organizational changes. This interest was further fostered by invitations to workshops, seminars and feedback sessions. As an indication of success on this issue, every interview went beyond the requested one hour. Indeed a number lasted well over two hours.

The attainment of interviewer proficiency is vital to the success of this methodology. The researcher had considerable experience of interviewing managers, clinicians and nursing staff (obtained during study for the Institute of Management Services Diploma, and later as an integral part of his previous position with Dinas Health Authority). This experience led the interviewer to develop various styles of interviewing staff, and the ability to tackle potentially contentious or difficult areas. For example, a less academic and more relaxed style line of enquiry was adopted when interviewing nurses as opposed to senior clinicians. This was rewarded by the absence of anti-academic feeling. The researcher did however, feel that his knowledge, experience and status were sometimes, implicitly called into question when interviewing senior medical staff. This situation was handled by the careful management of personal style, which generally involved an informed but unpretentious approach, coupled with a willingness to learn and general good nature. As part of this strategy the researcher wore a sober suit and tie for interviews with managers and senior clinicians. Nurses however, appeared sensitive to the sight of a suit, immediately associating it with medical representatives or management consultants. As part of a conscious policy to blend in with the way of life of the organization the suit was abandoned for subsequent interviews on wards and with auxiliaries. More relaxed interviews and a much warmer reception (often including tea and biscuits) resulted.

As all interviews were held at the Units, they had the added advantage of illuminating the internal context of the hospitals. This sensitivity to, and contextualisation of, issues that delved deeply into the social world of the respondent also helped to avoid losing (or not picking up on) particular interview data. It was also often possible to follow-up formal interviews with informal discussions and conversations, over lunch for example, in order to expand certain points and to develop further emergent themes.

In gathering data, the agreed use of an unobtrusive tape recorder suited the objectives of the investigation. The interview transcripts allowed the storage of very rich qualitative data, including nuances of language and stories particular to the context under investigation. The use of tapes also facilitated a natural conversation and guarded against the reactivity which may have resulted from note taking. Moreover, on playback of the tape, any undue bias could be addressed as could the interviewing style and technique. The tapes therefore provided feedback both on the interview and the conduct of the interviewer.

Interview content   The interviews covered three main areas; the environmental context of the units, the content of changes and the processes of change. From such broad questions, it was possible to give the respondent a large degree of freedom when answering. Such freedom invariably led to the raising of other issues and opinions, not only as an individual, but often and very importantly, as a group member. In achieving this, the values of the respondent were at least partially revealed. At all stages, the use of language was monitored in order to compare rhetoric and reality; an essential task in a study committed to interpretation and context.

Observation

After several months of interviews at Marw, the gatekeeper invited the researcher to take part in a number of marketing-based management projects. This golden opportunity, presented the chance to conduct observation and participate in the focal world under observation. Rather than maintaining the exclusive role of interviewer, the researcher began to spend more time at the unit and to adopt different roles in the field. These roles varied between complete observer to complete participant, involving interplay between the two.

The projects that the researcher became involved in centred on the installation of two major information systems (to monitor Extra Contractual Referrals and establish a Capital Asset Register). As these assignments were of direct relevance to the research, it was also possible to gain instant reactions to, and interpretations of, change initiatives at ward, theatre and office level; it was also possible to explore the linkages between individual factors in the organization through informal conversations.

The principal early task was to move from the position of stranger to that of someone who could be trusted (Fairhurst, 1983). This was largely achieved, to the extent that after a couple of weeks, staff tended to greet the researcher with a jovial 'in today are you?'. After a suitably light-hearted reply a relaxed personal conversation would often ensue. It seemed almost to be expected that they should be asked questions, and they all appeared to be happy to answer. The explicit nature of involvement meant that there was no need for deception. On the few occasions when the researcher's role was questioned, an honest if incomplete answer was given for example, 'I'm helping so and so out, I'm not based in this department'. So successful was the period of fieldwork and involvement, that after the initial three month period had elapsed it was agreed that it should continue for a few weeks to complete one project.

Both Unit gatekeepers invited the researcher to attend a range of meetings, seminars and workshops related to the reforms. These events afforded valuable insights into the political workings of the unit. Most members of the hospitals seemed to feel comfortable with the researcher in attendance and a great deal of information regarding the personalities and informal working of the organization was collected over lunch. At Marw, after declining several offers to 'go for a drink on a Friday', it was judged prudent to do so when it coincided with a member of the staff's 'leaving do'. This presented the opportunity to interact with many of the respondents in different surroundings, so providing an alternative view of the organization 'at play'.

Throughout the investigation a diary was maintained which included: contextual details, such as indications of cultural values (for example the age and content of notices on boards), settings, conversations overheard, and emergent ideas. This method of documenting a whole range of feelings and observations allowed them to be recorded as soon as possible after they where encountered and could be used by an external auditor to assess how far the fieldworker's bias influenced the outcomes. Even if not used in this way, the notebook proved enormously useful in jogging the memory during subsequent research phases.

Data Analysis Obtaining systematic observations of a strategic change process over time, using multiple methods, quickly produced a potentially overwhelming quantity of rich, qualitative data. Through a constant comparative analysis approach, incidents and statements occurring in the raw data were compared, classified and categorized in various combinations.

Initially, all of the interviews were partially transcribed (1/3 average) by the researcher, within hours of the session. Great care was taken to include the transcription of opinionated and attitudinal material, which was seen as particularly important to capture subjective responses to the change process. Any interpretations that emerged during transcription were noted either on the transcripts or in the field diary. After initially segmenting the data by unit of management, a chronological listing of 'events' was developed by combining the analysis of data collected through the adopted multiple methods (Van de Ven, 1987). An event is defined as a point in time where a change occurs in either the content, process or context of the management of the focal organisation. From this process, conceptual themes emerged which served to provide a first ordering of the data.

An adaptation of Miles and Huberman's (1984, p. 28) qualitative analysis technique was then adopted to further probe the data, through the regular and careful development of conceptual frameworks, which were viewed as 'boundary devices' rather than 'straight jackets'. The threat of these early categories becoming fixed frameworks was avoided by the re-definition of these pigeon-holes as issues emerged and altered in complexion. The enquiry was continued by listing emergent topics on a specially prepared analysis sheet. Alongside the topics, evidence was referenced by means of a cataloguing system that used key words or phrases with an interview code, or a document reference. Each emergent theme was then coded into multiple time-tracks which uncovered clues as to the progression of the changes. This method, which is based on that advocated by Poole (1983), avoided the problem of preordaining the existence of stages or phases to the process. In addition, the approach provided a way of identifying cycles and transitions among activity tracks from which case reports were later prepared.

Whilst this proved an effective method of qualitative data analysis it has borne out Miles's (1979) 'attractive nuisance' label. Miles warned that while the quality and depth of data that can result from interpretative research is appealing, the analysis can prove to be extremely labour intensive, especially for the single researcher. Indeed, during this investigation, a typical one and a half hour interview required approximately 14 hours to transcribe and analyse.

Reflection upon qualitative data

The epistemological and ontological stance of this research rendered many of the positivistic based procedures inappropriate for conducting 'validity' checks during this study. As Morgan points out, to judge one perspective in terms of the assumptions of another quite different view is not feasible or desirable (Morgan, 1983, p. 15). Instead, this investigation has operationalized criteria more in keeping with the objectives of the naturalistic paradigm, such as credibility, transferability, dependability and confirmability (Lincoln and Guba, 1985, p. 42). This section will describe the process of reflection upon the data in terms of these objectives.

Credibility

Many of the strategies and tactics identified by McKinnon (1988) for retaining the credibility (a term preferred to validity by many interpretative researchers) of research have been used. The following provides illustrations of the measures that were taken to ensure the credibility of the study.

The gatekeepers and other members of staff were developed as key informants, (Tremblay, 1982) through the deliberate development of close extra-interview relationships over informal exchanges and during lunch breaks. These willing informants provided much contextual information, useful future respondents and issues to pursue. These contacts also provided the opportunity to ask questions, such as those regarding well-known events like the Trust application process, that may have appeared naive and tiresome to others. In this respect the using of key informants was a tactic that was used to safeguard the credibility of the research and the dependability of the data.

The consistent attention that was paid to the context of the investigation, through the 'prolonged engagement' approach - involving a high number of lengthy interviews over time - and the triangulation of methods has done much to mitigate the threats to the data that are caused either by insufficient time spent in the field or poor access. In order to further protect the credibility of this study, member validation, the joint effort technique and seminars were used to feedback the multiple constructions of reality to their creators. As part of the interview process, the 'joint effort' technique involved using the researcher's perspective to probe and draw incidents and situations to the attention of the insider. Once this was done a checking procedure including on-going feedback of summaries to the interviewees (member validation), was followed to protect against the imposition of categories of meaning on to observed events. This cycle gave the respondent the opportunity to add further information and allowed the re-interrogation of interpretations. It also produced an agreed record which forms a defence against later possible claims of error and/or misunderstanding.

In the interests of naturalism, interviews were carried out in surroundings and at times that were familiar and part of the respondent's working day. This meant that interviews took place in hospitals, laboratories, managers' offices and wards during working hours. For the same reasons, respondents were not specifically requested to block out a period of time solely for the interview. However, most managers did. Unsurprisingly, interviews involving healthcare professionals were often interrupted by telephone calls or people entering the room on urgent business. This was welcomed as observations and contacts were made from these episodes. Such experiences were fertile ground in terms of indirect observation and bought the observer much closer to the phenomena being studied. When dealing with any response the social location of the respondent within the organization has been taken into account and indicated on interview transcripts or in the research journal.

It is also worth mentioning how important working experience of the NHS proved to be in fostering trust within fieldwork relationships. The comprehension of the language used by respondents allowed sensitive issues to be identified early and sensitively handled. For example, the researcher's familiarity with language widely understood within the context, such as 'housekeeping', 'contracting' and 'the sharp end', facilitated the understanding of the respondent's social world. Such knowledge also aided the adoption of a quasi-insider approach whilst operating with a stranger's perspectives.

Reactivity and confidentiality

The extent to which the research process affects responses is termed reactivity (Webb et al., 1966). If left unaddressed this issue can undermine the reliability of the data. While a number of the checks against this occurring have been discussed elsewhere in this paper, this investigation's view of bias, use of recording equipment and handling of the issue of confidentiality deserve detailed description.

Because this study's epistemological and ontological stance involved viewing bias as a phenomenon that needed to be managed, as opposed to eradicated (McKinnon, 1988), conceptual levers (in this case the methodological perspective and the concepts of change and market-orientation) were used both to distance the analyst from the data and to provide a new perspective on it. The researcher's formal interview training and experience also proved very useful in for example, the timing of interventions and the de-sensitising of issues using hypothetical questions. Given that a position of trust and rapport was established within the organizations, it was felt the researcher's presence was unobtrusive and often largely unnoticed, so that he did not materially affect either the object's actions or the other results collected. Respondents commented that this may have been aided by the fact that hospitals are now accustomed to having unfamiliar 'visitors' wandering around such as management trainees, management consultants and seconded regional staff.

At the beginning of every interview, permission to use the recorder was sought. Once agreed, (100 per cent acceptance) it was removed from sight as much as sound quality permitted. Reactivity was also reduced by careful management of the following issues. Only very few notes were taken, so allowing a normal speed conversation without obvious pauses and official barriers. A recorder was chosen that had a virtually inaudible mechanism, a strong pick-up was used to ensure the 'hiding' of recorder and the use of c60 tapes minimized changing of cassettes. Every interview began with an assurance of confidentiality. This was followed by information on the nature of the project, and an assurance that respondents were not being judged. Hence, prior to the start of the interview much effort was made to foster trust and openness from the respondent. This 'impression management' and attention to reactivity was essential in preparing the ground for interviews.

In each hospital, data were gathered on the change processes over time through interviews and documentary archival evidence (Doz and Prahalad, 1987). Interviews took place at different times as the change process evolved within each organization, with some key personnel interviewed repeatedly over several years. Where appropriate some respondents were interviewed repeatedly over the three year duration of the project. When this was not possible, documentary evidence and cross-checking between responses (member validation) was used to evoke or challenge recollections from participants to try and overcome *ex-post* rationalisation and selective recollection.

Most studies of organizational change to-date have been conducted after the outcomes were known, so biasing the outcomes. Although this study - which was initiated before the implementation of the reforms - made use of historical data, a major focus of the research entailed regularly scheduled and intermittent real-time field observations of the organizational developments as they unfolded over time, without knowing a priori the outcomes of the actions taken. This reactivity check involved observing key committee meetings and conducting informal discussions with key participants over the course of the change process.

Assurances of confidentiality were made for both ethical and methodological reasons. In the case of the latter, it was necessary to distinguish what was said by a respondent in private from what was said publicly. With confidentiality assured, the interviewees responded openly, providing sometimes intimate insights into their social world. External, sometimes 'political' confidentiality posed further constraints since issues of competitive advantage were increasingly involved.

Transferability

Much of the scepticism towards the case study approach largely rests on the view that generalizing from the results of one study is not possible. Drawing on the work of Mitchell (1983) and Yin (1984), Bryman argues that case studies should instead be:

> evaluated in terms of the adequacy of the theoretical inferences that are generated. The aim is not to infer the findings from a sample to a population, but to engender patterns and linkages of theoretical importance. Bryman (1989, p. 172)

On arrival at the stage when little new data emerged from the research process, 'saturation of categories' (Glaser and Strauss, 1967, p. 70) was achieved. It was at this point that careful attention had to be paid to the question of 'inferring logically' from the results of the investigation beyond the scope of the organizations studied. Using the results of the comparisons with other UK sites and inter-regional and district comparisons, informed by interview data and documentary evidence, the findings from this study would appear to be most relevant to hospitals within the unique Welsh set-up. However, in recognition of the similarities between many public sector organizations in terms of diffused accountability and unclear objectives, elements of the findings may have a wider relevance within the UK public sector.

Conclusions

This paper has used an investigation of NHS marketing change to illustrate a systematic and pragmatic research methodology. The approach has been shown to be aware of context, congruent with this researcher's epistemological values and sensitive to the nature and aims of the project. However, far from suggesting that this method is easy to manage, the paper has been at pains to indicate potential pitfalls and the intensity of effort required. Moreover, whilst a particular attempt has been made to manage the process, it must be remembered that no amount of re-interrogation or triangulation of methods can ever compel the reader to agree with the researcher - persuasion is the best that can be hoped for (Lincoln and Guba, 1985). Persuasion is however, more compelling when a systematic approach is adopted.

This paper has indicated a number of features that may be of interest to researchers using case studies to investigate organizational change in the NHS and elsewhere in the public sector. First, the nurturing of key informants pays handsome research dividends. They can for example, inform the vital tasks of gatekeeper selection and access negotiation. These missions are further eased when researching an organization from a position of some experience. Second, the use of methodological triangulation can help to counterbalance the inadequacies of single research methods, and add variety to research activity. Third, whilst conducting this type of research, the issues of image and relationship management become vital. Maintaining credibility, confidence and respect of those under investigation is cardinal.

Fourth, the adoption of an holistic, comparative-intensive case study research has produced a more comprehensive understanding of the longitudinal, NHS organizational change process than has been achieved from previous studies. For example, the longitudinal lens of the approach has aided the development of a Three Paradigm Model of Organizational Change. This model views the introduction of a market-orientation into the NHS as the third UK health care paradigm shift. The first is viewed as the birth of the NHS in 1946, and the second is depicted as emerging from Griffith's introduction of managerialism (DHSS, 1983). The adoption of this method has also uncovered a number of important, micro-political elements of the NHS change process which have previously been missed or ignored. For example, evidence from this study indicates that some hospital managers have manipulated existing quality-oriented organizational projects to provide a convenient intellectual technology and legitimating rhetoric for the emerging market-oriented paradigm. Overall, this paper has tried to show how a systematic implementation of a research methodology based on the comparative-intensive case study can be used to uncover not only, deeply-embedded longitudinal features of change, but also to capture the subtle, and therefore frequently overlooked, nuances of change processes.

References

Abrahamson, M. (1983), *Social Research Methods*, Englewood Cliffs, Prentice-Hall, N.J.

Berger, P. and T. Luckmann (eds.) (1989), *The Social Construction of Reality*, Penguin, Harmondsworth.

Bryman A. (1989), *Research Methods and Organization Studies*, Unwin, London.

Burrell. G. and G. Morgan (1979), *Sociological Paradigms and Organisational Analysis*, Heineman, London.

DHSS Management Inquiry Report (1983), (Griffiths Report), Report of the Health Advisory Service.

Doz, Y. and C.K. Prahalad (1987), 'A process model and strategic redirection in large complex firms: The case of multinational corporations', in Pettigrew, A. (ed.), *The Management of Strategic Change*, pp. 68-83, Basil Blackwell, Oxford.

Emmerson, R.M. (1983) (ed.), *Contemporary Field Research*, Little Brown & Co., Boston.

Fairhurst, E. (1983), 'Organisational rules and the accomplishment of nursing work on geriatric wards', in S. Fineman and I. Mangham (eds.), 'Qualitative approaches to organisations', *Journal of Management Studies*, Special Issue, Vol. 20, No. 3, July, pp. 315-32.

Glaser, B.G. and A.L. Strauss (1967), *The Discovery of Grounded Theory - Strategies For Qualitative Research*, Aldine, Chicago.

Gummesson, E. (1990), 'Marketing-orientation revisited: The crucial role of the part-time marketeer', *European Journal of Marketing*, Vol. 25, No. 2, pp. 60-75.

Hirschman, E. (1986), 'Humanistic inquiry in marketing research: philosophy, method and criteria', *Journal of Marketing Research*, Vol. 23, August, pp. 237-49.

HMSO (1989), *Working For Patients*, London.

Honigmann, J.J. (1982), 'Sampling in ethnographic fieldwork' in Burgess, R.G. (ed.) (1982), *Field Research: A Source Book and Field Manual*, Allen & Unwin, London.

Lincoln, Y.S. and E.G. Guba (1985), *Naturalistic Inquiry*, Sage, Beverly Hills.

McKinnon, J. (1988), 'Reliability and validity in field research', *Accounting, Auditing and Accountability*, Vol. 1, No.1, pp. 34-55.

McNulty, T., R. Whipp, R. Whittington and M. Kitchener (1993), 'Putting marketing into NHS hospitals: Issues about implementation', forthcoming in the *Journal of Public Money and Management*.

Miles, N.B. (1979), Qualitative data as an attractive nuisance: the problem of analysis', *Administrative Science Quarterly*, Vol. 24, No. 4, pp. 590-601.

Miles, N.B. and A.M. Huberman (1984), *Qualitative Data Analysis: A Source Book of New Methods,* Sage, London.

Mintzberg, H. (1983), *Power in and around Organisations*, Englewood Cliffs, Prentice Hall, N.J.

Mitchell, J.C. (1983), 'Case and situational analysis', *Sociological Review*, Vol. 31, No. 2, pp. 186-211.

Poole, M.S. (1983), 'Decision development in small groups III: A multiple sequence model of group decision development *Communication Monographs*, Vol. 50.

Read, S.M. (1989), 'Management changes in the National Health Services: nursing and organisational theory in relation to the development of a new unit of health care', University of Sheffield, Unpublished Ph.D Thesis.

Schatzman, L. and A.L. Strauss (1973), *Field Research: Strategies for a Natural Sociology*, Englewood Cliffs, Prentice Hall, N.J.

Scrivens, E. (1991), 'Is there a role for marketing in the public sector?', *Public Money and Management*, Vol. 11, No. 2, pp. 17-25.

Sheaf, R. (1991), *Marketing for Health Services*, Open University Press, Milton Keynes.

Smith-Easterby, M., R. Thorpe and A. Lowe (1991), *Management Research: An Introduction*, Sage, London.

Todd, D.J. (1979), 'Mixing qualitative and quantitative methods: triangulation in action', *Administrative Science Quarterly*, Vol. 24, December, pp. 602-11.

Tremblay, M.A. (1982), 'The key informant technique: A non-ethnographic application', in Burgess, R.G. (ed.) (1982), *Field Research: A Source Book and Field Manual*, Allen & Unwin, London.

Van Maanen, J. (ed.) (1983), *Qualitative Methodology*, Sage, Beverly Hills.

Watson, T., S. Riggs and N. Fook (1991), 'Participant observation research and managerial work', Paper presented to the British Academy of Management Conference, University of Bath.

Webb, E.J., D.T. Campbell, R.D. Schwartz and L. Sechrest (1966), *Unobtrusive Measures: Nonreactive Research in the Social Sciences*, Rand McNally, Chicago.

Webb, D. and N. Morgan (1992), 'Identifying and addressing strategy, implementation barriers in marketing', *MEG Conference Proceedings*, University of Salford, pp. 734-751.

Whipp, R. and A. Pettigrew (1991), *Managing Change for Competitive Success*, Basil Blackwell, Oxford.

Yin, R.K. (1984), *Case Study Research: Design and Methods*, Sage, Beverly Hills.

Zajac, E.J. and E.H. Bowman (1985), 'Perspectives and choices in strategy research', Working Paper 85-15, Reginald H. Jones Centre for Management Policy, Strategy and Organisation, Wharton School, University of Pennsylvania, Philadelphia

Part 3

Applied Research

9 Acquiring Expertise for a Knowledge-based System in Tourism Marketing

PAULO RITA

Introduction

This chapter focuses on the development of the research methodology that underlies the knowledge acquisition process to build TOUREX. TOUREX is a knowledge-based expert system designed to assist senior managers from national tourism organizations on promotion budget allocation decisions among international travel markets.

This chapter derives from doctoral research on the application of expert system technology to marketing decisions (Rita, 1993). In section 8.2 the three major conceptual constructs underlying the research project are identified: the organization - national tourism organizations; the marketing problem - promotion budget allocation decisions; and the information technology tool to solve the problem - expert systems. The development stages of building the system are described and discussed in section 8.3. Thereafter, in section 8.4, a thorough analysis of the issues involved in developing the research design for knowledge acquisition is presented.

Rationale for developing the system

Tourism is the world's largest industry and is of key importance for many countries. It creates wealth, sustains a great number of jobs and can be used to vivify regions, cities and towns with poor physical resources or declining industries. In addition, international tourism can make an important contribution to foreign currency earnings.

National tourism organizations (NTOs) are the statutory agencies of governments responsible for discharging the tourism marketing function in foreign markets. They are the agencies who undertake overall destination marketing, creating an 'umbrella campaign', under which, at the second level, the various individual providers of tourist services can market their own components of the total tourist product. The second level of marketing covers the full range of mainly commercial marketing initiatives in which airlines and other transport operators, hotel groups and tour operators, can promote their individual services to a market of potential buyers already aware of, and predisposed towards, the destination.

Every year NTOs spend vast amounts of money on promoting their countries as tourist destinations in selected markets abroad. This involves the allocation of funds among those markets. Generally speaking, a country's tourism development will be commensurate with the amount of its marketing budget. It is very difficult to demonstrate a correlation between spending in marketing and earnings from tourism because external factors, especially economic and political factors, also influence travel patterns. However, in the case of NTOs, there is evidence to suggest that where marketing expenditure has been cut back, there is a consequential loss of market share (Ahmed and Krohn, 1990).

A systematic evaluation of travel markets is a prerequisite of rational decision making in respect of allocating marketing inputs to specific countries. However, the use of econometric models to generate forecasts of international tourism demand, and to assess the consequences of possible changes in determining factors ('what if' forecasting), does not constitute per se enough information on which to base promotion budget allocation decisions (Mazanec, 1986a). Alternatively, a market response model which links promotional expenditures to tourism sales or market share, for each country, could be used to derive promotional budget allocation decisions. An assessment of market attractiveness is made implicitly by relating market output (number of visits, bed nights, receipts) to promotional input. However, modelling market input and output relationships alone is not sufficient since national tourism promotion is not the only determinant of tourist expenditure in any one country (Uysal and Crompton, 1984). A superior method of evaluating tourism markets would be to develop a decision support system (Mazanec, 1986b). Nevertheless, these systems do not account for the expert's knowledge. An expert system would combine the two sources of knowledge, that is would incorporate specialist knowledge of the tourism market as well as managerial judgement and expertise.

An expert system is a computer program that uses expert knowledge to solve problems in a specific domain. The representation of marketing knowledge in computer systems enables the dissemination of marketing expertise, making it available where it is likely to have an impact, namely at the point of decision making. Expert systems might force managers to consider factors that they may otherwise overlook, making them more aware of how and why they make decisions. In addition, managers would be able to combine their expertise with that of other experts, and with the accumulated empirical and theoretical knowledge in the domain.

In the case of NTOs, an expert system can aid the preparation and planning of an optimal budget allocation for each market, i.e. one which will maximize the yield gained by the destination country from its portfolio of tourist markets. Expert knowledge about different markets can be amalgamated in order to advise on an optimal budget to be allocated to each market. This essentially fills the gap of having to employ different experts for different markets each time a budget allocation decision is to be made, effectively reducing the relative cost and effort required in budget allocation decision.

Building the TOUREX system

The major goal for building TOUREX was to assist NTOs' senior managers in allocating more effectively promotion budget sums to international markets. Constructing a knowledge-based expert system, such as TOUREX, is a five-stage process, as shown in Figure 9.1 (Hayes-Roth, Waterman and Lenat, 1983).

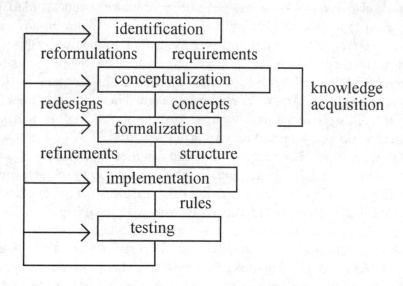

Figure 9.1 Stages of knowledge-based systems building

Identification

The first step in developing a knowledge-based system is to characterize the important aspects of the problem. This involves identifying the participants, problem characteristics, resources and goals. The researcher played the role of the knowledge engineer who designs and builds the expert system. The domain experts were senior managers from NTOs responsible for the allocation of promotion budgets to foreign markets. The participants (knowledge engineer and domain experts) had to identify the key elements of the problem and knowledge relevant to solving that problem. The sources of knowledge available to the knowledge engineer included experience of analogous problems and knowledge about methods, representations and tools for building expert systems. The sources of knowledge gained from the domain experts included their own and others past problem-solving experience and textbooks examples of problems and solutions in the domain.

Knowledge acquisition

The conceptualization and formalization stages constitute what is called knowledge acquisition (see Figure 1). Conceptualization, also known as knowledge elicitation, involves collecting the information, decision criteria and relationships in the knowledge domain primarily by interviewing an expert or experts. Formalization, also called knowledge analysis, is the process of representing that knowledge in a structured form. Knowledge acquisition is a difficult task since knowledge is rarely formulated in a fashion that permits simple translation into a program. In fact, knowledge acquisition is considered the bottleneck in the construction of expert systems (Cullen and Bryman, 1988). The research design that underlies the acquisition of knowledge for TOUREX is described in section 4 below.

Implementation

Implementation involves mapping the formalized knowledge from the previous stage into the representational framework associated with the tool chosen for the problem. The domain knowledge made explicit during the formalization stage includes, in a structured form, a set of inference rules and the control strategies. TOUREX, the expert system used to represent this knowledge, is implemented by using a knowledge engineering aid called Leonardo. Leonardo is an expert system development tool (shell) which features its own procedural programming language and offers the benefits of an object-oriented approach. Leonardo has rule-based facilities as well as more powerful concepts such as frames and classes.

Testing

Finally, the testing stage involves evaluating the knowledge and the representational forms used to implement it. TOUREX will be evaluated in two ways: (1) its performance will be assessed by using past data from NTOs to compare outcomes of the system with past results; and (2) questionnaires will be sent to NTOs' senior executives for managerial evaluation of the system.

A research design for knowledge acquisition

Marketing research has historically relied upon one theoretical tradition - the 'quantitative' paradigm (Deshpande, 1983). While quantitative methods have been developed most directly for the task of verifying or confirming theories, qualitative methods were purposely developed for the task of discovering or generating theories (Reichardt and Cook, 1979). Consequently, marketing science has grown much more rapidly in the area of hypothesis-testing than in the development, on an inductive basis, of new theories. More recently, this has become a common method of collecting primary data for marketing decisions.

The research design underlying the knowledge acquisition to develop TOUREX, although based on a survey approach, combines qualitative and quantitative methodologies in the form of in-depth interviews and a mail questionnaire respectively. This combination of research methodologies sought to achieve the systematic gathering of information regarding budget allocation decisions from NTO managers in order to develop the expert system.

In the first instance, library and desk research was undertaken in order to gain information on theoretical knowledge already established in the literature. The second phase of the research design comprised in-depth interviews with NTO managers who were responsible for promotion budget allocations. The purpose of these were to extend and qualify established theories in marketing. A mail survey formed the third phase of the research design. A survey which collects quantitative data over a large sample would provide statistical evidence relating to hypotheses developed during the first two phases of the research, for example, of associations between variables. Here the researcher must consider sampling, questionnaire design, questionnaire administration, and data analysis (see Chapter 4 of this volume). This research design, one that combines a qualitative technique, i.e., the interview approach to generate hypotheses, and a quantitative technique, i.e., the mail survey questionnaire approach, to test and modify these hypotheses, has its origin to some extent in the triangulation technique (Fielding and Fielding, 1986). The implementation of these distinct phases are described below.

Library and desk research

The definition of the research problem involved specifying the types of knowledge that are needed by the NTOs' senior managers for promotion budget allocation. Alternative models describing the desired outcomes, the relevant variables, and the relationships of the variables to the outcomes were developed by the author (e.g., Rita 1991 and 1992) from previous studies, trade journals, tourism statistics, official bulletins, and so on. These models list variables relevant to the promotion budget allocation problem and some tentative sets of relationships between the variables. However, the bulk of the knowledge acquisition was based on primary data collection which comprised two survey research techniques: in-depth interviews and mail questionnaires.

In-Depth interviews

The purpose of this phase of the research design was to develop the knowledge base for the expert system beyond the relationships established in the literature. Informal semi-structured interviews were conducted with 22 managers from 12 European NTOs which were involved in promotion budget allocation decisions. These managers/experts were decision makers on promotion budget allocation to international markets: heads of strategic planning, marketing directors, and research directors. The interviews, generally lasting between one-and a-half and two hours, were conducted at the managers' offices (head offices in the destination countries).

The interview schedule was a flexible tool for acquiring data to develop and extend marketing theory in the context of tourism. The idea of simply devising a questionnaire directly from the existing literature was unacceptable because of the incomplete nature of the literature. An interview, where the interviewer (knowledge engineer) asks questions of the respondents (domain experts) in a face-to-face situation, is the most desirable method to acquire expert knowledge for a knowledge-based system, especially where extensive and in-depth knowledge about complex domains is required (Hayes-Roth, Waterman and Lenat, 1983). In this case knowledge comprises an understanding of the ways the domain experts rationalize their promotion budget allocation decisions. Personal interviews enable richer, deeper and more insightful information to be collected than with a self-completion questionnaire.

The main objective of the interviews was to identify and analyse the most relevant variables and relationships affecting promotion budget allocation decisions to international travel markets. These variables, and their relationships to budget allocation decisions, form the hypotheses which are subsequently tested using a mail survey. During the interviews, information about aspects of budget allocation practices which were unique to individual NTOs was collected. Moreover, managers were able to explain the rationale underlying their own practices in the light of each NTO's contextual characteristics.

In accordance with the inductive objective of the research, and in order to reduce interviewer-interviewee biases as much as possible, managers were allowed to talk openly on what they thought was important, rather than fitting their thoughts into any rigidly fixed format. However, a broad interview schedule was adhered to in order to form a feasible structure for content analysis. Without a uniform structure of responses, comparisons across NTOs would have been impossible to make. Therefore, the interviews were semi-structured using an interview schedule to guide the direction of discussion. This type of interview combines the advantages of structured and unstructured interviews; it minimizes interviewer bias, elicits new knowledge, allows more freedom to explore the decision making of each organization, facilitates experts answering questions in their own words, and avoids suggesting answers to the experts.

Pilot testing is an important aspect of survey research (Oppenheim, 1992). The semi-structured interview schedule was pilot-tested with senior managers from two NTOs and three academics in the field. As a result of the pilot test, and taking into consideration the objectives set, the original interview schedule was slightly amended.

In extracting knowledge from the domain experts, three complementary techniques were used: problem discussion, problem description and problem analysis. The problem discussion technique was used to explore the kinds of data, knowledge and procedures needed to solve specific problems in the domain. The experts were also asked to describe a typical problem for each category of answer in the domain (problem description). Finally, the experts were presented with a series of realistic problems (scenarios) to solve aloud, probing for the rationale behind the reasoning steps (problem analysis).

The author took notes during each knowledge acquisition session and wrote out a report of his impressions and conclusions following the session. The report followed the format of the semi-structured questionnaire to provide comparability across respondents. These reports were sent back to those interviewed, so that experts could check that the knowledge supplied had been correctly recorded and understood by the author. This also allowed the experts an opportunity to add further information that had not been thought of during the interviews. The interviews were also tape recorded so that additional notes and quotes could be taken. In each session the consent of the experts was sought before using the tape recorder. Examination of relevant document, reports, and memoranda of NTOs also took place.

A qualitative content analysis of the interview data was used instead of formal statistical techniques due to the small sample size, non-random method of sample selection, and nature of the data collected.

Analysis of the interview data revealed a number of useful results. The findings suggested that some variables could be dropped from the model and system, and replaced by new ones. The knowledge (variables and relationships) gathered from the literature search were amended and extended on the basis of the results of this phase of the fieldwork. In addition, some important 'if-then' rules and 'what-if' scenarios were added to the knowledge base (Rita and Moutinho, 1994). This extended knowledge base was tested, and where necessary amended, using large scale survey data.

Mail questionnaires

Since research results should be characterized by both internal and external reliability and validity, a large-scale mail survey questionnaire was developed and applied to all NTOs (a census survey). Questionnaires were used to discover additional variables of the domain and in order to establish relationships between variables. They are an efficient way to gather further knowledge on the basis of existing hypotheses.

The hypotheses and propositions developed from the interviews formed the basis for the questionnaire survey. The objectives of this second survey were to test and refine these hypotheses and propositions. This survey comprised a closed question self-completion questionnaire based on the information obtained in the interviews. In this way, a mail survey questionnaire was used to generate information about a number of major areas, identified from the interview data from a statistically significant sample of NTOs in order to validate and expand the knowledge base of the expert system. The areas covered by the questionnaire are listed below:

- what marketing objectives are defined?
- what market segmentation techniques are used?
- what marketing and promotional strategies are formulated?
- what critical steps are considered for promotion budget allocation?
- what variables are considered for promotion budget allocation?
- what relationships and inference procedures are considered for promotion budget allocation (if-then rules/scenarios)?
- what promotion effectiveness measures are used?

Mailing to the NTOs required a population frame composed of names and addresses. However, since it was difficult to determine an individual's exact sphere of responsibility from his or her job title, mailing addressed to a specific individual or job title might not reach the manager who was most relevant for the survey. Therefore, the NTOs' chief executives constituted the target group and were asked to pass on the questionnaire to the most appropriate manager in the organization.

In recognizing the importance of a well-designed questionnaire as a research instrument, every effort was made to ensure the validity of the questions in respect of the respondents and the data including a pilot-test to 20 NTOs. As with the construction of hypotheses, it underwent several revisions. The results of this pilot-test, and subsequent refinement of the questionnaire, gave the author the needed assurance to proceed implementation of the full-scale survey.

The questionnaire was sent to each of the 172 NTOs throughout the world. After this mailing and two follow-up letters, a total of 88 questionnaires were returned. This represents a response rate of 51.2 per cent: over half of the NTOs participated in the study - a highly satisfactory result for a world-wide survey.

Nearly 100 variables were measured in the questionnaire, including marketing objectives, market segmentation techniques, marketing and promotion strategies, promotion effectiveness, and factors determining budget allocation. Each was measured by the means of a five-point rating (importance) scale. Variables and groups of variables were ranked in terms of their influence on promotion budget allocation. Statistical analysis techniques were used to analyse the results and included multivariate analysis of variance (MANOVA), paired t-test, and Newman Keuls test, as well as Cronbach's α to analyse the reliability of the construct used (see Table 9.1).

The original variables were reduced to 30 underlying sets of representative factors by using a principal components analysis. These groups were used by a cluster analysis to categorize the organizations into three major groupings. Some organizational characteristics were tested as predictors for cluster membership using a multivariate discriminant analysis technique. Organizational profiles were developed on the basis of a number of organizational characteristics of the NTOs. Two major clusters were identified - developed and less developed organizations - and their difference established by means of a set of diagnostic tests. The data generated by the questionnaire allowed for the testing of the hypotheses previously formulated, a comparison with the results from the interview data, and the improvement and expansion of the knowledge base.

Table 9.1
Statistical analysis techniques used in the research

Step	Statistical Techniques
1	Descriptive statistics Frequency tables Measures of central tendency
2	Reliability analysis Cronbach's α
3	Rank order of means Means scores Multivariate analysis of variance (MANOVA) T-Test / Newman-Keuls test
4	Principal components analysis Varimax rotation
5	Cluster analysis Agglomerative hierarchical clustering using Ward's method
6	Multivariate discriminant analysis
7	Measuring associations Chi square Cramer's V Lambda

The analysis of the surveys' results, together with the knowledge established during the desk research, provide the knowledge base for

TOUREX which was built around the 12 principal components which were found to be important determinants of promotion budget allocation decisions in NTOs. The original variables were also included in the system for user selection and input and were assigned weights which took into account each variable's relative importance, as measured by the rank mean score derived from the survey responses and the number of times a variable was referred to in the entire set of rules. Component weights and ratings, as well as rule and scenario attributes, were also introduced into the system. TOUREX also allows the user to develop his/her own rules. The system is capable of giving advice in any situation: (1) either through the means of rule pattern matching; (2) or by matching the list of components used in the scenario to a rule in the knowledge base and determining both scenario and rule attributes; and (3) as a last resort, by looking at the average percentage means of budget allocation for primary, secondary, and tertiary markets. Finally, the system provides a recommendation which comprises the priority that should be attached to each market, its budget allocation, the confidence level and justification for this decision. It also informs the user about the profile of the organization from which the particular decision rule was elicited (Rita, 1994).

Conclusion

TOUREX is a knowledge-based system designed to assist senior managers from national tourism organizations in the allocation of promotional budget sums to international travel markets. Developing such a system comprises three phase knowledge: acquisition, implementation and testing. This chapter has described the research design used in the knowledge acquisition phase to this project. The research design comprised two research methodologies; the first used in-depth interviews in an inductive approach to hypothesis generation while the second generated quantitative data from mail questionnaires. The combination of these two techniques in a hybrid design proved to be extremely effective in gathering data from experts. Hypotheses were developed from data generated from interviewing experts in the field, while data collected from the mail survey was used to expand and test these hypotheses. In this way an attempt is made to gain the twin benefits of both internal and external validity and reliability in the data.

References

Ahmed, Z. and F. Krohn (1990), 'Reversing the United States declining competitiveness in the marketing of international tourism: A perspective on future policy', *Journal of Travel Research*, (Fall), pp. 23-9.

Cullen, J. and A. Bryman (1988), 'The knowledge acquisition bottleneck: time for reassessment?', *Expert Systems*, Vol. 5, No. 3 (August), pp. 216-24.

Deshpande, R. (1983), 'Paradigms lost - on theory and method of research in marketing', *Journal of Marketing*, Vol. 47 (Fall), pp. 101-10.

Fielding, N. and Y. Fielding (1986), *Linking Data*. Sage Publications, Beverly Hills, California.

Hayes-Roth, F., D.Waterman and D. Lenat (eds), (1983), *Building Expert Systems*, Addison-Wesley, Reading, Massachusets.

Mazanec, J. (1986a), 'How to evaluate a travel market: econometric modelling versus multi-attribute decision making with management estimates', *Cahiers du Tourisme*, Serie C, No. 48, Centre des Hautes Etudes Touristiques, Aix-en-Provence, France.

Mazanec., J. (1986b), 'A decision support system for optimizing advertising policy of a national tourist office: model outline and case study', *International Journal of Research in Marketing*, Vol. 3, pp. 63-77.

Oppenheim, A. (1992), *Questionnaire Design, Interviewing and Attitude Measurement*, Pinter Publishing, London.

Reichardt, C. and T. Cook (1979), *Qualitative and Quantitative Methods in Evaluation Research*, Sage Publications, Beverly Hills, California.

Rita, P. (1991), 'Expert systems and marketing strategy: an application to portfolio management decisions in tourism', in N. Piercy et al. (eds), *Preparing Marketing for the New Millenium*, Proceedings of the 24th

Annual Marketing Education Group Conference, University of Wales College of Cardiff, United Kingdom.

Rita, P. (1992), 'An expert support system for promotion budget allocation in National Tourist Offices', *S.I.M.R.U. Working Paper Series*, Vol. 2, No. 4, Cardiff Business School, University of Wales College of Cardiff, United Kingdom.

Rita, P. (1993), *A Knowledge-Based System for Promotion Budget Allocation Decisions by National Tourism Organisations*. PhD Thesis, University of Wales College of Cardiff, United Kingdom.

Rita, P. (1994), 'TOUREX: an expert system application to international tourism marketing', in *Moving Toward Expert Systems Globally in the 21st Century*, Proceedings of the Second World Congress on Expert Systems, Lisbon, Portugal.

Rita, P. and L. Moutinho (1994), 'An expert system for promotion budget allocation to international markets', *Journal of International Consumer Maketing*, Vol. 6, No. 3 (forthcoming).

Uysal, M. and J. Crompton (1984), 'Determinants of demand for international tourist flows of Turkey', *Tourism Management*, (December), pp. 288-97.

10 Validating Prototype Development: The COMSTRAT Survey

FIONA DAVIES

Introduction

A team at Cardiff Business School is currently researching the uses and applications of expert computer systems in the field of marketing. A prototype system, known as COMSTRAT, is being developed, with the aim of assisting managers in strategic marketing decisions (Moutinho, Curry and Davies, 1992). Part of the development includes validation of the prototype, and this was done by a face-to-face survey of potential users.

An expert system could be defined as a piece of computer software which contains the knowledge or expertise of a human expert, and which can employ this knowledge to provide recommendations and advice to non-experts. The most common method for representation of such knowledge, and the one used by COMSTRAT, is in the form of a set of 'if ... then' rules, nested at several levels. Expert systems were first developed for medical diagnosis, where they were used for training purposes, and are now used in many electronic and industrial applications, such as fault diagnosis, and in financial areas such as tax

251

assessment. The aim of current research with the COMSTRAT prototype is to determine how useful such systems can be in the strategic marketing area, where knowledge is less structured, experts may disagree on courses of action and factors affecting choice of strategy are constantly changing.

The building of the prototype relied heavily on textbook marketing theory, in particular that of Porter (1980 and 1985) and the findings of the PIMS (Profit Impact of Marketing Strategy) studies (Buzzell and Gale, 1987). Users of the expert system are required to input information about the current market structure in their industry, with respect to evolutionary stage, competitive intensity, market leadership, use of new technology, and potential for deriving competitive advantage, and to provide figures for the market share and return on investment of the top three firms. In addition, data concerning their company's and competitors' market share and return on investment is required. Finally, each user must rate their company and competitors on the aspects of vertical integration, productivity, company growth, and quality of product or service. These variables are those identified by PIMS as having most bearing on a company's success. The system would then output advice, based on the input data and textbook theory, as to the best strategies for the company to implement. It would also show positioning graphs for the company and competitors and offer advice on how to react to specific moves by a competitor.

Expert systems, such as this, could serve a number of important functions for marketing managers. First, they encourage managers to explore new options, challenge assumptions, play 'what if' games, and critically assess their own strategic marketing expertise. Second, they provide a means by which the knowledge of an expert, whether an academic or a practitioner (even possibly a more experienced marketer in the company), can be transferred to people with less marketing knowledge or experience. In a large and decentralized company such a system could help to ensure uniformity of decision making. Finally, such systems may be used as training tools for new or inexperienced managers.

However, the most vulnerable part of the model is the expertise which it contains. Responsible managers would be reluctant to trust strategic advice if it was based on complex calculations which they could not understand, or theories put forward by an academic they had never heard of, especially if this advice disagreed with their intuitive reaction. McDonald (1990) argues that, 'in no other discipline outside marketing is the gap between theory and practice so great' - so it is likely that many potential users would place little reliance on a system whose advice is derived totally from academic theory. Herein lies the objective of the exercise of prototype validation.

The research design employed to achieve this objective comprised a sample survey where information was obtained from semi-structured interviews together with a demonstration of the prototype. Marketing practitioners in successful companies were interviewed to obtain information regarding the competitive strategies they would employ in various situations. This information was used to validate and expand the rules used by the system. The survey also provided an opportunity to obtain marketing managers' reactions to the prototype and suggestions for its amendment, and to gauge market potential for a finished product.

The following discussion describes and explains the research objectives and the research design which was employed in order to realise these objectives. In section 2, the choice of research design is justified while in section 3 the problems encountered in implementing the chosen design are described.

Choice of research design

The purpose of the research was to validate and develop an expert system prototype, more specifically to:

(a) validate the rule base of advice built into the prototype;

(b) generate further rules for this rule base, based on marketing practitioners' expertise;

(c) feedback on how the prototype would need extending to become a working model, and on the usefulness of such a model;

(d) feedback on managers' general perceptions of computer systems.

A survey of a sample of potential users of the expert system was chosen as the most appropriate research design to achieve these results. The data were gathered using personal interviews together with a demonstration of the prototype. The main factor determining choice of research design was that the respondents had to be able to test the prototype and give feedback to the research team. So, either interviews had to be carried out in person, or a working version of the model had to be sent to each respondent. The latter course was impractical due to software licensing rules and the possibility of users having problems in using the prototype. Carrying out personal interviews also gave more scope for probing the respondents' strategic thinking.

Selection of companies and respondents

As the prototype had to be shown to respondents, this afforded the opportunity to interview potential users in person rather than by postal or telephone questionnaire. Constraints on time and money meant that 20 was the maximum number of interviews possible, but it was thought that with careful selection this number would be adequate to ensure a representation of companies across different industries and with varying market positions.

It was important to choose successful companies in order that the marketing expertise contributed by interviewees would have some validity. This was achieved by selecting companies from the 'Excel Top 200' list of companies who were successful in the sense that both their market share and their profits were increasing. This did not of course guarantee that their marketing was effective, but made it much more likely.

Forty companies, within reasonable daily travelling distance of Cardiff and covering as wide an industry range as possible, were selected initially. A member of the research team telephoned these companies to ascertain the name of the Marketing Director or Manager. It was decided to try to interview the most senior person with responsibility for competitive strategy, on the grounds that they were likely to have most marketing experience and expertise. Letters were then sent explaining the project, asking for a one hour appointment to carry out the interview and demonstrate the prototype, and saying that a researcher would telephone during the next week to arrange the appointment. The letters emphasised that information collected would be confidential and that participating companies' names would not be divulged. Due to companies' refusals or inability to schedule suitable appointment times, the final 20 selected themselves from the initial 40.

Interview format

A semi-structured interview format was adopted where the interview schedule included several straightforward classification questions, e.g. type of industry, company's market share, but where the main purpose of the interview was to discuss what competitive strategies the company employed, both generally and in specific situations, how these were formulated, and the reasoning behind strategic decisions. It was important that respondents were encouraged, by appropriate questioning, to expand on their replies in order to obtain additional valuable information. The questionnaire comprised:

(a) a number of questions which could be easily answered in a few words, e.g. What is your main product/service area of responsibility? What market share does your company have in that product/service?

(b) other questions to probe the respondent's strategic thinking, e.g. which companies do you consider your main competitors? In what ways are they similar/dissimilar to you? Why are they threats?

(c) a multi-part question putting forward various 'scenarios' as to actions that might be taken by a competitor, and asking the respondent to explain his/her likely response to such action, e.g. In your type of market or industry, how would you compete against a competitor, with similar share, aggressively price cutting?

All questions were open-ended rather than pre-coded in order that interviewees would not be constrained by any preconceptions on the part of the research team. The interviews were taped, where the respondent agreed to this, in order that all information given could be retained and the interviewer could give full attention to the conversation.

Implementing the research design

Obtaining interviews

Four companies refused to be interviewed - two because it was company policy not to participate in such research, one because it felt it was approached for too many surveys, and one because it was developing its own expert systems, details of which were not to be revealed outside the firm. This latter company did not feel that it could participate in the survey without the risk of inadvertently revealing information on its own expert system.

Another three companies could be classified as 'implicit refusals'. Despite numerous telephone calls to the potential respondents, and promises from their secretaries that they would ring back, no contact could be made.

Three companies contacted proved to be groups of companies, with marketing functions separate for each company in the group. The Group Marketing Director suggested the most appropriate companies to contact in his group, and so a further three letters had to be sent. This could have been a problem if time deadlines had been tight.

In several companies the Marketing Director/Manager receiving the letter did not feel that he/she was the most appropriate person to respond to the survey, usually because they dealt only with high level corporate strategy. Decisions relating to strategy in specific markets or for specific product areas were the responsibility of a marketing manager or product manager at a lower level. In such cases the letter was passed on, sometimes two or three times, without a record being kept of this. This led to a great deal of time being spent on the telephone trying to track down the potential respondent.

Scheduling interviews

It was originally envisaged that two interviews could be carried out a day, making ten days' work in all (preferably not consecutive, to allow time in between interviews to transcribe tapes). Many of the selected firms were in London, with a few in the Home Counties and a small cluster around Manchester. This seemed to give reasonable scope to organize in this way and thus minimize travel and accommodation costs. However, this did not work out - the survey covered 15 days, on five of which two companies were seen. The causes were numerous including:

(a) many companies were decentralized, and where the letter had been passed on to a lower level manager, this person might work at a branch away from Head Office;

(b) in one case where a company was found to be a group, the member company suggested for contact was nowhere near either London or Manchester;

(c) respondents' diaries were very full, and it was not always possible to schedule two appointments within reasonable distance on the same day;

(d) several respondents had to change appointments already made. In two cases this occurred the day before the original appointment.

In ten cases it proved to be impossible, due to the director's/manager's commitments and previously booked interviews, to schedule a date during the survey period when the interview could be carried out.

Demonstration of the prototype

As a portable or laptop computer was unavailable, all respondents were asked to provide a suitable personal computer for the demonstration, and the technical requirements were specified in writing. Three companies did not have a suitable personal computer (PC) available. In three more companies, the PC provided was unable to run the program, as the technical requirements had not been checked. As a result, much time was spent either clearing the disk to give room for the prototype to run, or finding another PC. Several companies expressed concern about a program being installed on their PC, even for the short time required for the demonstration, due to the risk of viruses. One company had all the program disks checked by their own computer department, but the others accepted assurances that the disks were 'clean'.

All these problems could have been avoided if a portable or laptop computer had been available for the researchers' use.

Reactions to the prototype

Respondents were shown the prototype and encouraged to input data relevant to their own situation. At this stage they were asked what other input factors they felt would be necessary to enable the best strategic decision to be made, and whether they had any criticism of the way data was input. Then, at the output stages, they were asked for their opinion on the output format and the validity of the advice. All comments were recorded. In later interviews, suggestions given by previous respondents were then put to the current respondents to see if they agreed or disagreed. This prompting often led to further opinions being offered. It was useful to have as many ideas as possible for the further development of the prototype.

In half the interviews where the prototype was demonstrated this was done before interview, and in the other half after, in order to see if there was any difference in managers' reactions.

The questionnaire

The semi-structured interview format worked well, and most respondents talked very freely about all aspects of their strategy. Most did not object to being taped, and taping made it easier for the interviewer to follow the flow of talk, prompt with appropriate questions, realise where the answer from one question had strayed onto another relevant topic, and ensure that all questions were covered, albeit not in the set order. Where notes had to be taken, either because the respondent wished this or because the interview was taking place in a noisy open plan office, it was harder to pay attention and ensure that all topics were covered.

There were difficulties with some specific questions. It had been assumed in drawing up the questionnaire that it would be easy to ask respondents to relate their answers to the market for their product or service (or one of those for which they were responsible). But many managers were concerned with several markets, with vastly differing characteristics. For the purposes of the interview, the market in which the company was most successful was taken. In some cases the respondent was unable to give accurately the company's market share in that market, as figures were only available for the company as a whole, or for some business unit covering several markets. Financial figures, again, were sometimes only available at company level. Some respondents did not know market shares and/or financial figures for competitor companies because they were not made publicly available. Two companies, despite the assurance of confidentiality, were not prepared to reveal financial figures - this was company policy.

Timing

The time for appointments was generally underestimated at one hour. Several interviews took longer than this as managers were very happy to discuss their strategies at length, and prototype demonstration took on average a further half hour, and longer if there were problems in finding a suitable machine or a machine had to be set up. This resulted in one interview having to be followed up by telephone, as after providing a very full assessment of the prototype, the manager was unable to finish the questionnaire before his next appointment. Also two managers, after answering the questionnaire fully, did not have time to view the prototype. Actual lengths of time spent with managers ranged in length from one hour to three hours.

Analysis of findings

Taped interviews were transcribed, not completely word for word, but ensuring that no relevant information was lost. Suitable categories of answer were then set up for the open-ended questions, e.g. for response to the scenario 'competitor investing in new product development' possible categories were 'leapfrog', 'match', 'monitor', or 'ignore'. Transcripts were then scanned to classify each company's answers. This allowed the possibility of a wider range of answer categories than if these had been pre-set prior to the interview. The interview format also allowed respondents to explain their reasons for taking a certain course of action.

From each questionnaire values were extracted for 12 explanatory variables (e.g. industry type, potential for differentiation, relative market share compared to average of top three in market), and for nine dependent variables (e.g. reaction to prototype, reaction to competitor's price cutting). As most of these were categorical variables, e.g. values of HIGH, MEDIUM, LOW, or reactions of CUT PRICES, EMPHASISE VALUE, etc., it was decided that cross tabulations would be the most appropriate method of analysis. The numerical values were categorized into appropriate ranges, cross tabulations were carried out, and the diagnostic χ^2 test was applied to test for significant associations.

The team had realized at the start of the project that, with the small sample involved, it was unlikely that results of statistical significance would be produced. This was confirmed by the findings, and the number of pieces of 'missing data' meant that there were often far less than 20 answers for a particular question. For instance, only 17 companies knew their own market share, and only 14 that of their leading three competitors. Only nine felt that the scenario 'competitor investing heavily in new technology' could be relevant in their industry, and only 13 felt that the scenario 'competitor diversifying into related products' could be relevant in their industry.

However, as one of the reasons for the survey was to find out how closely strategies used in practice accorded with those which would be recommended by academic theory, the existence of missing values was valuable in itself. If firms do not know their own market shares or those of competitors, theories which assume that decision makers possess such knowledge or that such variables influence decisions require some modification.

The survey findings were printed in report form for the participating companies, and also expanded into an academic paper. The survey achieved the primary objective of furthering the development of the COMSTRAT expert system, as the following pointers to development were drawn from it:

(a) There is enough interest in this type of system in the marketing field, to make it worthwhile continuing development. Seven respondents would consider using a final version in the course of their work, and a further three for training purposes.

(b) There is little consensus of opinion on suitable strategies across industries thus further development should be geared to a specific industry.

(c) Industries which sell to a mass market would be more suitable for consideration than those where individual company/customer relationships are of paramount importance and strategic approaches may be based on one-to-one negotiating techniques.

(d) Companies operating in one clearly defined market, with a clearly thought out strategy, see less of a role for a COMSTRAT-type system than companies operating in diverse or changing markets where company strategy has to be constantly refined to suit individual markets.

(e) Text book theory can provide a basis for the system's rule base, but the guidelines currently given in the prototype are too simplistic and need to be much more detailed to be useful to managers.

(f) Companies using formal theory felt that graphical representations such as Boston Consulting Group matrices would be useful, but as less than half the companies used such methods, explanation would be required.

Conclusion

The selection method, both of companies and respondents within companies, produced 20 useful interviews. It was somewhat fortunate that the 20 companies willing and able to participate covered a broad cross section of industry types (leisure, manufacturing, consumer goods, financial and business, retail, public sector). There is a possibility of bias in that those willing to take part were those more favourable to technological development, but it is also likely that at least two refusals were from companies already at the forefront of such development who did not wish to reveal their secrets.

The sample size was obviously too small for results to be of statistical significance, and if such results were required, a much bigger survey would be necessary, especially to allow for the high percentage of missing data encountered on some responses.

The format of the questionnaire was satisfactory for the purpose. A possible alternative would be to have sent a pre-interview questionnaire asking for details such as markets operated in, market share, financial figures, etc. - this might have given a more complete picture by allowing respondents to find out information which was not readily available, but could have had the disadvantages of losing data on how many companies did not hold such information, or possibly of inaccurate figures being given, e.g. those relating to whole company's market share instead of that for a specific market.

Taping of interviews proved essential in this type of survey where the respondent is encouraged to expand on answers. Comprehensive note-taking is impossible without the risk of interrupting the respondents' reply. If taping is impossible, two interviewers are required - one to question and listen and one to take notes, preferably in shorthand. There was no noticeable difference in respondents' willingness to answer frankly and openly between those who agreed to be taped and those who did not. Those who were taped were assured they could ask for the tape to be switched off if there was any particular information they did not wish to be recorded but nobody asked for this.

All problems connected with prototype demonstration could have been eliminated if the researchers had had access to a portable or laptop computer.

The technique of showing the prototype alternately before and after interview indicated that the discussion of strategy beforehand could influence respondents favourably towards the idea of such a system - five who saw it after interview said they would consider using a final version, as opposed to two who saw it before interview.

Finally, the time for appointments was underestimated. The obvious solution on another survey of this type would be to give a longer estimate, but managers may be reluctant to give a longer appointment. The pre-interview questionnaire suggested above, and/or use of a portable computer, could also help to solve this difficulty.

References

Buzzell, R.D. and B.T. Gale (1987), *The PIMS Principle: Linking Strategy to Performance*, New York Free Press.

McDonald, M.H.B. (1990), 'Technique Interrelationships and the Pursuit of Relevance in Marketing Theory', *Quarterly Review of Marketing*, Summer 1990, pp. 1-11.

Moutinho, L., B. Curry, and F. Davies (1992), 'The COMSTRAT Model: Development of an Expert System in Strategic Marketing', Academy of Marketing Science Annual Conference Proceedings, San Diego, CA.

Porter, M.E. (1980), *Competitive Strategy,* New York Free Press, Macmillan.

Porter, M.E. (1985), *Competitive Advantage: Creating and Sustaining Superior Performance*, New York Free Press.

Part 4

Wider Issues in Research

11 Methodology and the Target Audience

PAUL NIEUWENHUIS

Introduction

A small, but growing number of publications tackles the pitfalls resulting from the differences between academic and commercial consultancy (Boyer and Lewis, 1984; Harman, 1989; and Furnham and Pendleton, 1991). However, as yet, little has been published regarding the extent to which research methodology is shaped according to the ultimate target recipients. Consequently, this paper draws largely on personal research experience and observations over the past decade or more. During this period the author has been involved in both commercial consultancy and academic research. This includes research for commercial clients as well as research for books, both academic and commercial, i.e. a book aimed at the general public.

The researcher's product is the result of a research process. The market for this product is the target audience. As the target audience for each research project varies, the product and hence the research should be tailored to fit its intended target audience or readership. In a sense, research is research: objective observation and experimentation, which is

265

then compared with work carried out in the same field by others previously. The researcher aims to try and find out new facts based on the facts he or she already knows. However, I would argue that the actual methods used can - and probably should - vary considerably between distinct readerships. In this paper, three different target audiences are distinguished - the academic, institutional or commercial and finally, the general public. The paper will analyse the different expectations of these three groups, especially in terms of the amount of new material expected, and also the differences in presentational expectations. Differences in the amount of innovation expected will influence the extent to which the research relies on either desk or field research. It will be argued that the ratio of desk to field research for a given project varies according to the target audience. This has clear implications for the relative cost of the different types of research.

The target audience

A manufacturer nowadays considers the market in developing a new product. Similarly, for the output of our research we must consider the intended market. The target audience is the market for our products. Three major types of target audience are identified:

ACADEMIC
INSTITUTIONAL or COMMERCIAL (i.e. industry, government, public bodies)
THE PUBLIC

Although each of these categories could be subdivided and refined (e.g. industrial/business vs. public bodies), on the whole, the broad categories hold true. Each of these groups has quite different expectations and it is important to recognise this before even starting the research.

Academic

Traditional academic research in countries within the Anglo-Saxon tradition is largely based on Cartesian principles and tries to emulate the positivist methods of the natural sciences (see Chapter 1).[1] Within the arts and social sciences these methods do not always transfer smoothly, however. In general, the principal aim of a piece of research within this framework is usually one of the following two:

(1) testing new data against an existing model
(2) using new data to try and change an existing model

In terms of presentation, accessibility is often not a high priority and this has implications for the language used in terms of style and terminology. Presentational accessibility has a relatively low priority as there is no need to explain jargon or complex material to a lay audience. This makes the researcher's job easier in many ways.

On the other hand, standards of research have to be very high especially in terms of the principle of 'innovation'. This term is used to denote the important academic notion that what one has to say has to be new in some way. This means, in practice, that either the data is new or whatever one has to say about the data is new. The 'innovation' or originality principle ensures that the field in general is able to progress by means of the regular addition of new data and new conclusions about known data.

Institutional and commercial audience

The author's experience of this sector stems from work as an industrial analyst and consultant, involving the production of research reports for vehicle and component manufacturers, dealer organizations, management consultants and financial institutions as well as bodies such as the European Commission.

Their requirements as a target audience are different in that the products of research normally provide input into a strategic decision-making process. They are therefore a means to an end, rather than an end in themselves. As Furnham and Pendleton (1991, p. 16) put it, '[this group] ... wants to use the knowledge ... unless the solution is usable, it is near worthless'. This is especially true when reports are produced for a single-client, rather than as publications, although ultimately both fulfil this same purpose.

Clearly the fact of a practical real world application has to be borne in mind from an early stage as this affects not only the way in which information is gathered but also the type of information that is gathered. In general, this target audience is interested in two things:

(1) the market
(2) the competition

These two main areas have to be tackled in terms of the present situation, but especially from the point of view of likely future developments. The two key areas outlined above, therefore, have to be considered within the context of:

(a) the present
(b) the future

Commercial organizations are not normally interested in the past; nevertheless, historical analysis is still an important part of the research as it can often give at least some indication of likely future developments, as well as enhancing our - and the client's - understanding of the present. This should therefore be included in the initial proposal and costings, even though it may not figure in the final written report or presentation.

The importance of forecasting future events for this audience cannot be overstated, as planning for several years ahead is one of their principal concerns. In order to avoid too strong a commitment on the part of the researcher to one particular set of speculations on future events, but also in order to allow a number of different possible events and research findings to be accommodated, the concept of the scenario has been developed. This is rarely used within the academic environment.

It is wise to present a number of quite different scenarios, each incorporating different possible future events based on the research findings. This allows the researcher or presenter of the information some scope for including personal favourites or even intuitive reactions to the data, which would not be permissible in a more rigorous academic document. Such seemingly subjective elements are legitimate as the researcher in this context often relies on his or her experience and expertise in a particular field and as such his or her views are valued by the recipient. However, each of the scenarios has to be backed up by relevant real world data to enable the recipient to assess their relative merits. The client is often not only interested in conclusions, but also in how these are arrived at.

The researcher may have to limit his or her input to the interpretation of data provided by a third party, or even the client. This can entail a certain degree of doubt on the part of the researcher about the validity of the data provided. However, one key difference here is that in the commercial context, personal experience and expertise are often valued more than raw data. In order to work seriously for this group, some direct experience is therefore essential. Unfortunately, as Furnham and Pendleton (1991, p. 16) point out '..., the direct experience of the academic is frequently second-hand or tangential ...'.

Presentation of the data and research findings becomes more important for this target group than it is for an academic audience. This target audience wants material presented in an easily digestible form. Language and presentation have to be particularly user-friendly and visual appeal is important. The written document may often play a secondary role, with the most senior players relying very largely on an audio-visual presentation format, something to which many academic researchers and their employers are not necessarily attuned. A summary of information in a more user-friendly format than was previously available is also welcomed. The main priority is the tailoring of the information presented to the needs of the target group. This may present problems. The requirements can, at worst, seriously bias the results as only data is sought that coincides with the purpose of the project. Projects can on occasion be commissioned from a neutral source with a view of making a political case, either for internal or external consumption. This may lead to ethical problems as outlined in the next chapter.

However, one of the main potential dangers for the quality of research is the fact that this group often wants instant results. Although public bodies may take a more leisurely approach to deadlines, private companies usually want the report at short notice. Indeed, as Furnham and Pendleton (1991, p. 16) argue when assessing the differences between an academic and consultancy approach, 'expectations about time and its use are indeed a major difference between these worlds'. This clearly has implications for methodology in that corners may have to be cut. It may, for instance, be more efficient to fly over to a distant location for a few days to talk to a few people, rather than spend a week in local libraries digging out the same data. This can obviously affect quality as the quality of data may be lower or more biased. Additionally, the researcher is often not provided with the necessary time to interpret and consolidate the information gathered.

The principle of innovation has some relevance here too, as this audience likes to hear things it did not know and welcomes a new angle on known facts, although on the whole, innovation is less important than for the academic target group.

The public audience

The general public - for our purposes - consists of the intelligent general reader of non-fiction. He or she is accessed via the written media of newspapers, magazines and commercial books as well as radio, video and television. The present analysis is limited to the target audience as readers of books or articles.

The main task of the researcher in addressing this target audience is in translating, interpreting, synthesizing, simplifying or summarizing existing sources and in presenting them in an accessible manner. Totally new data rarely enjoys a first launch in a commercial book, its launch medium is one of the two earlier categories. The principle of innovation is therefore of limited importance here. Limited in that a work for this market should not directly duplicate an earlier publication for the same audience. This is really the only requirement.

Presentation in terms of language and visual appeal become more important here as we are dealing with a generally non-expert lay audience. Fulfilling this criterion is more difficult than it at first appears in that it is not always easy to assess how much the reader knows about the subject. As readers will vary greatly in this respect, we must expect to some extent to alienate the extremes within our readership, i.e. the experts on the one hand and those who fail to grasp the basic principles on the other. It is important, however, to make these extremes as small as possible without debasing the chosen subject.

It is also important to avoid the classic academic's gaffe of patronizing readers, as this will most definitely have the effect of alienating them. In general, this audience will expect an overview of the topic under discussion and it will want some clear conclusions at the end of it to be used in conversation. It is important for the reader to learn something from the book or article, but also to recognise some of it as coinciding with views already held or facts already known. All this has to be achieved by the writer without any real knowledge of the reader and this is a major difference from the other two groups outlined above.

Having established the characteristics and expectations of the three target audiences, some of the implications of these differences for the research methodology are analysed in the next section. The main difference lies in the varying proportions of desk and field research required by each of the three groups.

The desk to field ratio

Research can be of two types. These are often known as: (a) field research or (b) desk research. Desk research consists basically of using the results of previous field research carried out by another researcher or even previous desk research carried out by another researcher. However, it should be possible - ultimately - to trace back every source to an original piece of field research carried out by someone somewhere at some time. The main danger of desk research is clearly that mistakes and misinterpretations once duplicated can lead a life of their own and can be difficult to separate from fact. However, original field research has its own problems too, as highlighted in some of the other papers in this volume.

Not all research projects necessarily use both types of research; it is possible to use only one type for a particular project. On the whole, each project normally involves some of each. However, the typical ratios of desk to field research do tend to vary depending on the target audience. These differences in the desk to field ratio are investigated further below.

Academic research: DESK greater than or equal to FIELD

In academic research, desk research tends to be greater than or equal to field research. However, it is important to recognise that different disciplines and indeed individual projects will vary considerably in this respect. Thus, history, literature and mathematics will have a very strong desk research bias. Anthropology or geology will have a stronger field bias. Within the social sciences too there are differences, with business and management research for example often favouring a relatively strong field research bias, perhaps reflecting its closeness to the commercial target audience. However, within the academic context, even largely field-based projects will relate their findings to previously published work or operate within a model whose parameters are laid down in existing written sources. This aspect is virtually unique to research for the academic target audience and for this reason this audience has been allocated the relatively strong desk bias.

Research for institutional audiences: DESK smaller than FIELD

In research carried out for the institutional and commercial target group, the bias tends to be towards field research. This relates mainly to the interest in future events of this target group, as well as the time pressures outlined earlier. To the extent that written sources essentially belong to the past, however recent, they are automatically relegated to a secondary role. In practice, the typical research for this target group consists of face-to-face interviews, telephone interviews, informal conversations with 'contacts', etc. One could add to this factory visits and visits to trade shows or conferences.

Even the written sources used for the desk research for this group consist of the more immediate media of newspapers, magazines, published statistics, industry databases etc. rather than books. Some reference can be made to works containing vital theoretical background information, but mostly they are just that: background to the real essence of the report or presentation.

Research for the public audience: DESK greater than FIELD

As pointed out above, the third target audience, the general public, requires less innovation but more interpretation of existing, often academic sources. In view of this, desk research must be more important than field research. Although field research can dominate in some cases - such as travel books and guides - overall, this is a desk research area. Many commercial books rely exclusively on previously published material and this is acceptable in view of the relative lack of importance of the innovation principle mentioned earlier.

Unlike the academic audience, and to a lesser extent the institutional audience, the commercial book or article does not require detailed source references. Instead, a list of further reading is often more helpful in allowing the reader to pursue certain areas in greater detail. This also allows vital sources to be acknowledged by the writer.

The cost of research

Market principles are increasingly being applied to the area of research both inside and outside the academic world. This has clear implications both for the quality and the nature of the research carried out. Research can be expensive, but it can also be remarkably cost-effective. In practice, the cost is closely related to the desk to field ratio in that the more field research is required, the higher the cost. With limited funding, the bias moves more and more in favour of desk research, with a consequent lack of new field research. This could ultimately damage the important innovation or originality principle outlined earlier, while also damaging the researcher's credibility with the institutional or commercial audience which values direct knowledge more than the other two target groups.

Another implication is a close relationship between the target audience and the cost of research. The costs of researching a commercial book are normally lower than those for an academic project, which are in turn lower than those for a commercial or institutional project. This is essentially due to the increasing importance of both the innovation principle and the desire for information about the future as one moves through the three target audiences from the Public through the Academic to the Institutional and Commercial. Unfortunately, this fact is not always recognized by those who provide or can be expected to provide the funding for research.

Figure 11.1 attempts to summarize the findings of this paper. The core of data is interpreted by the researcher in three different ways, according to the target audience; this is represented by the three outgoing arrows. Each of the three target audiences analysed earlier is represented by a satellite. Each satellite has a major force on each side embodying the main priorities guiding its expectations from research output. Outgoing arrows from the satellites indicate the desk to field ratio most likely to be used in the research for this target audience. Tapered arrows around the data core indicate the degree to which presentational and cost factors vary according to the target audience. For example, research targeted at the general public carries a high desk to field ratio, consequently, the cost of that research is relatively low. The tapered arrow representing increasing cost is narrower here than for research for an academic or institutional audience. Conversely, use of language is extremely important. The tapered arrow representing use of language expands the wider the target audience.

Conclusions

Although this analysis may paint a relatively simple picture of the differences between different target groups or recipients of research output, it is increasingly important for researchers to be aware of the fact that differences do exist and to learn to cater for these differences. It is also important to avoid value judgements, especially from a - perhaps elitist - academic viewpoint, as there are good reasons for the different expectations of the three principal target groups identified in this paper.

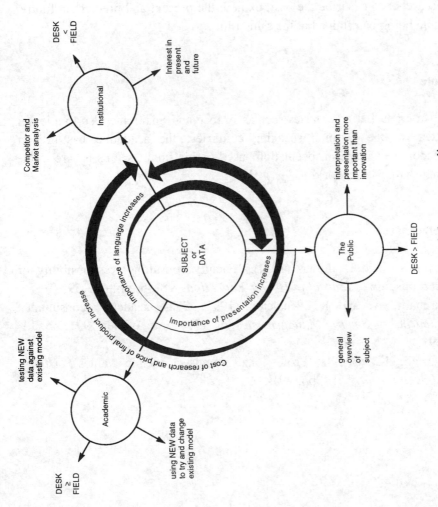

Figure 11.1 Cost, innovation and presentation and the target audience

Despite the differences in target audience, there are common factors. Whatever the audience, the researcher's role is to act as an interpreter between the subject or data and the audience, the reader of his or her writings. The researcher's role combines that of the historian, the storyteller and the astrologer, as large parts of the audience expect the researcher to describe the past, explain the present and predict the future, while being entertained at the same time.

Note

1. In many Latin countries such as France and Spain and also to a lesser extent in the German speaking countries, the academic has greater freedom to engage in speculation based on his findings; this is rare in the English-speaking world

References

Boyer, C. and D. Lewis (1984), 'Faculty consulting: responsibility or promiscuity', *Journal of Higher Education*, Vol. 5, pp. 637-59.

Furnham, A. and D. Pendleton (1991), 'The academic consultant', *Journal of General Management*, Vol. 17, No. 2, Winter 1991, pp. 13-9.

Harman, K. (1989), 'Professional versus academic values', *Higher Education*, Vol. 18, pp. 491-509.

12 Ethics in Business and Management Research

PETER WELLS

Introduction

What is a discussion on ethics doing in a book about practical research methods in management and business? After all, researchers, as socialized human beings, will already have a well established and implicit code of ethical behaviour. Moreover, there are prevailing norms within academia which inform personal actions and attitudes, norms essentially couched within a 'professional' ethos. However, this set of norms in practice conceals a wide diversity of implicit ethical stances; it also tends to obscure the extent to which ethical standards could and should underpin our work. This question of ethics is not simply a minor distraction, to be subsumed within a footnote and passed over. The personal values we bring to research both shape and are shaped by the nature of the work we do. A more rigorous and honest account of our own ethical stand-point, with all the contradictory and unresolved elements which this entails, is an important pre-requisite in establishing our academic integrity, our purpose, our goals, and our means of attaining them.

277

Clearly academic life currently brings with it certain behavioural norms which are expected of individuals, including those engaged in research. There is a broad consensus, for example, that academics should not steal others' work and present it as their own; should not show favouritism when assessing student performance or refereeing academic papers and research proposals; should not invent data when conducting research. Many of these norms are deeply entrenched, as the discussion on plagiarism below shows. Yet if research is, at least in part, about challenging conventional wisdom, it should also be about challenging the prevailing (implicit) ethical system.

This chapter seeks to outline ethical issues in business and management research. Firstly, the context within which an ethic of research in business and management might be developed is discussed. Attention is drawn to those academic and professional areas where a framework of ethical behaviour is already established. Here two questions are of interest: what is the nature and content of ethical guidelines and practices? To what extent could these guidelines and practices be relevant to ethics in business and management research? Secondly, a more direct consideration of ethical standards in business and management research is presented, with a focus on illustrative ethical issues in four key researcher activities: fund raising; theorization; the application of research methodologies; and publishing. Here attention is drawn to the way in which ethical standards are unevenly developed, and also to the extent to which ethical standards may be circumscribed and contradicted by the demands placed on researchers. Finally, in the conclusions, it is argued that the development of a unified, written code of ethics underpinned by an ethos of professionalism is an unsatisfactory and unrealizable goal. Rather, we would argue that the debate on ethics in business and management research, currently very poorly developed compared with that in other disciplines, should become a central part of the discourse which informs academic work in general.

Ethics within other discourses

Ethics have an important part in the teaching and practice of other subjects. Of particular note are the discourses associated with medicine and the law, both of course vocationally-orientated with a well established body of practitioners. Moreover there is a concern with ethical issues in other social sciences research, notably geography and sociology, a concern which perhaps more closely reflects the situation in economics and related disciplines.

Medical ethics

Medical ethics are perhaps the best known and established, dating back to the original Hippocratic oath of 5 BC. This earliest statement contained much of the basic elements which are still to be found today; in particular the inextricable link between relations with others (i.e. good conduct) and the wider prosperity and status of the profession. An updated part of the oath, written in 1947, states, 'I solemnly swear to consecrate my life to the service of humanity. I will practice my profession with conscience and dignity' (quoted in McClean and Maher, 1983).

Medical ethics takes as its starting point the sanctity of human life. Phillips and Dawson (1985) list several written international codes of ethics for medical practitioners which attempt to develop basic ethical principles. These codes essentially define the relationship of the practitioner to his/her patient, colleagues, and governing body. They take the form of prescriptive statements; the doctor shall or shall not do x, y and z; for example the doctor shall preserve patient confidences; the doctor shall not steal another doctors' patients. These normative statements are then applied to the practice of medicine. McClean and Maher (1983) identify ten key issues or contexts where ethical problems are especially acute: sanctity of life; abortion; euthanasia; terminating treatment; consent; experimentation; sterilization and contraception; negligence; confidentiality; and decision making.

While there are important ethical issues arising from research in medicine, especially with respect to experimentation and human subjects, the main concern is with the application of knowledge and theories arising from research. In this regard, it is interesting that Pond (1987) and Phillips and Dawson (1985) argue that ethics in medical practice require greater attention because of medico-moral dilemmas posed by scientific and technical advances. Equally the social dimension of medical technology is often overlooked. McEwan (1993) contends that the 'biological vision' that has dominated medical thinking this century has led, for example, to the possibility of sex selection in babies but that this does not address the social dimension of gender and power relations which bring women to desire sons rather than daughters. Thus, even in medicine which has the best developed written code of ethics, and the greatest tradition of facing ethical issues in practice, it is clear that there are clear limitations on the usefulness of a written code of ethics. Indeed, in a study of the teaching of medical ethics in the UK, Pond (1987) argues for an approach which is 'exploratory and analytical rather than hortatory' (p. 35).

Aside from a written code of ethics, medicine is of interest for the way in which ethical practice is regulated, and the link between ethical (professional) behaviour and the overall status of the profession. The British Medical Association (BMA), for instance, was established to, '... promote the medical and allied sciences, and to maintain the honour and interests of the profession' (BMA, 1988, p. 1).

The General Medical Council provides for self-regulation of the profession, it has the power to suspend or erase the registration of any registered medical practitioner judged guilty of serious professional mis-conduct. Thus medical ethics are referred to as, '... the standards of professional competence and conduct which the medical profession expects of its members' (Pond, 1987, p. 1).

The BMA, and equivalent bodies in other countries, has considerable control over the profession as a whole. The professional association is able to regulate the numbers of practitioners, the standards of the profession, and to remove practitioners who contravene accepted behaviour. Much of the ethical code of conduct is concerned with these aspects - for medical ethical discourse the main concern is with either the patient or with fellow practitioners. A similar situation prevails in legal ethics, which is discussed next.

Legal ethics

Hazzard (1978) notes that, in the context of the legal profession, '... professional ethics gives priority to an 'other' who is a client and in general require subordination of everyone else's interests to that of the client' (p. 15).

Part of the establishment of the law as a 'reputable' profession has been the concern with defining a clear code of conduct for members of the profession. This is largely because, 'The ethics of lawyers in general, and those serving powerful clients in particular, have always been the subject of popular anxiety and suspicion' (Hazzard, 1978, p. xiii).

Those in the legal profession have to deal with much of the unsavoury side of human life and events - which clearly brings with it certain ethical difficulties. As Mellinhoff (1973) argues, there are some situations which are more or less irreconcilable with ethical norms. For instance, it is widely held that everyone has a right to a trial, and hence to representation on legal matters at that trial, but equally a 'good' lawyer should only speak on those causes that he or she believes in - thus creating a danger that some individuals will not be effectively represented.

It is interesting however that the written codes which guide legal practice are more orientated to the status of the profession than those which guide medical practice. The American Bar Foundation (ABF), for instance, defines nine basic rules of professional responsibility (ABF, 1979). These are:

(i) Maintain the integrity and competence of the profession.
(ii) Ensure legal counsel is available to all.
(iii) Prevent unauthorized practice of law.
(iv) Preserve client confidences and secrets.
(v) Exercise independent professional judgement on behalf of the client.
(vi) Represent the client competently.
(vii) Represent a client 'zealously' within the bounds of the law.
(viii) Assist in improving the legal system.
(ix) Avoid 'even the appearance' of professional impropriety.

Only four of the above 'canons' are explicitly about the client, the rest are more concerned with ensuring the status of the profession as a whole. Such general principles are usually subject to interpretation, elaboration and amendment. In the UK for instance the written code of conduct is highly detailed, giving a 'blow-by-blow' account of guidelines for conduct in all the key aspects of legal life likely to be met. For example, speaking about a lawyer representing a guilty client, 'If the confession [of guilt] has been made before proceedings have been commenced, it is most undesirable that an advocate to whom the confession has been made should undertake the defence', Boulton (1975).

Ethics is thus associated with professionalism, with a code of practice or acceptable behaviour. It is frequently the central part of an administered ethical regime, with a written code of practice and some form of sanction via self-regulation. Much of legal and medical ethics is about practice rather than research per se, practice which has quite tightly drawn boundaries of operation.

In so far as there are ethical issues raised in medical research, there may be parallels which could be relevant to the social sciences. New research within medicine raises new ethical issues, and in so doing a sort of case-law of ethical decisions is established. Medical research for instance raises all sorts of ethical questions which had not been previously addressed, mainly in relation to the ethics of using knowledge rather than the ethics of how that knowledge is obtained, simply because in the past such ethical choices were impossible. With modern medical technology it is possible to, for instance, prolong an individual life for a greater period than previously which, in the case of coma patients, leads to questions about when such medical support should be removed. In the realm of health research a primary concern is with safeguarding individual health records, with a range of rules designed to decide when personal health records will be made available to researchers. The development of new treatments, operating procedures and drugs also can be considered research - where again the main issue is the legitimacy of experimentation on human subjects.

However, it remains the case that the bulk of ethical issues in the two disciplines discussed above are related to practice rather than research. Indeed, there are real limitations to the extent to which the 'role models' of ethical behaviour developed within medical and legal disciplines can be successfully applied to the social sciences in general, and to business and management research in particular. In effect, this problem reflects and reinforces the problems which have accompanied the uncritical adoption of 'scientific' philosophies and methods in the social sciences (Outhwaite, 1987). The difficulty of applying positivist and empiricist approaches to social science is in part attributable to the rather different ethical issues which arise in social science. The role models of ethics developed in the law and in medical subjects as outlined above consist of two basic elements: a narrowness of scope within a 'disinterested' professionalist ethos; and a written code of behaviour with the possibility that unethical behaviour could be detected and sanctioned. In terms of narrowness of scope it is clear that, for example, in the medical ethical discourse there is a closely defined range of activities that come under consideration. Both legal and medical ethics are more concerned with practice, with the application of knowledge to human subjects, than with the process of research. In business and management research however the scope and character of the work undertaken is enormously varied. This diversity mitigates against a written code of ethics for such a written code would have to be so generalized it would be devoid of substantive meaning. The professionalist ethos must also be questioned, for it is essentially based on self-interest: the supply of 'professionals' within such occupations is managed and regulated by the relevant professional association and the state with a view to ensuring that rewards are high. There is no equivalent professional body within the realm of business and management research to that of the BMA. While associations do exist they do not control the profession as a whole. Moreover, the concept of professionalism carries with it the notion of neutrality and 'disinterestedness' in which the professional is separate from social and personal values. That is, the professional conducts his or her work in a dispassionate, scientific manner. Yet it is clear that many researchers in business and management (as with any other discipline) have strong value-based reasons for conducting research; frequently researchers are far from neutral.

Ethics in the social sciences

Of course ethics may also be studied within the realm of philosophy, but this dimension is not addressed within this chapter. That is, we are not concerned with ethics as the philosophical study of the moral value of human behaviour. Rather, we define ethics in terms of a code of behaviour appropriate to academics and the conduct of research. Ethics in this sense is most well established in the physical sciences, and in the social sciences is most prevalent where the personal interests of individuals are at issue. This is clearly the case in subject areas such as psychology which are quasi-medical in outlook and practice, and in more vocationally orientated subjects such as social work where again the direct interests of individuals and their welfare is at stake. It has also been a consideration in sociology, which tends to confront such issues as inequality and the distribution of wealth that highlight ethical problems (Harrison and Lyon, 1993) or which tend to confront the human as subject of research directly in particular methodologies (Hart, 1970; Klockars and O'Conner, 1979; Kimmel, 1988). Bulmer (1982), for example, is concerned with the ethical implications of covert participant observation. This form of ethnomethodology is seen as problematic, especially where the research is of an applied or policy-orientated nature, because it demands a degree of duplicity on the part of the researcher. In a sense this is a question of means and ends - do the ends justify the means. Bulmer argues that there are research contexts in sociology which demand covert participant observation, and with due safeguards this can be carried out. A similar line is taken by Klockars and O'Conner (1979), who they argue that research into difficult aspects of social behaviour demand that the researcher be very careful in reaching ethical judgements about their subjects. In a similar vein, Harrison and Lyon (1993) point to ethical issues related to the use of autobiographical source material; in this instance the authors' essentially are arguing a position similar to that which pertains to medical and legal concepts of client confidentiality.

In a more general view, Ansof (1986) contends that in the social sciences, '... we select our research projects according to our scientific value systems and not according to societal relevance and the importance of the problem' (p. 21). Ansof laments the end of an era (which possibly never existed) when, '... the ethic of research was the business of researchers and that this ethic was pursuit of knowledge for its own sake' (p. 20).

This is an interesting point because it alludes to some deep-seated changes underway in academic social science research. On the one hand there has been a sustained attack on academics to improve relevance, research needs to be useful with greater 'real world' applicability. Heller (1986) identifies 12 types of research ranging from basic research entirely within academia with no intention to seek applications in the real world, through to a client-dominated request for specific advice and information. As Heller notes, 'Client funding can create difficulties since power relationships are always present within the client system' (p. 7).

It could be argued that business and management research, which tends to be of a more applied nature than some social science areas, would face more of the ethical difficulties associated with the client system. Moreover, the growing significance of contract researchers within the university system (see Wells, 1992) will also make a difference. Contract research staff have strictly limited periods of appointment and rather less discretion over the source of funding than securely tenured academics, and are perhaps more susceptible to the pressures which clients can bring to bear.

More recently, research associated with radical feminist perspectives in sociology, geography and related disciplines have fostered an ethic of care and responsibility (Lowe and Short, 1990; Crush, 1991; Curry, 1991; Reed and Slaymaker, 1993). In part at least, this is an attempt to shift the largely human-centric character of ethics which has been prevalent to date in the social sciences and replace it with something which encompasses a far broader set of relationships, so taking humanity off 'centre stage'. Reed and Slaymaker (1993), for example, take the view that in order for geographers to contribute to the growing debate on humanity and the environment it is necessary to develop explicit ethical statements, 'A discussion of the roles of culture and ethics in issues of environmental quality, social equity, and sustainability is urgently needed' (p. 738).

It is perhaps too soon for such perspectives to become established in business and management research. However, it does suggest that there is a growing discourse from within other social science disciplines which could usefully inform debate in business and management research. A simple transposition of ideas from these related disciplines is likely to be problematic. As is shown below it is not always easy to reconcile moral imperatives with the practical realities of business and management research.

There are then some grounds for suggesting that ethical issues in business and economics research have been substantially neglected and cannot be addressed simply by recourse to the measures adopted elsewhere (Punch, 1986). It could be argued that the ethical issues in business and management research are less significant and less worthy of attention that those in other disciplines, because, for example, that research does not deal with the 'life or death' situations faced in medicine, or with the personal issues faced in law. In the following section some illustrative ethical issues are raised to show that there is indeed a need to face these problems.

Ethics within business and economics research

While it is not the intention here to create a definitive code of practice on ethical behaviour in the course of research, it is useful to identify the main areas where ethical questions may arise and the sort of questions which have to be faced. To facilitate this it may be useful to segment research into four activities and consider some of the ethical questions which may arise in each. Such a division of activities is somewhat arbitrary but does allow the identification of ethical issues at key points in the research process. The point here is not to be prescriptive, but rather to indicate where some of the starting points for a discourse on ethics may lie in business and management research.

Raising funds

In order to conduct research in business and management it is usually necessary to have funding. There is an implicit view that some sources of funding are more desirable or prestigious than others, or alternatively that some sources are more 'suspect' or 'tainted'. Underpinning this view is a conceptualisation of academia being separate and aloof from the mundane and the day-to-day in order to concentrate on higher issues. The most valued source of funding, in the UK, are the Research Councils - in particular the Economics and Social Research Council (ESRC). On the other hand industry funding is viewed as more constrained, less innovative, and 'tainted' by narrow commercial considerations. That is to say, academic freedom is held to be impaired by the exegesis of near-market research when the client sets the research agenda, defines the methodology, and determines much of the character of the output. Moreover, it may be the case that commercially funded research carries restrictions over the publication of results and thus contributes less to the expansion of the frontiers of knowledge. In the worst case, the so-called impartiality of academic credibility is undermined by funding which, in effect, legitimises a corporate view of real-world phenomena (corporate can mean the private sector, but it can also mean state Departments and organisations). Given the changes to research funding in the UK over the last ten to 15 years, with a greater emphasis on research which yields direct policy results or is of value to business, the distinction between working for private capital and working for the state has been somewhat eroded anyway. In either case it is not usually possible for researchers to work on something which has no interested party involved in the funding.

In between these two extremes lies funding from other government sources (e.g. Ministries; local or regional state bodies; and government agencies such as the police) and quasi-commercial sources such as foundations and charities. Of course, in many instances, especially if the researcher is relatively 'junior', there may be little choice involved. They are simply contracted in to work on subject x funded by agency y; the only choice comes in whether to apply for the work in the first place. Equally, in business and management research at MBA level many researchers have to work in the area that their sponsor firm dictates. It is also the case that an increasing number of contract research staff in universities face a rather different context within which they work and this too has practical and ethical implications (Wells, 1992). Contract researchers, often working to very short contract life-spans of under three months, have grown rapidly in numbers over the last ten to 15 years. From being a marginal and exceptional case they have become one of the most important groups on the new academic scene. However, contract researchers do not have the job security of full-time tenured staff, a fact which must surely influence the nature of the work they do and the ethical outlook they use. Where researchers are expected to be 'self-funding' (i.e. generating enough income for the institution from research to pay for their own jobs) it may be the case that they cannot afford the luxury of ethical choices over which projects and funding sources they take on - it is rather easier for a tenured academic to pontificate on the morality of research!

There is some truth in the view that state funding is less encumbered, but from an ethical perspective it is by no means clear that funding given by the state is, by definition, less of a constraint on the impartiality of academic freedom. Neither is there any guarantee that this research is more defensible in ethical terms; after all the state in all its forms may also be a mechanism of power and control. In this context it is worth noting that the most 'circumscribed' research project I have undertaken was one for the European Commission. This was a project undertaken by institutions in all 12 member states, led by a team from Germany. In this project I had no influence over the subject of study, the research design, the questions to be asked, and even the structure and content of the written report. Moreover, the research carried with it no rights to the data so that it was not possible to publish the work in the ordinary way. Indeed, the UK report to the German central team (an internal document which the German team used to create a final report for the EC) was also vetted by the UK Department of Employment who changed several critical items in the text. In this context the contract researcher is little more than a well-informed drone!

The development of theories and explanation

In a related manner, the theories which we deploy and develop to explain phenomena also carry ethical implications. It is now widely accepted that the 'value-free' assumptions of positivism in fact conceal an ideological view of the world which - in so far as those ideologies are not made explicit - can lead to an instrumentalist and authoritarian social science.

Theories which deny human diversity and individual rights can lead to social science which suppresses emancipatory efforts, and reinforces the social position of academics as part of an elite 'meritocracy' with a functionalist mission to make society more efficient or 'better'. This is a technocratic vision of the role of social science in which the researcher either seeks to de-politicize (or legitimize) real world phenomena by explaining events in terms of 'natural' and inevitable laws, or the researcher seeks to manipulate the real world in a form of social engineering. In more recent years researchers in the social sciences involved in this empiricist tradition have sought to develop a more sensitive and appropriate set of methodologies. Fothergill and Gudgin (1982), in the realm of industrial geography, argue that their methodologies carry no explicit policy implications, there is no ethical accompaniment to their work. It is also the case that, as Wass demonstrates elsewhere in this volume, it is possible to pursue a radical research agenda in conjunction with traditional, positivist methods.

The development of critical social theory and, following this, 'realist' philosophies of social science, can be seen in part as a response to the ethical and political content of theories which embody a positivist approach - and the recognition that social science can all to easily be abused (Heller, 1986). As Levy-Leboyer (1986) argues, it is the misuse of theories and techniques which is more important than non-use.

At the least this suggests that researchers need to consider with care the ethical implications of their theories. What do these theories say about our relation to others and to the non-human ecogeosphere? (see for instance Reed and Slaymaker, 1993). The relevance of research is thus a critical consideration. In many instances the 'world view' which underpins research methods is implicit only. Reed and Slaymaker (1993) do not seek to develop one prevailing ethic to encompass all research - they recognise this as an impossible mission. On the other hand, they do argue that it would be fruitful for researchers to examine more closely the ethical antecedents of their theories.

Research methodologies

In some research perspectives it is clear that ethical issues must be faced and certain positions taken. In general, the closer the research is to actual individuals in real-world settings, the more likely are ethical questions to be raised.

In ethnography for instance, it is impossible to ignore the ethics of research. In the most problematic area, that of covert participant observation, the researcher is essentially a 'spy', albeit one with the best of motives, who records the actions, words and attitudes of people without their knowledge or consent (Kimmel, 1988; Hart, 1970; Bulmer, 1982). In a very real sense the researcher is deliberately dishonest, the true purpose of the research is concealed. On the other hand, the researcher in this situation may argue that the academic integrity and validity of the work would be jeopardized if the observed knew the purpose of the observer, the behaviour of the observed persons would change accordingly and thus be unrepresentative of 'normal' behaviour. Much depends upon the actual context of the research and the intended use of the empirical material. Clandestine participant observation may be used to inform policy making for example, and in so far as it does will have a material impact upon the people concerned. Even where the participant observation is done with the full knowledge of the observed the researcher is only a temporary participant, able to withdraw or transfer out of that context in a manner which the observed may not. That is, the researcher is only 'playing' at a life which others cannot escape from.

However, it is also the case that other types of business and management research carry ethical dimensions. It is common in the case of survey work (questionnaires, interviews, etc.) of both individuals and state or corporate entities that confidentiality is promised by the researcher. That is, the researcher obtains information which could cause damage if released or published, especially in the case of firms where information could be of value to competitors. This implies an ethic of honesty and integrity. Yet often the researchers do reveal identity, at least to those with a general knowledge of the subject. For instance, in industrial research the name of the firm may be omitted or disguised but description of the case leaves little room for doubt. Such a description may be very useful, indeed vital, for the overall case to be made. By not naming names, the researcher has kept within the strict terms of confidentiality, but in spirit the trust has been broken.

In the case of 'benchmarking' research for instance, firms may release or allow to be measured details of performance which are of immediate competitive interest to their rivals in the marketplace. Benchmarking consists of creating a series of measures of corporate performance, and then comparing those measures with other similar companies to identify 'best practice'. Benchmarking figures may also be of interest to firms considering acquisition. It would be considered by most to be unethical to release that information to a third party for gain (or even for no immediate reward) as it breaks a promise (i.e. the confidentiality clause evident in medical and legal ethics). The academic community enjoys unusually free access to many parts of the business world simply because it is seen as impartial, offering no competitive threat. Thus, research in business and management 'benchmarking' needs to find a balance between the demands for research which yields useful applications (and is therefore of material interest in terms of competitive performance), and the demands for unbiased and neutral work which allows academics privileged access.

Publication, references and intellectual property rights

The concept of plagiarism is clearly dependent upon the concept of intellectual property rights (IPR). In almost all cases IPR is regarded as cherished, pertaining to an individual, group or organization. Yet IPR is in direct conflict with the concept of academia as a social resource which expands knowledge for the general good of society. It is a reflection of a long-standing and deeply rooted tradition in western civilisation which emphasises the individual and material wealth ownership. IPR is achieved via publication, though the legal realities of copyright in academic publishing are confused to say the least. For example, academic journals are not simply repositories of professional knowledge, they are also commercial ventures - the late Robert Maxwell built his early fortune on publishing academic journals. Authors give their work to journals freely, and journals sell the work for profit. Is this an ethical situation?

Of course, in reality most knowledge builds upon existing knowledge. To make progress we need to know what questions to ask and this supposes a degree of knowledge. In a very real sense, research is a collective endeavour. The use of references acknowledges the contribution of previous academic papers and books which have enabled us to get this far. It also serves to guide readers to other published work on subjects of related interest, or perhaps giving details of a particular point which is made briefly in the text. Moreover, it enables researchers clearly to distinguish the contribution they have made, where originality is to be found. It is perhaps right that we should recognise our debt as researchers to those that have gone before us, and to explain in what ways we believe we have expanded the frontiers of knowledge. But this practice is in reality little more than a stultifying convention in which form is more important than substance (see Curry, 1991 for an interesting account of the ethical dilemmas involved in writing and publishing). I am surely not alone as a researcher who has had papers submitted to journals rejected or returned for amendment because they were 'under-referenced' or failed to take account of a particular facet of the literature in the field. In leading academic journals it is not unusual to find over one hundred references which, while testimony to academic diligence, tends to reinforce the elitism and impenetrability of academic work.

Plagiarism in the context of group research work is more problematic. There has been an observable tendency for research in business and management to become dominated by large, multi-individual (and often multi-establishment) research projects. A junior researcher may often be recruited into such a project, while more senior researchers are involved in establishing and managing these projects. In the largest projects there will also be multiple funding agencies and an international dimension. In this context, it is far more difficult to identify with precision which individual contributed which aspects to the work. In the physical sciences, the usual way around this problem is to credit all those involved in a project as authors but the individual who actually wrote the paper is credited first. It can be a real issue for researchers in business and management who may feel that their work has been taken by somebody else (i.e. somebody more senior such as a supervisor) who has published it in their own name. The division of labour in business and economics research, with the more junior research staff doing much of the actual data gathering and manipulation, and the more senior staff undertaking more of the writing is largely unavoidable. However, great care is needed to ensure this position is not exploited by the more senior researcher. Alternatively, the abilities and attributes in some individuals may be better suited to aspects of the research other than writing - for example organising the research or processing the information. Their contribution may be vital to the overall research project, but is easily neglected or underplayed at the writing stage.

An issue related to that of the use of references is that of the way in which we communicate business and management research. Large numbers of references, the use of highly specialized terms, the convoluted and often pedantic nature of academic language, the growth of increasingly specialist journals with their own style and form which need to be adhered to all serve to mystify and obscure (Curry, 1991). In this sense, the character of communication may serve to reinforce the ethos of professionalism noted above. A progressive and emancipatory research ethic should surely seek to bridge the chasm between academic theorization and everyday life, and the form and content of text is a critical means of achieving this (Lowe and Short, 1990). Certainly this paper is not immune from the use of over-elaborate construction! But it should at least be recognised that there are some very real ethical issues about the way in which we present and communicate our research.

The problem lies in the dual purpose of references and publications. On the one hand, there is the 'frontiers of knowledge' aspect alluded to above. On the other hand, publications output and citation are increasingly used as a crude measure of individual academic worth, as well as establishment-level performance (e.g. University Funding Committee ratings). Thus, the practice of publishing, and of citations, has assumed a rather different role. The 'measurement' practice, for example, provides a rationalization for self-plagiarism and for the development of 'citation circles' in which several authors cite each others' work and thus inflate the importance of the group overall. In relation to the above point on referencing papers in academic journals, a more pragmatic attitude recognises that certain references are essential (for acceptability to the editors) and others are very helpful, even where they are not needed in the text as such. Ironically the one strong feature to emerge from citation analysis is that the majority of academics do not write for journals, do not read journals, and do not cite journals. In every discipline the picture is dominated by a few leading authors which are regarded as 'de-rigour' in almost any paper, and then there is an enormous body of published work which is not referred to at all.

Self plagiarism also raises ethical questions. As noted above, with the continued pressure for publications there is generally an incentive to 'recycle' research work into as many publications as possible. In so far as new audiences are addressed, or new themes to a particular piece of work raised, then such a practice is generally considered reasonable. However, there is no clear boundary between this and a ruthless self-plagiarism which extracts the maximum 'mileage' possible from a given piece of research. In any case, the definition of the problem of self plagiarism tends to emphasise the publication only of work which can report new findings; that is to say, work which is more reflective, developing ideas over a long period of time, and seeking to bring together a series of related themes is less likely to be published.

Ultimately, it is difficult to separate the above issues from the position of most researchers within the established academic system of hierarchy and control. The use of citation indices and the overwhelming importance of a good publications record all too easily leads to a situation where researchers are taught that the way in which publications are achieved is more important than the content of those publications or their intrinsic merits. Ironically, the proliferation of journals has resulted in a situation where, in many disciplines, it is relatively easy to publish work and this in itself has diluted the importance of publishing, or at least made it more difficult to evaluate the quality of publications.

Finally, on the issue of how to go 'public' with research, it should be noted that ethical questions may arise because of the subject of research. As Berry et al. (1986) show, it is entirely possible that researchers interested in social phenomena are not passive observers of the scene but could contribute significantly to the social debate surrounding key issues which they are researching. As Berry et al. explains, 'our responsibility as scholars went beyond our immediate interests as researchers'. That is, in the interests of research it could be argued that they should have kept out of the contentious debate (in this instance on the closure of public enterprise facilities) where they would inevitably be seen as taking sides. However, the research team here felt that the debate over closures was misinformed, a facet the researchers could do something to address.

Conclusion

Ethical issues are to be found in many aspects of research in business and management, although rarely explicitly discussed. Young researchers face a rather different context to many of their more senior (and safely entrenched) colleagues. Perhaps as a consequence, they face greater moral dilemmas in the course of their work. There remains an implicit stereotype of academic endeavour which includes an ethic of impartiality, the researcher is a dispassionate observer, reporter and analyst and thereby occupies a sort of 'ethical' high ground in which the motivations and applications of the work is not challengeable.

This is a position which is not really sustainable under detailed analysis. Several aspects of ethical issues were outlined above in a brief review of the context within which economic and management research is conducted. This showed that there are serious ethical issues to be addressed, even if a resolution of those issues is not straightforward and may indeed be impossible. That is, currently many ethical choices are made implicitly and almost by accident. There is a clear need for a more positive view. A comprehensive business research ethic seems unlikely and unreasonable. A written code of ethics appears impracticable. Nevertheless, there is a case for all researchers to recognise the ethical positions they have taken in their work. It may not be possible to justify those ethical positions unambiguously, but further debate around ethical themes would certainly sharpen understanding of the role and meaning of research.

References

ABF (1979), *Annotated code of professional responsibility*, Chicago: American Bar Federation.

Ansof, H.I. (1986), 'The pathology of applied research in social science', pp. 19-23 in F. Heller (ed.), *The use and abuse of social science*, Sage, London.

Berry, A.J., T. Capps, D. Cooper, T. Hopper, and E. Lowe (1986), 'The ethics of research in a public enterprise', pp. 85-98 in F. Heller (ed.), *The use and abuse of social science*, Sage, London.

BMA (1988), *Rights and responsibilities of doctors*, British Medical Association, London.

Boulton, W. (1975), *Conduct and etiquette at the bar*, Butterworths, London.

Bulmer, M. (1982) (ed.), *Social research ethics: an examination of the merits of covert participant observation*, Macmillan, London.

Crush, J. (1991), 'The discourse of progressive human geography', *Progress in Human Geography*, Vol 15, No. 4, pp. 395-414.

Curry, M. (1991), 'On the possibility of ethics in geography: writing, citing, and the construction of intellectual property', *Progress in Human Geography*, Vol. 15, No. 2, pp. 125-47.

Fothergill, S. and G. Gudgin (1982), 'Ideology and methods in industrial location research', pp. 92-115 in D. Massey and R. Meagan (eds.), *Politics and method: contrasting studies in industrial geography*, Methuen, London.

Harrison, B. and E.S. Lyon (1993), 'A note on ethical issues in the use of autobiography in sociological research', *Sociology*, Vol. 27, No. 1, pp. 101-9.

Hart, C.W. (1970), 'Some factors affecting the organisation and prosecution of given research projects', pp. 531-39 in N.K. Denzin (ed.), *Sociological methods: a sourcebook*, Butterworths, London.

Hazzard, G.C. (1978), *Ethics in the practice of law*, Yale University Press, New Haven and London.

Heller, F. (1986), *The use and abuse of social science*, Sage, London.

Klockars, C.B. and F.W. O'Conner (1979), *Deviance and decency: the ethics of research with human subjects*, Sage, Beverly Hills.

Kimmel, A.J. (1988), *Ethics and values in applied social research*, Sage, Newbury Park, CA.

Levy-Leboyer, C. (1986), 'Applying psychology or applied psychology', pp. 24-35 in Heller, F. (ed.), *The use and abuse of social science*, Sage, London.

Lowe, M. and J. Short (1990), 'Progressive human geography', *Progress in Human Geography*, Vol. 14, pp. 1-11.

McEwan, P.J. (1993), 'The biological vision: triumphs and hazards', *Social Science and Medicine*, Vol. 37, No. 7, pp. v-ix.

McClean, S. and G. Maher (1983), *Medicine, morals and the law*, Gower, Aldershot.

Mellinhoff, D. (1973), *The conscience of a lawyer*, West Publishing Co, St Paul, Minn.

Outhwaite, W. (1987), *New philosophies of social science*, Macmillan, London.

Phillips, M. and J. Dawson (1985), *Doctors' dilemmas: medical ethics and contemporary science*, Harvester Press, Brighton.

Pond, D. (1987), *Report of a working party on the teaching of medical ethics*, Institute of Medical Ethics, London.

Punch, M. (1986), *The politics and ethics of fieldwork*, Sage, Beverly Hills.

Reed, M.G. and O. Slaymaker (1993), 'Ethics and sustainability: a preliminary perspective', *Environment and Planning A*, Vol. 25, No. 5, pp. 723-40.

Wells, P. (1992), 'The contract researcher and the university system, *Area*, Vol. 24, 2, pp. 5-8.

13 Concluding Remarks

VICTORIA WASS AND PETER WELLS

The process of compiling this book has not been without difficulty, not least in terms of the practical issue of ensuring that all contributions were submitted. More importantly, the editors have been confronted with a central question: what constitutes academic research in a Business School environment? By this we do not mean, what is the possible subject domain of business and management research? for, as our contributions clearly show, there is an enormous diversity of phenomena considered legitimate objects of enquiry. Rather, the key issue is to define how quality is measured in business and management research, and by what standards we might evaluate that research.

The process of compiling this edited volume, which encapsulates the diversity and range of research carried out within a Business School, has served to highlight just how varied standards are. There is no common standard or quality measure which embraces all types of research within the business and management area. For the postgraduate researcher, this is an issue of some importance, because it goes to the heart of how far a piece of work can be said to merit the award of a postgraduate degree.

As was indicated in the introduction, as editors we did not feel it was our place to make judgements as to the superiority of any particular set of philosophical assumptions, scientific objectives or methods of implementation. Rather, we sought to interpret methodology in the context of business and management research. The multi-disciplinary, and often inter-disciplinary, nature of business and management research distinguishes it from research undertaken in the traditional disciplines, such as economics and sociology. As a result, methodology is not dictated by the subject of study; rather it is the subject of choice. We argued in Chapter 1 that this choice should be a conscious choice; that is, explicitly justified with reference to alternatives. In placing methodology within the context of a distribution (see Table 1.1) and emphasizing the relationship between a methodology and the philosophical foundations upon which it is premised and the techniques by which it is implemented, we sought to assist the process of conscious choice.

The potential for inter-disciplinary research in business and management gives rise to methodological pluralism. Here, techniques which are generally considered to be confined to specific methodologies are combined within a single study. Such an approach is justified in terms of triangulation, that is the confirmation of research results under one technique by those created under another, and by the ability to address many facets of the phenomena under investigation in order to reveal a more comprehensive picture. This approach is illustrated in a number of chapters (see Stiles, Kitchener and, in particular, Lowe) all of whom use a combination of techniques deployed at different stages during the research project. While the adoption of many techniques may appear to offer a flexible research design, the researcher risks exhibiting a lack of understanding of the status of the knowledge created. There is an implicit danger of ontological conflict (i.e., using techniques which derive from different understandings of the nature of human action) and epistemological conflict (i.e., using techniques which derive from different definitions of what constitutes scientific knowledge). In general, multi-method research does not address the problem of contradictory methodologies. In part, this is due to the pragmatic as opposed to paradigmatic nature of much multi-method research.

The orientation towards addressing practical problems encountered in the business and management arena, as opposed to questions of a conceptual nature, is a second distinguishing feature of business and management research. Many of the chapters of this book provide examples of applied research. Of particular note in terms of market orientation are the chapters by Rita and Davies, both of whom emphasise the direct utility of their research. Research is seen as the means by which existing models may be adapted to fit in with the empirical world. Immediate application is the main objective of the research and also the measure of the achievement of a satisfactory standard. For Rita and Davies then, discussions on epistemology and ontology are of little relevance; the scientific basis of the models and the theories of knowledge upon which the research is founded are taken as pre-established and beyond the realm of debate. While there are great strengths in this problem solving perspective, there is also a danger that applied research fails to meet the standards of rigour and validity expected within more traditional, well established, and theoretically driven disciplines.

For more 'mainstream' academic research (Delbridge and Kirkpatrick; Anderson; Wass; and Healey and Rawlinson) the issue of standards is more a question of being cognisant of the strengths and weaknesses of the methodologies employed, and of the relationship between those methodologies and the theories deployed. Research seeks robustness and validity in terms of a set of criteria established within the particular paradigm from which the research derives. The achievement of an academic standard is through the identification of sources of distortion in the data. For positivist research, distortions constitute bias which prevents the researcher from revealing the 'truth' about a subject. The objective of the research is to eliminate, or failing this control for, sources of bias. For the naturalist, distortion is an inevitable and 'natural' feature of research and the objective is to recognise and reflect upon the sources distortion when interpreting the data.

The contributions from Nieuwenhuis and Wells, in their different ways, are also about standards. For Nieuwenhuis, the key point is that different audiences have differing expectations in terms of how research is conducted and presented - though all audiences expect consistency, rigour, and accuracy. This is not to suppose that research for a business audience is of a lower standard of accuracy or diligence, and it may be the case that an 'academic' research training is of value in sustaining those standards. For Wells, the theme of standards is pursued more widely to encompass ethical norms and expectations. Here, it was argued that the pursuit of academic standards should be paralleled by the pursuit of wider moral standards.

Thus, academic standards are not reducible to a single theoretical perspective or methodology; standard does not mean standardized. This leads us as editors to the slightly uncomfortable conclusion that it is almost impossible to provide a comprehensive definition or codification of academic standards. The creation and reproduction of academic standards lies within the subjective interpretation of individuals in the light of their experience and perception of prevailing practice. The research process itself is, in part, about discovering answers to the questions posed in the introductory chapter, even if this is only an implicit undercurrent to the stated research objective of answering questions or hypotheses on a specific subject. As a last resort, the researcher can adopt a pragmatic solution to the problem of defining standards where the most critical decision which the research student makes is that of the choice of supervision, closely followed by that of external examiner. For the researcher intending to publish in the academic press, where each journal defines its own set of standards, the critical choice is reduced to a choice of journal. Yet, it is clear from the chapters in this book that researchers seek to rise above pragmatism, such that a commitment to the work brings with it a commitment to go beyond what is sufficient, to an exploration of wider issues.

Index